The **Good** Book

The **Good** Book

40 Chapters That Reveal the
Bible's Biggest Ideas

DERON SPOO

David C Cook®

transforming lives together

THE GOOD BOOK
Published by David C Cook
4050 Lee Vance Drive
Colorado Springs, CO 80918 U.S.A.

David C Cook U.K., Kingsway Communications
Eastbourne, East Sussex BN23 6NT, England

The graphic circle C logo is a registered trademark of David C Cook.

The website addresses recommended throughout this book are offered as a
resource to you. These websites are not intended in any way to be or imply an
endorsement on the part of David C Cook, nor do we vouch for their content.

LCCN 2016958397
ITPE ISBN 978-1-4347-1150-2
eISBN 978-1-4347-1098-7

Published in association with the literary agency of Ann Spangler &
Company, 1415 Laurel Avenue Southeast, Grand Rapids, Michigan 49506.

The Team: Tim Peterson, Nick Lee, Jennifer Lonas, Andrew Sloan,
Helen Macdonald, Abby DeBenedittis, Susan Murdock
Cover Design: Amy Konyndyk
Cover Photo: Getty Images

Printed in the United States of America
First Edition 2017

1 2 3 4 5 6 7 8 9 10

010817

To Paula, my wife, my best friend.
I am grateful daily that God has
given us the gift of life together.

Contents

Foreword   11

Acknowledgments   13

Introduction   15

In the Beginning

1. You're More Like God Than You Think
    Genesis 1   27

2. When Everything Broke—Including You
    Genesis 3   35

3. Staying Afloat in Troubled Times
    Genesis 6   43

4. Faith Isn't Safe
    Genesis 12   51

5. When God Asks Too Much
    Genesis 22   59

God Is Good When Life Gets Messy

6. On a First-Name Basis with God
    Exodus 3   69

7. When Life Seems Out to Get You
    Exodus 14   77

8. Ten Keys You Can't Live Without
    Exodus 20   85

9. God Can Use Even Your Failures
    Judges 16   95

10. Why Hard Times Help
    1 Samuel 17   105

God Is Big

11. Making Sense of Your Suffering
    Job 1   115

12. Forget the Funeral—This Is Life!
    Psalm 23   123

13. Guilty but at Peace
    Psalm 51   131

14. God Is Closer Than You Think
    Psalm 139   139

15. Words of Wisdom
    Proverbs 1   147

Tough Love, Troubled Times

16. The Real Face of Jesus
    Isaiah 53   157

17. Inferiority and Obedience
    Jeremiah 1   165

18. Whose Side Is God On?
    Daniel 3   173

19. Integrity under Fire
    Daniel 6   183

20. Man on the Run
    Jonah 1   191

Why Two Testaments?   197

Jesus Has Just Entered the Building

21. Jesus—God with Skin On
    John 1   207

22. Welcome to Our World
    Luke 2   217

23. What Does Jesus Want?
Matthew 5   227

24. Why Worry Never Works
Matthew 6   235

25. Life over the Long Haul
Matthew 7   243

Jesus Won't Leave Us as We Are

26. Is Jesus Strong Enough?
Luke 8   255

27. The Original Come-to-Jesus Meeting
John 3   263

28. God Is Looking for What He Loves
Luke 15   271

29. Every Scar Tells a Story
Mark 15   281

30. Beating Death
Matthew 28   289

Following Jesus

31. Where Is Jesus Now?
Acts 1   299

32. Happy Birthday to Us
Acts 2   309

33. When Jesus Interrupts Your Life
Acts 9   319

34. God Loves the People You Can't Stand
Acts 10   329

35. What Heaven Holds in Store
Revelation 22   337

God's Message for You

36. Is God Ever Mean?
   Romans 8   347

37. More Than a Feeling
   1 Corinthians 13   355

38. Can God Change Your Character?
   Galatians 5   363

39. Straight Talk
   James 1   371

40. Becoming Your True Self
   1 John 3   379

Epilogue   385
Notes   389
About the Author   399

Foreword

I think we need a little help here. Something's broken. For a lot of people these days, life isn't making a whole lot of sense. The age of connected living, online profiles, and Internet interactions isn't all that was promised. And all this pressure to keep up appearances ... it's just weighing us down.

At the heart of all this, we find a messed-up idea that says we're in control. It says that we get to *want* it all and to *have* it all. It isn't working; it's leaving people deflated or discouraged. But is this really anything new? Haven't we been here before? Isn't the history of humanity a repeating tale of the same mistakes—misplacing our hopes?

And that's the truth right there. Though we've never lived in times quite like these, we're still walking with the same limp or talking with the same stutter.

In the Bible, you will find God's truth, which is both timely and timeless—for your today and all your tomorrows. You will find the story of our failures—namely, cowardice and greed, anger and self-interest. There are everyday people living everyday lives and some with epic falls from grace. And I can see a bit of myself in all those stories.

But I can see something else too. I can see that the story doesn't end there.

That's why *The Good Book* is so helpful. It makes the Bible personal. It brings the characters to life. It takes you on a journey through the forty most essential themes in Scripture. It connects the dots between the lessons taught thousands of years ago and the realities of life today.

Deron Spoo is a pastor and a friend. And you can trust Deron to guide you well. If you're new to all this and don't know where to begin, or if you're an old hand wondering how to restart a good habit, Deron's going to help you. He'll leave you with a deeper understanding of God's story, stir up a greater thirst for Scripture, and show you how to apply it to your daily life.

The Good Book is more than just a great resource. This book you are holding is an opportunity for you to begin a journey of transformation. Maybe you'll enjoy it with others from your church, explore it with folks from your small group, or simply savor it in personal study. Know this: it is designed to change your life—you won't be the same again.

Kyle Idleman, author of
Not a Fan and *Grace Is Greater*

Acknowledgments

I must give special thanks to several important people without whom this book wouldn't be. Each person mentioned here has not only encouraged this project but has also enriched my life.

My family—Paula, Kira, Caleb, Seth, Mom, and Dad. You are the most important people in my life. You're my foundation and my inspiration from which my best efforts spring.

My church family—First Baptist Church of Tulsa. How we've grown together! Daily I'm thankful God saw fit to have us partner together in his kingdom work. I'm especially grateful for the small group of friends—you know who you are—who prayed me through this project.

My agents—Ann Spangler and Linda Kenney. You believed in the value of this project when few saw it. Your resolute conviction strengthened me when my own confidence wavered. Ann and Linda, you have my trust and my deepest respect.

My publisher—David C Cook. What a talented team! I'm especially grateful for the expertise Verne Kenney brought to bear on this project. Also, I appreciate my editor, Timothy Peterson, whose keen eye added to the clarity of this volume.

And finally, a special word about Calvin Miller, my mentor, professor, and old friend. Calvin encouraged me to write and to write according to my passions. And so here it is! Heaven is richer for Calvin's presence there today, and I'm richer for having spent twenty years learning from his intimate relationship with Christ.

Introduction

The Holy Scriptures are the highway signs: Christ is the way.

—Søren Kierkegaard

The young woman standing before me was a spiritual blank slate. She had no reference point to begin her journey toward God, no experience, no context. She approached me after a worship gathering on a Sunday morning. This was her first time in church. Not her first time in *this* church, but her first time in any church … *ever*.

In a matter of seconds, she gave me a rough idea of her thoughts about God. It wasn't that she didn't believe *in* God; she didn't know what to believe *about* God. From her point of view, God had never struck her as urgent, relevant, or worth serious consideration. In short, she had no God history. Certain unwelcome events in her life had recently prompted her to consider the Christian faith. So she found herself in church, talking to me.

More than two decades ago, George Hunter coined a term for people with no God history and "no christian memory." Based on the word *agnostic*, a term for those who view God as unknowable, Hunter came up with the word *ignostic* to describe someone who is ignorant about the subject of God.[1] An ignostic may willingly admit that God is knowable, but he or she doesn't have the first clue about how or where to begin a search for him.

The young woman's first question for me was simple: "Is there a book I can read that can tell me what you believe about God?" The answer, of course, was the Bible. It was the right answer, yet I secretly wondered whether it was the best answer to give her.

If the Bible intimidates even the most adept readers, imagine how intimidating it would seem to this young woman, a first-time Bible reader. On top of that, the Bible is notoriously easy to misinterpret, especially when lone verses are lifted out of context.

Scripture is an infinite resource for knowing God and understanding life, but practically speaking, where should a new Bible reader begin? And how can anyone decipher the bizarre names, faraway places, and cultures of the distant past? Who is qualified to guide us in our quest to grasp the simple truths of God's love, the necessity of a life-changing experience with him, and the promise of forgiveness and a fresh start?

The Bible is like the ocean, according to an old metaphor. The ocean is so deep in places that no person, however capable a swimmer, could survive its extremities. But at the same time, when the ocean touches the land, the water is so shallow and the waves lapping the beach are so gentle that even a toddler can safely play there. Anyone who has visited the beach has seen firsthand that the ocean is both intimidating and approachable.

The same is true of the Bible. Like the ocean, its depths can never be fathomed. Even after a lifetime of study, the most brilliant theologians admit they've only begun to plumb its depths.

Centuries of Christian scholarship haven't been able to chart its vast expanse. The Bible can be intimidating and yet approachable at the same time. Anyone can pick up a Bible and encounter simple truths that are nothing short of life changing.

Since no single book can fully explore the depths of the Bible, in this volume we'll focus on the best-known passages of Scripture that form the basis of the faith we know as Christianity. Consider this your guidebook to the Bible. Throw a beach towel over your shoulder and take a stroll in the surf.

For those of you who are experienced Bible readers, I offer a word of advice: Reject the tendency to be satisfied with your current understanding of the Bible. Refuse the temptation to think that what you grasp of the Scriptures today is somehow enough. Don't just settle for wading in the surf. Dive deeper! Untold riches await your discovery.

Many years ago, the evangelist Robert Sumner told the story of a man from Kansas City who was involved in an explosion. The accident left him badly burned. Tragically the man lost the use of his hands and the sight in both eyes. He had recently become a Jesus follower and had discovered the joy of reading the Bible. But now he was unable to see or use his hands to read braille.

One day the man learned of a woman in England who had taught herself to read braille using her lips. He tried this approach as well, but the nerve endings on his lips were too damaged to distinguish the characters. As he made a final attempt to read braille with his lips, the man's tongue happened to brush the page. Instantly he realized he had found a way to read the Bible after all.

Since then, he has read the Bible cover to cover four times, using only his tongue.[2]

Given the obvious barriers to reading the Bible, why didn't this man simply read it once and be done with it? Why read the Scriptures again and again? Simply put, each time we read the Scriptures, our understanding is expanded and our love for God is deepened. So if you're a more experienced Bible reader, these forty chapters will not only help you explore the Bible's biggest ideas, but they'll also enable you to grasp afresh the greatness of God.

Selecting the Bible readings for this book was more art than science. My experience as a pastor, my journey as a follower of Jesus, and many conversations with people informed my choices. Often, people who didn't grow up in church complain about the challenge of understanding the Bible. I asked a number of them to give me insight as to what they don't comprehend about Scripture. I also talked with parents who confessed that their children know more about the Bible than they do, and these parents wished they had a safe place to ask questions in a judgment-free environment.

These people even confessed to feeling ignorant when everyone else seems to be in the know about well-known passages in the Bible. Psalm 23 is often quoted at funerals, but what does it really mean? And 1 Corinthians 13 is recited during many wedding ceremonies, but who wrote these words and where are they found in the Bible?

The Scripture passages you're about to encounter could be considered absolutely essential for understanding big ideas of the Bible. To understand the Beatles, it's essential to be familiar with the *White Album*. To know the Eagles well, listening to "Hotel California" is a must. To recognize Beethoven, you first have to get acquainted with his piano sonatas. In other words, to know these artists well, you must be able to readily recognize their signature pieces of music.

(Likewise, the Bible contains signature chapters that every follower of Jesus should recognize instantly.) You not only *should* know these chapters, but you *can*. After understanding these chapters, you'll be able to recognize the rhythm of the Scriptures and tap your toes to the cadence. As I've taught these chapters in my church, I've enjoyed watching faces light up when, for the first time, people experience reading the Bible with understanding instead of insecurity.

As a matter of good practice, I encourage you to read the Bible selections first. Each chapter will take about five minutes to read. Then, after reading the entire Bible passage, read my brief exploration of that passage. Finally, I encourage you to reread the Bible chapter with the benefit of knowing more about the context and content.

Before you dive into the breakers of the Bible, I wish to highlight two important terms that will not only serve beginners well but will also serve as valuable reminders for those with greater exposure to the Bible.

*Throughout this volume, I refer to the *Older Testament* and the *New Testament*. The Older Testament is the faith history of the Hebrew people. In our culture, *old* often means "obsolete," while *older* implies a bit of experience. The thirty-nine books of the Older Testament were written in the Hebrew language by the Jewish community that believed in God prior to the coming of Jesus. Without the Older Testament, we would have great difficulty appreciating and understanding the New Testament, a collection of twenty-seven books written in the Greek language by the first followers of Jesus. These books contain God's renewed plan to bring humanity into a relationship with him.

Because the Bible was originally written in ancient languages, we must rely on modern-language translations to make it accessible. For this guide, we'll use the Christian Standard Bible.

The forty Bible chapters we'll be discovering and discussing are broken down into eight sections. In each section, we'll cover five chapters of Scripture under one theme that is both biblical and applicable to real life. My hope is that you'll quickly realize that the terms *biblical* and *real life* aren't opposites but synonyms. The Bible is important not only because it's an ancient document but also because it enables us to meet the eternal God in the present moment.

If I had selected forty chapters of the Bible at random, you might arrive at the end of this book more confused than ever about what the Bible is all about. So what ties all forty chapters in *The Good Book* together? Allow me to answer that question with a story.

Early one morning I was waiting in line at my favorite coffee shop. Soon a blind woman entered the shop. As she walked across the room, tapping her walking stick on the floor, I decided to be helpful. When she was a dozen feet away, I told her that I was at her ten o'clock and was at the end of the ordering line. As we stood together in line, we struck up a conversation. She was on her way to the state capital with some colleagues to lobby for the visually impaired community.

"In fact, I'm meeting some friends here," she said.

With that, she tapped her walking stick on the tile floor. I then noticed three or four of her friends across the room. Instantly their heads swung around to look for her—even though they couldn't see. One of them took his cane and rapped it in response on the tiles under his table. They had found one another. Had I not been at the center of the action, I would never have observed their taps. I also learned what their taps meant. In three or four taps each, they had sent the message, "I'm here. I'm here."

The forty chapters that follow cover the most essential themes of the Bible. More than that, as you read them, I hope you sense a tap. In the pages of this book, I hope you sense the presence of God saying to you, "I'm here. I'm here."

As you begin, remember that the ultimate benefit of reading the Scriptures isn't greater familiarity with the Bible but deeper intimacy with God. The Bible, from the first word to the last, points to the person of Jesus. My prayer is that you'll encounter the eternal love of God by meeting Jesus in the pages of Scripture.

FOR REFLECTION

All Scripture is inspired by God and is profit-able for teaching, for rebuking, for correcting, for training in righteousness, so that the man of

God may be complete, equipped for every good
work. (2 Tim. 3:16–17)

Don't miss the promise and the importance of reading the Bible:
if you know the Scriptures, you'll never be at a loss for how to
handle life.

What do you believe will be your greatest challenge in reading
the Bible?

IN THE BEGINNING

Genesis 1

¹ In the beginning God created the heavens and the earth.

² Now the earth was formless and empty, darkness covered the surface of the watery depths, and the Spirit of God was hovering over the surface of the waters. ³ Then God said, "Let there be light," and there was light. ⁴ God saw that the light was good, and God separated the light from the darkness. ⁵ God called the light "day," and the darkness he called "night." There was an evening, and there was a morning: one day.

⁶ Then God said, "Let there be an expanse between the waters, separating water from water." ⁷ So God made the expanse and separated the water under the expanse from the water above the expanse. And it was so. ⁸ God called the expanse "sky." Evening came and then morning: the second day.

⁹ Then God said, "Let the water under the sky be gathered into one place, and let the dry land appear." And it was so. ¹⁰ God called the dry land "earth," and the gathering of the water he called "seas." And God saw that it was good. ¹¹ Then God said, "Let the earth produce vegetation: seed-bearing plants and fruit trees on the earth bearing fruit with seed in it according to their kinds." And it was so. ¹² The earth produced vegetation: seed-bearing plants according to their kinds and trees bearing fruit with seed in it according to their kinds. And God saw that it was good. ¹³ Evening came and then morning: the third day.

¹⁴ Then God said, "Let there be lights in the expanse of the sky to separate the day from the night. They will serve as signs for seasons and for days and years. ¹⁵ They will be lights in the expanse of the sky to provide light on the earth." And it was so. ¹⁶ God made the two great lights — the greater light to rule over the day and the lesser light to rule over the night — as well as the stars. ¹⁷ God placed them in the expanse of the sky to provide light on the earth, ¹⁸ to rule the day and the night, and to separate light from darkness. And God saw that it was good. ¹⁹ Evening came and then morning: the fourth day.

²⁰ Then God said, "Let the water swarm with living creatures, and let birds fly above the earth across the expanse of the sky." ²¹ So God created the large sea-creatures and every living creature that moves and swarms in the water, according to their kinds. He also created every winged creature according to its kind. And God saw that it was good. ²² God blessed them: "Be fruitful, multiply, and fill the waters of the seas, and let the birds multiply on the earth." ²³ Evening came and then morning: the fifth day.

²⁴ Then God said, "Let the earth produce living creatures according to their kinds: livestock, creatures that crawl, and the wildlife of the earth according to their kinds." And it was so. ²⁵ So God made the wildlife of the earth according to their kinds, the livestock according to their kinds, and all the creatures that crawl on the ground according to their kinds. And God saw that it was good.

²⁶ Then God said, "Let us make man in our image, according to our likeness. They will rule the fish of the sea, the birds of the sky, the livestock, the whole earth, and the creatures that crawl on the earth."

²⁷ So God created man in his own image;
he created him in the image of God;
he created them male and female.

²⁸ God blessed them, and God said to them, "Be fruitful, multiply, fill the earth, and subdue it. Rule the fish of the sea, the birds of the sky, and every creature that crawls on the earth." ²⁹ God also said, "Look, I have given you every seed-bearing plant on the surface of the entire earth and every tree whose fruit contains seed. This will be food for you, ³⁰ for all the wildlife of the earth, for every bird of the sky, and for every creature that crawls on the earth — everything having the breath of life in it — I have given every green plant for food." And it was so. ³¹ God saw all that he had made, and it was very good indeed. Evening came and then morning: the sixth day.

1

You're More Like God Than You Think
Genesis 1

You're more like God than anything else he created. At times you might feel worthless. Perhaps this is why the first chapter of the Bible sends the unmistakable message that you are priceless. Even on days when you feel barely human, you are, in fact, more like your Creator than anything else in existence.

Speaking of feeling barely human, I assure you that I face my own set of challenges. No matter how much Scripture I read or how hard I pray, progress seems slow and halting when it comes to a problem that plagues me. What's my difficulty? My personality gravitates toward worst-case scenarios, leading me into worry and fear. My mind is adept at conjuring negative outcomes for any situation. I struggle even though the Bible is peppered with "fear nots"—the most common command in Scripture, and two words Jesus uttered often. My anxiety seems to have grown over the years. I'm constantly concerned for my family, about making ends meet, and about the group of people I help lead. I tend to obsess over all the things I can't control.

My lack of progress could be interpreted as a spiritual failure on my part. And perhaps in some ways it is. But in another way, this struggle offers me an ongoing opportunity to learn to depend on God each day. Without this tension, I might fall into the trap of thinking I can handle life without the Lord's help.

Even on days when I face my worst bouts of worry, I'm still the closest representative of God in all creation. And the same is true of you. Even in your worst moments, you're more like God than the best of the rest of creation.

When we read Genesis 1, it's easy to become sidetracked from this truth by focusing on lesser ideas. For instance, people have long debated the age of the universe. If it were essential to our faith to know the exact date of creation, I suspect God would have shared it with us. He didn't. Nevertheless, many modern readers and heavy thinkers dig into Genesis 1 and immediately debate the age of the cosmos. Answers range from billions of years to a mere six thousand.

A seventeenth-century thinker by the name of John Lightfoot confidently stated that God completed the creation event in the year 3929 BC. How's that for accuracy! At this point there's little to be gained from such speculation. Entertaining such theories will distract you from the wonderful truth in the first chapter of the first book of the Bible: *you bear a striking resemblance to your Creator.*

Instead of the *when* of creation, Genesis 1 would have us focus on the *who* of creation. Though dates and statistics elude us, we're led to the certainty that there is a divine personality at work in creation: "In the beginning *God* ..." (Gen. 1:1).

The first glimpse we're given of God in the Bible leaves an indelible imprint on our souls: God is creative. His creativity is evident throughout the visible world. Creation is both infinitely large and infinitesimally small. And God is responsible for all of it!

The heart of a hummingbird "weighs a fraction of an ounce [and] beats eight-hundred times a minute." By contrast, the heart of a whale weighs one thousand pounds[1] and is the size of a compact car.

God's creation is vast. Imagine holding an atlas of the universe in your lap. Each page contains a picture of a single galaxy, some spiraled, others elliptical, still others irregular—all of them stunning. You flip through your universal atlas at the rate of one page every second. To go from cover to cover would require approximately ten thousand years.

God's creation also contains variety. When God created trees, he didn't merely create one kind of tree. In the Amazon jungle alone, there are thousands of known species of trees.

The only word that comes close to describing the fullness of God's creative genius is *majestic*. In its majesty, all of creation mirrors something of its Creator. The same whale mentioned earlier communicates with other whales via a low-frequency hum. Two whales are capable of carrying on a conversation even when they're separated by hundreds and perhaps thousands of miles of water.[2] Indeed, majesty does come to mind. And residing atop the majesty scale is humanity—you and me.

Along with the *who* of creation, Genesis 1 also addresses the *how* of creation. God spoke, and existence exploded into being. God's verbal big bang was the source for everything from quasars to quarks and lightning to lightning bugs.

As you read Genesis 1, notice the rhythm and order of creation. There's a beautiful arrangement and symmetry to God's creative activity. What he formed in the first three days, he correspondingly filled in the three days that followed. Day 1 found him creating light and dark. On day 4 he filled what he formed with sun, stars, moon, and meteors. On day 2 God formed the sky and sea, followed by filling creation with birds and fish on day 5. Day 3 witnessed God forming land and then populating it with all sorts of creatures on day 6. Forming and filling.

Included in day 6 was creating human beings. God started simple, creating light and darkness, but his formations became increasingly complex as his creative activity continued. God culminated with the creation of humanity, his most intricate invention.

Genesis 1 is clear: the pinnacle of God's creative work was man and woman. In God's eyes, nothing in the created order was more impressive. Nothing else could serve as the ultimate fruit of his forming power. Genesis 1:27 offers this observation: "So God created man in his own image; he created him in the image of God; he created them male and female."

What could it mean to be made in the image of God? Thinkers and theologians have wrestled with this question for centuries.

Here's a small example. Though I love my children equally, I have a unique relationship with my son Seth. In many ways—body build, attitude, humor, and appearance—Seth captures my essence in his smaller form. Sometimes I can almost read his thoughts. You could say that he bears my image.

So it is between God and human beings. We bear his image in our smaller frames. Internally we resemble him because we *have* a spirit and God *is* spirit. We're more than mere physical beings. This spiritual element (or soul, if you prefer) may be invisible, but it exists nonetheless.

Externally we bear God's image because of our capacity to experience relationships. That reflects God's own desire to be in relationship with us. We have a built-in need and desire to relate to God and other humans because we were created in his image. That's what allows us to enjoy intimacy with him.

Many people wonder whether Adam and Eve were the only people God directly created. In later chapters of the Bible, their descendants went off and met other people east of Eden. Where did these people come from?

[All history is selective. No history book in the world could possibly record every event surrounding a given historical occurrence. Likewise, the Bible is selective. But we trust that even though its content is selective, it's also significant. God shared the people and events that would lead us to a better understanding of him.]

Genesis 1 reveals two essential truths about who you are. First, you are not an accident. You are not the result of cosmic chance; you're an intentional and individual creation of God. Second, God created you as an act of love. God is far from indifferent when it concerns you.

We share ourselves with only those we care about. Just as we share ourselves with only those we care about, God shared the best part of himself with you and me. Nothing else in all creation can make this claim.

So relish this life, knowing that when God sees you, he can't help but see a reflection and resemblance of himself.

FOR REFLECTION

Acknowledging God as creator is a simple and sure way to remove the weight of stress from our lives. We're made according to God's design. And our designer has given us a destiny! Fulfilling that destiny is a matter of putting all of life and our future into his hands. We aren't expected to handle life on our own; we are God's responsibility.

What one action or attitude can you change today that will help you better reflect the image of God—your true identity?

Genesis 3

¹ Now the serpent was the most cunning of all the wild animals that the LORD God had made. He said to the woman, "Did God really say, 'You can't eat from any tree in the garden'?"

² The woman said to the serpent, "We may eat the fruit from the trees in the garden. ³ But about the fruit of the tree in the middle of the garden, God said, 'You must not eat it or touch it, or you will die.'"

⁴ "No! You will not die," the serpent said to the woman. ⁵ "In fact, God knows that when you eat it your eyes will be opened and you will be like God, knowing good and evil." ⁶ The woman saw that the tree was good for food and delightful to look at, and that it was desirable for obtaining wisdom. So she took some of its fruit and ate it; she also gave some to her husband, who was with her, and he ate it. ⁷ Then the eyes of both of them were opened, and they knew they were naked; so they sewed fig leaves together and made coverings for themselves.

⁸ Then the man and his wife heard the sound of the LORD God walking in the garden at the time of the evening breeze, and they hid from the LORD God among the trees of the garden. ⁹ So the LORD God called out to the man and said to him, "Where are you?"

¹⁰ And he said, "I heard you in the garden, and I was afraid because I was naked, so I hid."

¹¹ Then he asked, "Who told you that you were naked? Did you eat from the tree that I commanded you not to eat from?"

¹² The man replied, "The woman you gave to be with me — she gave me some fruit from the tree, and I ate."

¹³ So the LORD God asked the woman, "What is this you have done?" And the woman said, "The serpent deceived me, and I ate."

¹⁴ So the LORD God said to the serpent:

Because you have done this,
you are cursed more than any livestock
and more than any wild animal.
You will move on your belly
and eat dust all the days of your life.
¹⁵ I will put hostility between you and the woman,
and between your offspring and her offspring.
He will strike your head,
and you will strike his heel.

¹⁶ He said to the woman:

I will intensify your labor pains;
you will bear children with painful effort.
Your desire will be for your husband,
yet he will rule over you.

¹⁷ And he said to the man, "Because you listened to your wife and ate from the tree about which I commanded you, 'Do not eat from it':

The ground is cursed because of you.
You will eat from it by means of painful labor
all the days of your life.
¹⁸ It will produce thorns and thistles for you,
and you will eat the plants of the field.
¹⁹ You will eat bread by the sweat of your brow
until you return to the ground,
since you were taken from it.
For you are dust,
and you will return to dust."

²⁰ The man named his wife Eve because she was the mother of all the living. ²¹ The Lord God made clothing from skins for the man and his wife, and he clothed them.

²² The Lord God said, "Since the man has become like one of us, knowing good and evil, he must not reach out, take from the tree of life, eat, and live forever." ²³ So the Lord God sent him away from the garden of Eden to work the ground from which he was taken. ²⁴ He drove the man out and stationed the cherubim and the flaming, whirling sword east of the garden of Eden to guard the way to the tree of life.

2

When Everything Broke— Including You
Genesis 3

Genesis 1 leaves us with the sense that all is right with the world. God viewed the extent and expanse of his creation and stated his opinion that it was "very good" (v. 31). God didn't consider creation to be "good enough." Creation wasn't completed with an attitude that "this will do for now." Rather, God was delighted with all he had accomplished. He might well have said, "It can't get any better than this!"

I have a friend who is a gifted artist, specifically a painter. Over a period of months, he'll work, rework, and retouch a canvas. Then the day arrives when he senses that nothing of value can be added to the canvas, and to subtract anything would only diminish the work's impact. The eye of the artist is finally satisfied. So it was with the canvas of creation at the close of Genesis 1. It was all very good!

Imagine, if you can, a world with no pain, sickness, disease, discomfort, hunger, injustice, or death. This was the world God

originally intended. The universe operated exactly as God planned.
What for us is imagination, for God was original intent. Creation
was in perfect alignment with its Creator.

Obviously something went horribly wrong.

Genesis 3 is an account of a catastrophe. This chapter gives us
the framework to understand the perpetual pain of our planet. If
you've ever sensed that *something is not quite right* with the world,
Genesis 3 confirms your hunch. The Bible gives us a front-row seat
as evil enters the human experience.

God's commands to the first humans were simple: "Live. Take
care of things. Reproduce. The one tree in the middle of the garden
… don't eat from it!" Genesis 3 highlights something we'll find to
be true of the rest of the Bible: most of God's commands are simple and direct. (We'll see this again in the Ten Commandments.)
Our greatest challenge with God's commands isn't understanding
them but obeying them.

Genesis 3 also gives us our first exposure to the idea that evil
is personal. As there is a personal good—a personal God of the
universe—there also exists a personal evil. Satan is God's—and
our—ultimate enemy. The first description of the Devil found
in the Bible is the word *cunning* (v. 1). Satan's craftiness came
in the form of a question, the first question in recorded history:
"Did God really say, 'You can't eat from any tree in the garden'?"
(v. 1). With this question Satan managed to raise doubt as to the
goodness of God and the clarity of his commands. *Are you sure
you understood God correctly? If God really loves you, why would he
withhold anything from you?*

The story of Adam and Eve is our story as well. In fact, original sin is strikingly unoriginal. Disobedience to God follows a predictable pattern. As it was for Adam and Eve, so it is for you and me. Notice the oft-repeated cycle of sin.

First, there is temptation. It's worth noting that temptation rarely comes in the same way twice. Satan rationalized with Eve. He negotiated and finagled until she gave in. By contrast, Adam, who demonstrates little by way of impulse control, needed little convincing. His compromise appears almost instantaneous. The Devil tempted Eve directly, while he tempted Adam through the agency of Eve. Whereas Eve needed a debate, Adam was a pushover.

Second, the cycle of sin involves the act of disobedience itself. As a pastor, I field a frequent question: Are all sins the same, or are some sins worse than others? My answer is yes and no.

The Bible teaches that all sins are equally evil. Disobedience to God is disobedience, regardless of the specific details. However, some sins are worse than others in terms of their consequences. Gossip, for instance, can destroy a reputation, but murder destroys a life. Therefore, all sins are the same because all sins are opposite God's will, but some sins are worse in terms of outcome.

Following the first two acts in the cycle of sin is the grand finale of the blame game. Adam not only blamed Eve, but he also incriminated God: "The woman *you* gave to be with me—she gave me some fruit from the tree, and I ate" (v. 12). Adam seemed incapable of taking responsibility for his own actions (sound familiar?). Eve, in like fashion, attempted to blame the serpent: "The serpent deceived me, and I ate" (v. 13).

This sin cycle of temptation, disobedience, and blame is a predictable pattern we mindlessly repeat our entire lives. Have you ever had a strong desire for something you knew to be wrong, but try as you may, you could not resist it? Have you ever questioned God's character and commands, all the while knowing his ways are always best? Have you ever reacted to your own failures by claiming the real fault belonged to someone else? Only when we take responsibility for our decisions and actions do we open ourselves to God's forgiveness and restoration.

Adam and Eve's problem with evil affects us all. Genesis 3 doesn't merely record Adam and Eve's fall into sin. The chapter also highlights the failure of the entire human race to live up to God's original intent of an intimate, obedient relationship with him. Adam and Eve were damaged goods, a trait they passed on to us.

For centuries the largest man-made object on our planet was the Great Wall of China. Today that honor belongs to the Fresh Kills Landfill located on Staten Island, New York. Before its closure in 2001, Fresh Kills was receiving as much as twenty-nine thousand tons of trash each day. The heaps of trash cover thousands of acres with one mound standing some five hundred feet high, making it almost two hundred feet taller than the Statue of Liberty.[1]

It's been speculated that Fresh Kills holds the body of Jimmy Hoffa, but the only confirmed corpse is that of an elephant. In 1995, the Environmental Protection Agency (EPA) estimated that the Fresh Kills Landfill was responsible for generating close to 2 percent of global methane emissions.[2]

Isn't it telling that the largest man-made item on our planet is a pile of garbage? The point is clear: humans have made a mess of God's creation. What is more, we've made a mess of our own lives. This is the truth of Genesis 3, and that truth lingers even today.

We've mindlessly mutilated the world God intended to reflect his majesty. Sin has affected and infected every area of life. You won't be able to find one area that has escaped sin's negative impact. Power struggles, manipulation, and suspicion mark our relationships (v. 16). Work is more difficult because of sin (v. 17). Sin has shattered the perfect alignment of creation (v. 18). And not to be overlooked, the most devastating result of sin was the introduction of death into God's created order (v. 19). Anyone who has dealt with the death of a loved one will tell you that the event feels unnatural. That's because it is! God created us to experience unlimited life. Instead, we've settled for disobedience and its irreversible consequence, death.

Yet even amid the devastation and depression of Genesis 3, there is hope. God walked through the garden in search of the humans in hiding. When confronted and questioned, Adam replied, "I was afraid" (v. 10). Humans respond to fear in one of three predicable ways: we flee, fight, or hide. By running, we try to escape the fear. In fighting, we attempt to overpower our fear. When we hide, we admit the problem won't go away, so *we* try to go away. Consumed with the fear of being found disobedient, Adam and Eve hid from God, hoping to avoid his penetrating gaze.

Which tactic are you using to avoid God today? Are you running from him? Are you wrestling with God for ultimate control of your life? Or are you simply in hiding?

Whatever your tactic, God's presence in the garden sends us a clear message: God hasn't left us alone in our brokenness. He continues to search for hiding humans even today.

FOR REFLECTION

Over the course of history, Christian leaders produced a list called the Seven Deadly Sins. While this list isn't found in the Bible, there is wisdom in listening to the voices of the past. These sins are capable of causing incredible damage to our lives and destruction to our relationship with God. The Seven Deadly Sins are pride, lust, greed, gluttony, envy, anger, and sloth.

Which of these sins is the greatest source of temptation in your life? What excuses do you make for not ridding your life of this sin? What stands in the way of you taking responsibility for your actions and opening yourself to God's restoration?

Genesis 6

¹ When mankind began to multiply on the earth and daughters were born to them, ² the sons of God saw that the daughters of mankind were beautiful, and they took any they chose as wives for themselves. ³ And the LORD said, "My Spirit will not remain with mankind forever, because they are corrupt. Their days will be 120 years." ⁴ The Nephilim were on the earth both in those days and afterward, when the sons of God came to the daughters of mankind, who bore children to them. They were the powerful men of old, the famous men.

⁵ When the LORD saw that human wickedness was widespread on the earth and that every inclination of the human mind was nothing but evil all the time, ⁶ the LORD regretted that he had made man on the earth, and he was deeply grieved. ⁷ Then the LORD said, "I will wipe mankind, whom I created, off the face of the earth, together with the animals, creatures that crawl, and birds of the sky — for I regret that I made them." ⁸ Noah, however, found favor with the LORD.

⁹ These are the family records of Noah. Noah was a righteous man, blameless among his contemporaries; Noah walked with God. ¹⁰ And Noah fathered three sons: Shem, Ham, and Japheth.

¹¹ Now the earth was corrupt in God's sight, and the earth was filled with wickedness. ¹² God saw how corrupt the earth was, for every creature had corrupted its way on the earth. ¹³ Then God said to Noah, "I have decided to put an end to every creature, for the earth is filled with wickedness because of them; therefore I am going to destroy them along with the earth.

¹⁴ "Make yourself an ark of gopher wood. Make rooms in the ark, and cover it with pitch inside and outside. ¹⁵ This is how you are to make it: The ark will be 450 feet long, 75 feet wide, and 45 feet high. ¹⁶ You are to make a roof, finishing the sides of the ark to within eighteen inches of the roof. You are to put a door in the side of the ark. Make it with lower, middle, and upper decks.

¹⁷ "Understand that I am bringing a flood — floodwaters on the earth to destroy every creature under heaven with the breath of life in it. Everything on earth will perish. ¹⁸ But I will establish my covenant with you, and you will enter the ark with your sons, your wife, and your sons' wives. ¹⁹ You are also to bring into the ark two of all

the living creatures, male and female, to keep them alive with you. ²⁰ Two of everything — from the birds according to their kinds, from the livestock according to their kinds, and from the animals that crawl on the ground according to their kinds — will come to you so that you can keep them alive. ²¹ Take with you every kind of food that is eaten; gather it as food for you and for them." ²² And Noah did this. He did everything that God had commanded him.

3

Staying Afloat in Troubled Times
Genesis 6

When my wife and I were first married, we agreed on the importance of travel. Neither of us traveled much growing up, and we felt the poorer for it. So for two decades now, we've lived modestly in order to travel extravagantly. Once we've successfully saved for a trip, we're off! Our adventures have included a few months in Europe, time in Israel, a brief excursion to northern Africa, and countless expeditions across the Americas. For our family, travel is the perfect combination of education and entertainment. We learn so much, and we have fun doing it.

And then there are the cruises. I have to admit I was skeptical at first. I couldn't imagine a ship large enough to keep me from feeling confined. But after our first voyage, I was won over. The food, the dancing, the excursions, and the ability to sleep in the same bed every night made for the perfect blend of adventure and predictability.

Genesis 6 tells the story of a ship. But make no mistake; this was no pleasure cruise. For Noah, the man at the center of the story, these unprecedented events were on the extreme edge of adventure and offered no predictability or entertainment. Yet they taught Noah the greatest lessons of his life.

The story that begins in Genesis 6 is one many children learn from an early age. Some adults find it hard to consider plausible or even possible. It's difficult to imagine a ship large enough to hold the variety of animals Noah was commissioned to rescue. Not that I would dare speak for God, but perhaps accounts of this kind are in the Bible to remind us of his unlimited power and the possibilities he offers. He is in no way limited by what I believe is possible.

The story opens not with the roar of floodwaters or the crash of waves but with a moan. The earth was overgrown with evil. Genesis 6:6 says, "The LORD regretted" that he had made humanity. The word for "regret" is the Hebrew word meaning "to sigh." We can all identify with what God must have felt. Have you ever cared for someone so deeply that you hurt when that person made wrong choices? You might even have sighed because you cared more about the consequences than the other person did.

In his grief, however, God noticed Noah.

Noah lived a different kind of life. While the rest of the world was sinking, Noah was on the rise. While society wasted away, Noah's integrity gained strength. "Noah was a righteous man, blameless among his contemporaries; Noah walked with God" (v. 9). What an impressive description! We would do well to emulate Noah.

Noah's relationship with God was summed up in the word *righteous*. Although it sounds spiritual, this word is quite simple. Remove the suffix *-eous*, and the word *right* is readily revealed. Noah lived in right relationship with God.

Blameless summed up Noah's relationship with others. As wicked as the culture around Noah was, people couldn't help but acknowledge this man's good reputation and solid character.

Journalist Philip Elmer-DeWitt said, "Some people make headlines while others make history." Noah made history because he determined to be a man who lived in right relationship with God and in blameless relationships with others. Noah personified the greatest commands in the Bible. The most important commands, which Moses originally uttered and Jesus himself echoed and endorsed, are simply these: "Love the Lord your God with all your heart, with all your soul, with all your mind, and with all your strength. The second is, Love your neighbor as yourself. There is no other command greater than these" (Mark 12:30–31). Righteous before God and blameless among others—Noah embodied the essence of how a Jesus follower does relationships.

Genesis 6 teaches several powerful truths we would do well to apply to our lives. First, we capture a glimpse of *authentic obedience* in this chapter. In fact, Genesis 6 ends with the sentence, "[Noah] did everything that God had commanded him" (v. 22). The writer of the New Testament book of Hebrews applauded Noah for his obedience, which was evidence of his faith: "By faith Noah, after he was warned about what was not yet seen and motivated by godly fear, built an ark to deliver his family" (11:7).

Noah's story dispels the common myth that obedience to God makes our lives easier. Noah faced the overwhelming task of building a ship greater in length than a football field. No doubt the task of shipbuilding proved frustrating and at times overwhelming. If you've ever built an object of any size, you know that construction rarely stays on schedule or within budget. The wishful thinking that following Christ automatically makes the rest of life convenient is a cultural concept, not a biblical one. But be assured, while following God may be hard at times, it's the best decision you'll ever make.

The Scriptures are sprinkled with people living in obedience who also faced the greatest challenges of their lives. Daniel in the lions' den, Jeremiah in the bottom of a cistern, Paul in a jail cell, and Jesus on a cross are only a few of the many examples. Obedience doesn't translate into an easy life, but it's essential for a life well lived.

Second, the story of the flood (which continues through Genesis 9) is a profound picture of community. The word *ark* used in Genesis 6 was a word the Hebrew-speaking people borrowed from the Egyptian language. *Ark* has a subtlety of meaning that can be understood in two very different ways. First, it can mean "palace." When floodwaters rise, any dry boat will feel like luxury accommodations. Second, *ark* can also be understood as "coffin." Noah's ark was a big box, containing eight family members who lived together in tight quarters for more than a year. Yes, *coffin* comes to mind.

Such is the reality of community. In the floodwaters of life, people are a palace. But at the same time, the very people we love most will also demand our greatest patience. Community can make us feel like the wealthiest people alive and, at the same time, claustrophobic from close contact. The truth is that while community resembles both a palace and a coffin, Christ followers need community to stay afloat in the floodwaters of life.

A fitting example is the fire ant. Despite our dislike of them, fire ants exemplify the value of community. They're nearly impossible to drown because they've learned to stick together. If fire ants invade your yard, don't bother with the water hose. These aggressive ants have developed a response to rising water from their species' experience of surviving Amazonian flash floods. Fire ants link their bodies together to form a living life raft. Connected by jaws and claws, their bodies form a superstructure that can remain buoyant for weeks.[1] Evidence suggests that if one ant attempts to abandon ship, the others will forcibly hold the would-be defector in place to improve the group's chances of survival.[2]

What a picture of community! Whether we sink or swim in life may very well depend on the people we're connected to. We even hold on to those who try to slip away. We stay afloat by staying together.

Finally, Genesis 6 gives us a glimpse of trust. In the details of constructing the ark, notice the one part left out that is standard for outfitting boats: the rudder. The ark was designed to drift, not for Noah to navigate. Noah and his family put themselves fully into the hands of God. And perhaps this is the grand lesson we can take from Noah's great challenge. We may not always be able to fix the problems that present themselves to us, but it is always wise to surrender ourselves to the care of God.

FOR REFLECTION

When John F. Kennedy was president, among the items on the Oval Office desk was a coconut paperweight. During World War II, Japanese forces hit his PT-109 boat. Stranded in the Solomon Islands, Kennedy carved an SOS message on this coconut and gave it to two natives to deliver to a nearby base. That coconut is a reminder that there are times when we all need to be rescued. Noah's rescue was the result of simple trust in God, who provided the ark to save Noah and his family.

How do you need God to rescue you today? Even if you feel adrift, it's all right to ask God for his help. Have you asked? Once you do, wait in simple trust for God's response.

Genesis 12

¹ The LORD said to Abram:

Go out from your land,
your relatives,
and your father's house
to the land that I will show you.
² I will make you into a great nation,
I will bless you,
I will make your name great,
and you will be a blessing.
³ I will bless those who bless you,
I will curse anyone who treats you with contempt,
and all the peoples on earth
will be blessed through you.

⁴ So Abram went, as the LORD had told him, and Lot went with him. Abram was seventy-five years old when he left Haran. ⁵ He took his wife Sarai, his nephew Lot, all the possessions they had accumulated, and the people they had acquired in Haran, and they set out for the land of Canaan. When they came to the land of Canaan, ⁶ Abram passed through the land to the site of Shechem, at the oak of Moreh. (At that time the Canaanites were in the land.) ⁷ The LORD appeared to Abram and said, "To your offspring I will give this land." So he built an altar there to the LORD who had appeared to him. ⁸ From there he moved on to the hill country east of Bethel and pitched his tent, with Bethel on the west and Ai on the east. He built an altar to the LORD there, and he called on the name of the LORD. ⁹ Then Abram journeyed by stages to the Negev.

¹⁰ There was a famine in the land, so Abram went down to Egypt to stay there for a while because the famine in the land was severe. ¹¹ When he was about to enter Egypt, he said to his wife Sarai, "Look, I know what a beautiful woman you are. ¹² When the Egyptians see you, they will say, 'This is his wife.' They will kill me but let you live. ¹³ Please say you're my sister so it will go well for me because of you, and my life will be spared on your account." ¹⁴ When Abram entered Egypt, the Egyptians saw that the woman was very beautiful. ¹⁵ Pharaoh's officials saw her and praised her to Pharaoh, so the woman was taken to Pharaoh's household. ¹⁶ He

treated Abram well because of her, and Abram acquired flocks and herds, male and female donkeys, male and female slaves, and camels.

[17] But the LORD struck Pharaoh and his household with severe plagues because of Abram's wife Sarai. [18] So Pharaoh sent for Abram and said, "What have you done to me? Why didn't you tell me she was your wife? [19] Why did you say, 'She's my sister,' so that I took her as my wife? Now, here is your wife. Take her and go!" [20] Then Pharaoh gave his men orders about him, and they sent him away with his wife and all he had.

4

Faith Isn't Safe
Genesis 12

In the pages of the Bible, four personalities rise head and shoulders above all others. Imagine Mount Rushmore with its four faces of Presidents Washington, Jefferson, Lincoln, and Roosevelt. If we could carve a "Mount Rushmore of Scripture," the obvious choices would be Abraham, Moses, David, and Jesus. To comprehend the Bible, it's essential that we understand and appreciate the lives of these four men.

Genesis 12 gives us an introduction to the first of these pivotal personalities—Abram, whom God later renamed Abraham. Living some two thousand years before Christ, Abraham was as far on the before-Jesus side of history as we live on the after-Jesus side.

Abraham's home was Ur of the Chaldeans, located in what we call Iraq today. From what we can tell from ancient records and remains, Ur was a city of about three hundred thousand people. A megacity in its day, Ur was the center of finance, culture, art, and commerce for all of Mesopotamia.

Ur of the Chaldeans was part of the ancient Sumerian culture. Many historians credit the Sumerians with developing the first written language and for one of the oldest recorded recipes on the planet—beer. Besides being a social drink, beer was a useful way to preserve grain. Abraham came from this educated and sophisticated society. People viewed Ur as we would view New York City or Los Angeles in our day—trendy, metropolitan, and the place to be. But God asked Abraham to leave it all behind, proving yet again that following God means putting aside our tendencies to play it safe.

Linguists tell us that the most powerful word in any language is *home*. Home has an emotional, mental, and almost physical pull on our lives. In contrast, God's command to Abraham was "*Go.*" Challenge, not comfort, is the lifestyle of those who wish to follow God.

The best way to capture the essence of Abraham's life and lifestyle is with the label *faith*. When God invites us into the adventure of following him, he rarely tells us where we'll end up. The only way to discover the end of the story is to take the first step.

Consider the African impala. Despite its amazing ability to leap thirteen feet high, a zookeeper can keep it contained behind a small three-foot wall. Zookeepers know the impala will refuse to jump if it can't see where its feet will land.[1] We all have the instincts of the impala. "Look before you leap," we're taught. But the faith Abraham modeled shows us that once we've heard clearly from God, we are to leap and leave the looking up to him.

New Testament writers applauded Abraham for being a model of faith. James 2:23 says that "Abraham believed God, and it was

credited to him as righteousness, and he was called God's friend."
Romans 4:20–21 adds, "[Abraham] did not waver in unbelief at
God's promise but was strengthened in his faith and gave glory to
God, because he was fully convinced that what God had promised,
he was also able to do."

Also not to be overlooked is Abraham's age. Seventy-five is
hardly the age we think of when it comes to starting over (Gen.
12:4). It seems we never retire from the plans or purposes of God.
As long as he gives us breath, God asks for our obedience.

God responds to the faith in our lives with rewards called *blessings*. Genesis 12:2–3 details the blessing of God on Abraham's life.
In fact, there wasn't just one blessing but seven. The initial blessing
was "I will make you into a great nation" (v. 2). From our perspective four thousand years postpromise, we can see the fulfillment
of this statement. Nearly half of the people on our planet look to
Abraham as a father figure. Not only do nearly 14 million Jews
claim Abraham as their physical ancestor, but an additional 1.6
billion Muslims and more than 2 billion Christians see Abraham
as a spiritual ancestor.

These blessings bestowed on Abraham weren't given for selfish
purposes. The end result was that "all the peoples on earth [would]
be blessed through [him]" (v. 3). How is this even possible? It
seems unimaginable that one person could affect an entire planet.

Again, with the advantage of four thousand years of history,
we see the fuller picture. From one man named Abraham, a nation
would rise: the Jewish people. From this nation would emerge the
pivotal person of history, Jesus Christ. Through him would come

the hope of salvation for the planet through a restored relationship with God. And this gift is offered to all the people of the world! Promise kept.

If you take the time to read and reflect on the rest of Abraham's biography, you quickly discover that he was a deeply flawed individual. In fact, you won't make it out of Genesis 12 without seeing Abraham's compulsion to lie. His life was pot-holed with errors and inconsistencies. More than once Abraham disobeyed God and disappointed the people closest to him. This man of faith also tended to repeat the same mistakes over and over. Does this remind you of anyone? Perhaps yourself?

Our faith doesn't instantly free us from our faults. The promises of God over our lives don't translate into instant perfection. The standard we live by as we follow God isn't immediate perfection but continual progress. To remain in the struggle against sin is a winning strategy. To continue to strive and refuse to settle is the pattern of people making headway in their relationship with God.

Faith is anything but safe. As I write these words, a close friend lingers near death in a hospital. The trial of his life is marked with risks and restarts. Originally educated as a chemist, he left his first profession to pursue pastoral ministry. After starting two churches from scratch, both of which still thrive today, he again changed the direction of his life and became a professor. On more than one occasion, my friend intentionally uprooted his life from Ur. He never became so comfortable that he was unwilling to listen to God and lift his foot in response to the command to go. Now my friend's heart is simply giving out. It's ironic, since his life has been all heart—a heart wide open to God's fresh direction.

What a way to live! May we always endeavor to step out in faith, allowing God to lead us to a country on the far side of complacency. Playwright Neil Simon stated it well: "If no one ever took risks, Michelangelo would have painted the Sistine [Chapel's] floor." Following God involves taking chances. Blessings await us on the far side of risk. And it all begins with faith, which is anything but safe.

FOR REFLECTION

Abraham was a model of stepping out in faith. As we take steps to follow God, we grow in our friendship with him. In what way is God currently prompting you to step out in faith and trust him?

Consider Hebrews 11:6: "Without faith it is impossible to please God, since the one who draws near to him must believe that he exists and that he rewards those who seek him."

Genesis 22

¹ After these things God tested Abraham and said to him, "Abraham!"
"Here I am," he answered.

² "Take your son," he said, "your only son Isaac, whom you love, go to the land of Moriah, and offer him there as a burnt offering on one of the mountains I will tell you about."

³ So Abraham got up early in the morning, saddled his donkey, and took with him two of his young men and his son Isaac. He split wood for a burnt offering and set out to go to the place God had told him about. ⁴ On the third day Abraham looked up and saw the place in the distance. ⁵ Then Abraham said to his young men, "Stay here with the donkey. The boy and I will go over there to worship; then we'll come back to you." ⁶ Abraham took the wood for the burnt offering and laid it on his son Isaac. In his hand he took the fire and the knife, and the two of them walked on together.

⁷ Then Isaac spoke to his father Abraham and said, "My father."
And he replied, "Here I am, my son."
Isaac said, "The fire and the wood are here, but where is the lamb for the burnt offering?"

⁸ Abraham answered, "God himself will provide the lamb for the burnt offering, my son." Then the two of them walked on together.

⁹ When they arrived at the place that God had told him about, Abraham built the altar there and arranged the wood. He bound his son Isaac and placed him on the altar on top of the wood. ¹⁰ Then Abraham reached out and took the knife to slaughter his son.

¹¹ But the angel of the LORD called to him from heaven and said, "Abraham, Abraham!"
He replied, "Here I am."

¹² Then he said, "Do not lay a hand on the boy or do anything to him. For now I know that you fear God, since you have not withheld your only son from me." ¹³ Abraham looked up and saw a ram caught in the thicket by its horns. So Abraham went and took the ram and offered it as a burnt offering in place of his son. ¹⁴ And Abraham named that place The LORD Will Provide, so today it is said: "It will be provided on the LORD's mountain."

¹⁵ Then the angel of the LORD called to Abraham a second time from heaven ¹⁶ and said, "By myself I have sworn," this is the LORD's declaration: "Because you have done this thing and have not withheld your only son,

¹⁷ I will indeed bless you and make your offspring as numerous as the stars of the sky and the sand on the seashore. Your offspring will possess the city gates of their enemies. ¹⁸ And all the nations of the earth will be blessed by your offspring because you have obeyed my command."

¹⁹ Abraham went back to his young men, and they got up and went together to Beer-sheba. And Abraham settled in Beer-sheba.

²⁰ Now after these things Abraham was told, "Milcah also has borne sons to your brother Nahor: ²¹ Uz his firstborn, his brother Buz, Kemuel the father of Aram, ²² Chesed, Hazo, Pildash, Jidlaph, and Bethuel." ²³ And Bethuel fathered Rebekah. Milcah bore these eight to Nahor, Abraham's brother. ²⁴ His concubine, whose name was Reumah, also bore Tebah, Gaham, Tahash, and Maacah.

5

When God Asks Too Much
Genesis 22

The words that open Genesis 22 make a strong impression: "After these things God tested Abraham" (v. 1). These words, like the musical score of a movie, signal that something ominous is about to take place. What does it mean that God would test Abraham? And if God tested him, does that mean God might possibly test you and me?

The only survivor of a shipwreck washed up on a small, uninhabited island. Daily he cried out to God for rescue. The man built a small hut to protect himself from the elements. One day while he searched for food, his lean-to caught fire and was instantly engulfed in flames. The man was struck with grief, feeling anger toward God and pity for himself. Early the next morning, a ship drew near the island and rescued the man. When he asked how he had been found, the captain was surprised. "We saw your smoke signal yesterday," he offered, "and knew where to find you." God's testing is often his way of helping us, even if we don't fully appreciate it at the time.

In Genesis 22, God had begun to make good on his promise to produce from Abraham a great nation. By giving Abraham a child, God started the process of creating a nation from one man. Isaac was the long-awaited promise of God. Isaac himself would have two sons, Jacob and Esau. Jacob, in turn, would have twelve sons, who would become the fathers of the twelve tribes of Israel. Abraham, Isaac, and Jacob are collectively called the patriarchs.

No surprise, then, that Abraham must have found it difficult to reconcile God's promises with his command to sacrifice Isaac on a makeshift altar. From a logical point of view, God was asking too much.

As Isaac lay waiting for the knife in his father's hand to complete its task, God stopped Abraham and showed him a ram caught in a nearby thicket. The ram replaced Isaac on the altar and spared his life. As a result of this test of obedience, Abraham's understanding of God was expanded, and he "named that place The LORD Will Provide, so today it is said: 'It will be provided on the LORD's mountain'" (v. 14). The Hebrew phrase for "The LORD Will Provide" is *Jehovah Jireh*—a name for God well known to those who have experienced his provision in their own times of need.

What we find in Genesis 22 reveals at least two lessons of true faithfulness. The first is this: Abraham valued obeying God more than he valued understanding him. Think about the way we're naturally inclined to pray in uncertain and confusing times. Most often we find ourselves wanting God to make sense of the events around us. *Help me understand,* we plead with God. Perhaps it's time we take a cue from Abraham, a master of faith, and put our focus and energy into obedience rather than comprehension.

In the late 1990s, I served on a humanitarian-aid team that traveled to the Communist island of Cuba. Midway through the trip, I received a message that an emergency had occurred at home. When I finally succeeded in reaching my wife by telephone, I learned she had lost the baby we were expecting. My instinct was to fly home immediately to be near my wife. However, plane schedules and visa restrictions didn't work in my favor. My only alternative was to stay in Cuba and somehow remain engaged in the efforts at hand. I didn't understand God or his timing. I felt as though he was asking too much of me. My only alternative was to obey.

Never before had I felt so helpless. But I'm forever grateful for what my wife and I experienced in those days of our forced separation. A community of friends rallied around her, taking her to the doctor, babysitting our daughter, and providing food and comfort. My handful of friends in Cuba circled around me, steadying my stride as we walked through what remained of our task. My own sense of self-sufficiency was shattered. But what replaced it was something stronger: the power of community when circumstances were heavier than my ability to handle them. In my own family, we experienced *Jehovah Jireh*.

Are you willing to obey God even when—especially when— you don't understand what he is doing? When your answer to this question is a wholehearted yes, only then have you begun to experience the true essence of faith.

The second lesson of true faithfulness is the ongoing challenge to recognize the distinction between God and his gifts. While it's right and good to appreciate God for the good things he brings into our lives, it's vital that we worship the Giver and not the gifts themselves.

Here's a challenging question worth serious consideration: Would you love God and serve him even if he took from you every gift and blessing? If your only reward were God himself, would you still choose to be faithful?

One Christian thinker from the Middle Ages boldly admitted that humans are tempted to love God in the same way they love a cow. He said, "You love a cow for her milk and her cheese and your own profit. That is what all those men do who love God for outward wealth or inward consolation—and they do not truly love God, they love their own profit."[1] A more modern understanding of this idea would be to say that many love God as they love their cars. We love our cars as long as they are stylish and convenient and get us from point A to point B. To love God only for his gifts is, at best, a fickle faith. To love him whether we experience his gifts or not is a deep and full faith.

God will test each of us. He will test you. Be sure of it. God will bring into your life situations, strains, people, and events to challenge the development of your character and to test the resolve of your trust in him. By contrast, Satan's work is best described as temptation. The Devil's aim is to magnify the worst parts of your character and distract you from God.

It's important to keep the distinction between God's tests and Satan's temptations clear in our minds. Testing is God's method of bringing out our best, while tempting is Satan's method of reducing us to our worst. The New Testament addresses this distinction in James 1:13: "No one undergoing a trial should say, 'I am being tempted by God,' since God is not tempted by evil, and he himself doesn't tempt anyone."

In Bill Frey's book *The Dance of Hope*, he tells of a friend named John who was a classmate at the University of Colorado in the 1950s. An accident as a teenager left him both blind and bitter. He had given up hope. Finally John's father, fed up with his son's perpetual pity party, reminded him of the impending winter. He then ordered his blind son to put the storm windows on the house. He told John to get the job done before he got home or else. The father then left the room, slamming the door behind him.

John's rage boiled. Muttering curses, he felt his way through the house until he found the garage. Tools in hand, he mounted the stepladder. As he ascended, he found himself thinking, *[My dad will] be sorry when I fall off the ladder and break my neck.* But John didn't fall. Inch by inch he managed to put the storm windows in place. His father's plan worked. If he could install the storm windows, perhaps he could piece his life back together.

John discovered years later that at no time during that day was his father ever more than a few feet from his side.[2] John's father wasn't about to let his son fall. In the same way, our God, our Father, is our provider even today. *Jehovah Jireh.*

God isn't stingy. He doesn't delight in depriving us of good things. We need not view God's gifts as something to be pried from his closed hand. Instead, God opens his palms and provides all we need in life, beginning with our relationship with him.

In Genesis 22:12, God described Abraham accurately when he said, "Now I know that you fear God, since you have not withheld your only son from me." The event took place on Mount Moriah, predating the life of Jesus by two thousand years. It would be on another mountaintop two millennia later that another "only Son" would not be withheld. Ultimately, God's Son would be the sacrifice of the ages and for all eternity.

"It will be provided on the LORD's mountain" indeed.

FOR REFLECTION

Sacrifice is an important concept in the Bible. Abraham was willing to sacrifice his son Isaac as an act of obedience. Later in the Older Testament, an entire system of sacrifice was established to deal with the sins of the people. Ultimately, out of love God would sacrifice his Son, Jesus, for the salvation of humanity. In turn we're asked to sacrifice nothing less than our whole selves to God for his use. The apostle Paul brings the challenge to us in these words: "Therefore, brothers and sisters, in view of the mercies of God, I urge you to present your bodies as a living sacrifice, holy and pleasing to God; this is your true worship" (Rom. 12:1).

What is God asking you to sacrifice on his behalf today? What is one practical way you can move away from selfishness toward surrender to him and his purposes?

GOD IS GOOD WHEN LIFE GETS MESSY

Exodus 3

¹ Meanwhile, Moses was shepherding the flock of his father-in-law Jethro, the priest of Midian. He led the flock to the far side of the wilderness and came to Horeb, the mountain of God. ² Then the angel of the LORD appeared to him in a flame of fire within a bush. As Moses looked, he saw that the bush was on fire but was not consumed. ³ So Moses thought, "I must go over and look at this remarkable sight. Why isn't the bush burning up?"

⁴ When the LORD saw that he had gone over to look, God called out to him from the bush, "Moses, Moses!"

"Here I am," he answered.

⁵ "Do not come closer," he said. "Remove the sandals from your feet, for the place where you are standing is holy ground." ⁶ Then he continued, "I am the God of your father, the God of Abraham, the God of Isaac, and the God of Jacob." Moses hid his face because he was afraid to look at God.

⁷ Then the LORD said, "I have observed the misery of my people in Egypt, and have heard them crying out because of their oppressors. I know about their sufferings, ⁸ and I have come down to rescue them from the power of the Egyptians and to bring them from that land to a good and spacious land, a land flowing with milk and honey — the territory of the Canaanites, Hethites, Amorites, Perizzites, Hivites, and Jebusites. ⁹ So because the Israelites' cry for help has come to me, and I have also seen the way the Egyptians are oppressing them, ¹⁰ therefore, go. I am sending you to Pharaoh so that you may lead my people, the Israelites, out of Egypt."

¹¹ But Moses asked God, "Who am I that I should go to Pharaoh and that I should bring the Israelites out of Egypt?"

¹² He answered, "I will certainly be with you, and this will be the sign to you that I am the one who sent you: when you bring the people out of Egypt, you will all worship God at this mountain."

¹³ Then Moses asked God, "If I go to the Israelites and say to them, 'The God of your fathers has sent me to you,' and they ask me, 'What is his name?' what should I tell them?"

¹⁴ God replied to Moses, "I AM WHO I AM. This is what you are to say to the Israelites: I AM has sent me to you." ¹⁵ God also said to Moses, "Say this to the Israelites: The LORD, the God of your fathers, the God of Abraham, the God of Isaac, and the God of Jacob, has sent me to you.

This is my name forever; this is how I am to be remembered in every generation.

¹⁶ "Go and assemble the elders of Israel and say to them: The LORD, the God of your fathers, the God of Abraham, Isaac, and Jacob, has appeared to me and said: I have paid close attention to you and to what has been done to you in Egypt. ¹⁷ And I have promised you that I will bring you up from the misery of Egypt to the land of the Canaanites, Hethites, Amorites, Perizzites, Hivites, and Jebusites — a land flowing with milk and honey. ¹⁸ They will listen to what you say. Then you, along with the elders of Israel, must go to the king of Egypt and say to him: The LORD, the God of the Hebrews, has met with us. Now please let us go on a three-day trip into the wilderness so that we may sacrifice to the LORD our God.

¹⁹ "However, I know that the king of Egypt will not allow you to go, even under force from a strong hand. ²⁰ But when I stretch out my hand and strike Egypt with all my miracles that I will perform in it, after that, he will let you go. ²¹ And I will give these people such favor with the Egyptians that when you go, you will not go empty-handed. ²² Each woman will ask her neighbor and any woman staying in her house for silver and gold jewelry, and clothing, and you will put them on your sons and daughters. So you will plunder the Egyptians."

6

On a First-Name Basis with God
Exodus 3

Have you ever met someone famous? Someone with a big name?

I've had only a few encounters with well-known people. Among my most memorable was a backstage meeting with Don Henley of the Eagles. I met Don (that's what I call him now, *Don*) in his dressing room before an Eagles concert. A friend of mine happens to know a friend of Henley's family. Phone calls were made and backstage passes were arranged. My friend gave me the gift of meeting my favorite musician.

As I shook Henley's hand, I was genuinely nervous. I thanked him for providing the music my wife and I first dated and danced to. He seemed genuinely pleased to meet a Baptist who professed to loving dance. (By the way, it isn't a sin to dance; it *is* a sin to dance poorly.)

Afterward I couldn't stop thinking about our encounter. I told everyone I knew about it. Even today I recount the experience to others who share my love of the Eagles. There's something about a brush with greatness that elevates our own sense of importance. Big names make us feel bigger.

Moses is one of the biggest names in the Bible. Yet he met a name infinitely superior. Before we talk about this encounter, we must review a bit of Moses's story. Moses's life can be sliced into three segments. His first forty years were spent in Egypt. Although he was a lower-class Hebrew by birth, Pharaoh's daughter adopted him, which meant he enjoyed a privileged place in Egyptian society. Because he enjoyed the advantages of education and wealth, the first third of Moses's life was spent in luxury and affluence.

The second era of Moses's life was inaugurated with a serious mistake—the murder of an Egyptian. After the incident, Moses fled from Egypt into exile. Forty years in the desert was a sharp contrast to his earlier life of ease. Only later would Moses realize that God used this time in exile to equip him for the challenges ahead. A valuable lesson for us all: just because life isn't to our liking doesn't mean it's without purpose.

Philip Yancey observed that "Moses ... spent half his life learning leadership skills from the ruling empire of the day and half his life learning wilderness survival skills while fleeing a murder rap."[1] Moses was then prepared for the final and most important phase of his life—the exodus from Egypt. The last era begins in Exodus 3, when he was no less than eighty years old.

The problem Moses faced began long before he was born. More than four hundred years earlier, the Israelite people—the promised descendants of Abraham—had migrated to Egypt to escape the worst of a severe famine. As the Israelites grew more and more numerous in their temporary home, the Egyptians became more and more concerned. Eventually they resorted to oppression to keep the Hebrews from overpowering them.

Yet God wasn't absent in the Hebrews' crisis. When Moses encountered God in the wilderness, the Lord told him that he had "observed" and "heard" and "[known] about their sufferings" (v. 7). For all of us, the temptation we face in the midst of suffering is thinking that God has abandoned us. Pain skews our ability to perceive God's presence. But Moses learned that God is close to his people and personally concerned about their difficulties.

Moses met God at a burning bush. Brush fires weren't uncommon in dry weather, and no doubt in forty years, Moses had witnessed his fair share. But this fire was different. The flames neither consumed the bush nor spread. As Moses approached the burning bush, he was commanded to remove his sandals.

This seemingly peculiar command was rich in meaning. In Moses's day, people didn't dress up when they went to worship God; instead they dressed down. When worshippers approached God, they wore only the bare necessities. The removal of garments symbolized a desire to eliminate pretense and pride. In truth, there is only one requirement for approaching God—authenticity.

Also, among ancient peoples, slaves weren't allowed to wear shoes. Having bare feet was a sign of servitude. Likewise,

God asks us to approach him as servants, ready to submit and surrender to his perfect will and love.

Moses discovered two things at the burning bush. First, and most important, he met a big name. He asked the Lord, "If I go to the Israelites and say to them, 'The God of your fathers has sent me to you,' and they ask me, 'What is his name?' what should I tell them?" (v. 13).

Most names are nouns. But the name God shared with Moses was derived from a verb: "I AM WHO I AM." The Hebrew term could also be translated as "I WILL BE WHO I WILL BE."

This strange name "I AM" at once reveals and conceals God's true identity. God's self-given name reinforces the reality that he is always working, acting, and moving. Also, God's name sets his true identity apart from human expectations. God is as he chooses to be, not as we might wish him to be. God is somehow deeper than our efforts to define him. His identity is eternal. No single name is big enough to capture his full character.

In fact, in the New Testament book of John, Jesus used the I AM name of God seven times to refer to himself:

I am the bread of life. (6:35)

I am the light of the world. (8:12)

I am the gate. (10:7)

I am the good shepherd. (10:14)

I am the resurrection and the life. (11:25)

I am the way, the truth, and the life. (14:6)

I am the vine. (15:5)

These titles reveal not only Jesus's abilities but also his identity as God.

The second thing Moses discovered at the burning bush was his own destiny. Contact with big names enlarges our world with a sense of grander purpose. After the first forty years in Egypt and the second forty years of exile, Moses would spend his final forty years leading an exodus—the deliverance of Hebrew slaves from Egyptian oppression. Moses discovered that God's name brings fresh perspective and the opening of new possibilities. Moses's lifelong adventure began with knowing God's name.

Our culture is obsessed with celebrity. Knowing big names is seen as proof of our importance. But here is a secret every Christ follower knows: all big names are nothing when compared with the name of God. We have the privilege of knowing our Creator, which brings a sense of determination and destiny to our lives. We can say with all confidence that we share an intimate friendship with the God of the universe!

FOR REFLECTION

The three eras of Moses's life help us understand our own lives. Moses spent forty years in Egypt (a period of ease), forty years in exile (a season of difficulty), and forty years leading the exodus (a time spent fulfilling his life's mission).

What season are you in right now? How might God be using the present to prepare you for your future? Whatever your season, realize that God is both present and at work in your life.

Exodus 14

¹ Then the LORD spoke to Moses: ² "Tell the Israelites to turn back and camp in front of Pi-hahiroth, between Migdol and the sea; you must camp in front of Baal-zephon, facing it by the sea. ³ Pharaoh will say of the Israelites: They are wandering around the land in confusion; the wilderness has boxed them in. ⁴ I will harden Pharaoh's heart so that he will pursue them. Then I will receive glory by means of Pharaoh and all his army, and the Egyptians will know that I am the LORD." So the Israelites did this.

⁵ When the king of Egypt was told that the people had fled, Pharaoh and his officials changed their minds about the people and said: "What have we done? We have released Israel from serving us." ⁶ So he got his chariot ready and took his troops with him; ⁷ he took six hundred of the best chariots and all the rest of the chariots of Egypt, with officers in each one. ⁸ The LORD hardened the heart of Pharaoh king of Egypt, and he pursued the Israelites, who were going out defiantly. ⁹ The Egyptians — all Pharaoh's horses and chariots, his horsemen, and his army — chased after them and caught up with them as they camped by the sea beside Pi-hahiroth, in front of Baal-zephon.

¹⁰ As Pharaoh approached, the Israelites looked up and there were the Egyptians coming after them! The Israelites were terrified and cried out to the LORD for help. ¹¹ They said to Moses: "Is it because there are no graves in Egypt that you have taken us away to die in the wilderness? What have you done to us by bringing us out of Egypt? ¹² Isn't this what we told you in Egypt: Leave us alone so that we may serve the Egyptians? It would have been better for us to serve the Egyptians than to die in the wilderness."

¹³ But Moses said to the people, "Don't be afraid. Stand firm and see the LORD's salvation that he will accomplish for you today; for the Egyptians you see today, you will never see again. ¹⁴ The LORD will fight for you, and you must be quiet."

¹⁵ The LORD said to Moses, "Why are you crying out to me? Tell the Israelites to break camp. ¹⁶ As for you, lift up your staff, stretch out your hand over the sea, and divide it so that the Israelites can go through the sea on dry ground. ¹⁷ As for me, I am going to harden the hearts of the Egyptians so that they will go in after them, and I will receive glory by

means of Pharaoh, all his army, and his chariots and horsemen. ¹⁸ The Egyptians will know that I am the LORD when I receive glory through Pharaoh, his chariots, and his horsemen."

¹⁹ Then the angel of God, who was going in front of the Israelite forces, moved and went behind them. The pillar of cloud moved from in front of them and stood behind them. ²⁰ It came between the Egyptian and Israelite forces. There was cloud and darkness, it lit up the night, and neither group came near the other all night long.

²¹ Then Moses stretched out his hand over the sea. The LORD drove the sea back with a powerful east wind all that night and turned the sea into dry land. So the waters were divided, ²² and the Israelites went through the sea on dry ground, with the waters like a wall to them on their right and their left.

²³ The Egyptians set out in pursuit — all Pharaoh's horses, his chariots, and his horsemen — and went into the sea after them. ²⁴ During the morning watch, the LORD looked down at the Egyptian forces from the pillar of fire and cloud, and threw the Egyptian forces into confusion. ²⁵ He caused their chariot wheels to swerve and made them drive with difficulty. "Let's get away from Israel," the Egyptians said, "because the LORD is fighting for them against Egypt!"

²⁶ Then the LORD said to Moses, "Stretch out your hand over the sea so that the water may come back on the Egyptians, on their chariots and horsemen." ²⁷ So Moses stretched out his hand over the sea, and at daybreak the sea returned to its normal depth. While the Egyptians were trying to escape from it, the LORD threw them into the sea. ²⁸ The water came back and covered the chariots and horsemen, plus the entire army of Pharaoh that had gone after them into the sea. Not even one of them survived.

²⁹ But the Israelites had walked through the sea on dry ground, with the waters like a wall to them on their right and their left. ³⁰ That day the LORD saved Israel from the power of the Egyptians, and Israel saw the Egyptians dead on the seashore. ³¹ When Israel saw the great power that the LORD used against the Egyptians, the people feared the LORD and believed in him and in his servant Moses.

7

When Life Seems Out to Get You
Exodus 14

Though the name Moses is of Egyptian origin, it sounds like the Hebrew for "drawing out." This refers to the circumstance when Pharaoh's daughter found Moses as a three-month-old baby, floating in a basket in the Nile River and "drew him out of the water" (Exod. 2:10). Moses's name takes on even greater meaning given the miracles he experienced in Exodus 14.

As it was for Moses, so it is for each of us: God's work in our lives defines who we are. William Carey, a nineteenth-century Jesus follower, is remembered for saying, "Expect great things from God; attempt great things for God."

Moses was no stranger to attempting great things. He courageously confronted the king of the Egyptians and demanded the release of the Israelite slaves. As Moses led the Israelites to freedom, the Egyptian king felt the panic that accompanies a poor political decision. He regretted releasing the slaves and dispatched his national guard to restore the Israelites to their shackled existence. Suddenly Moses and his people were trapped between an approaching army and an unyielding sea. Moses had attempted something great—freeing his people. Now it was time to expect God to do something even greater. And God didn't disappoint.

A key to interpreting and understanding Scripture is to notice words and phrases that repeat themselves. Exodus 14:4 says, "I [God] will harden Pharaoh's heart so that he will pursue [the Israelites]. Then I will receive glory by means of Pharaoh and all his army, and the Egyptians will know that I am the LORD." It is this profound message of "glory," repeated twice more in verses 17 and 18, that dominates Exodus 14.

Simply put, to glorify an individual is to enhance a person's reputation. Glorifying someone means to intentionally make that person look good. For example, my wife is one of the most organized people I've ever known. A manifestation of her organizational prowess is her method of Christmas shopping. After we develop our gift-giving budget, she goes to work to find the best deals for everyone on our Christmas list. On a single day, Black Friday, she purchases every gift on our list. Only the task of wrapping remains. I admire my wife's gift of organization. With this simple account, I hope I've succeeded in glorifying her in your mind and enhancing her reputation.

God's purpose in the events of Exodus 14 was to make himself look good. This wasn't the work of ego. God *is* good. He simply wants us to recognize this truth. God's intent is to drive deep into his people's collective consciousness the fact that he can be trusted even when life seems out to get us. God can use anything to make himself look good, even a stubborn person (v. 4) and uncertain circumstances (vv. 17–18). It's critical that as followers of God, we keep our focus on Christ even as we deal with our critics and crises.

We would be wise to heed Moses's counsel to the panicking people: "Don't be afraid. Stand firm and see the LORD's salvation that he will accomplish for you today" (v. 13).

Don't be afraid. This simple charge happens to be the most frequent command in the Bible. One scholar concludes that it's used a total of 366 times—"one for every day of the year and an extra one for leap year!"[1]

The Baltimore Symphony Orchestra performed not long after 9/11. In the middle of the evening performance, the concert hall was plunged into darkness. As the people grew restless, fearing another attack had taken place, the orchestra continued playing. Near the end of the musical score, the lights came up again. As the orchestra finished, the audience responded with a standing ovation.[2] Courage isn't the absence of fear; courage is the decision to keep playing in the presence of fear.

Stand firm. A key to undoing our problems lies in making the decision to outlast them. Can you remember the greatest problem you faced 365 days ago? Chances are you can't. As surely as problems appear, they also vanish. Perseverance is the decision to stand firm until the storm has passed. A favorite quote from Winston Churchill hangs on the wall of both my office at work and my study at home: "If you are going through hell, keep going." Make the decision, with God's help, to outlast the adversities of life.

See the Lord's salvation. Public-opinion polls regularly report that while 90 percent of Americans say they believe in God,[3] only about 80 percent believe in miracles.[4] Miracles are another way of demonstrating that God is still interested, involved, and invested in what goes on in our world. Miracles carry the message that God isn't indifferent toward his creation.

Exodus 14 allows us to witness not one but two miracles God performed to save the Israelites. These twin miracles are meaningful especially for those who feel trouble coming hard on their heels. First, a barrier of fire and cloud stood between the Egyptian army and the Israelites. The barrier was nothing other than God's presence. God himself literally stood between his people and the approaching enemy.

Second, just as God protected the Israelites, he also provided a means of escape through the sea. A wind began to blow from the east, a wind strong enough to divide the waters of the Red Sea, creating a dry path for the Israelites. Once they crossed the sea, the Egyptians followed, only to find the walls of water collapsing on top of them.

The parting of a sea seems an unlikely story. Just because it's recorded in the Bible, does that mean it's true? I certainly believe it is. By disrupting the normal order of things, God reminds us that neither the natural world nor what we deem possible can limit his power. Again, the goal of miracles is for God to enhance his reputation in the midst of life's difficulties. Charles Spurgeon, a famous nineteenth-century pastor, applied the Red Sea miracle to all our lives when he said, "The Lord will make a way for you where no foot has been before. That which, like the sea, threatens to drown you, shall be a highway for your escape."[5]

Exodus 14 ends with these words: "When Israel saw the great power that the LORD used against the Egyptians, the people feared the LORD and believed in him and in his servant Moses" (v. 31).

The Bible in many places points to the fear of the Lord. To fear someone in the biblical sense of the word is to be in awe of that person. The ultimate application of Exodus 14 may be summarized this way: those who fear the Lord never have to be afraid of anything else. As we stand in awe of God—his love, kindness, and care—life loses any threat it might have held over us. Even when life seems out to get us, God is intent on saving us.

FOR REFLECTION

As the Israelites left Egypt, a pillar of cloud guided them during the day. At night they followed a pillar of fire. When the pillar stopped, they were meant to stop. When the pillar moved, they were to move. Even at night they were given enough light to travel. This valuable piece of wisdom helps us understand something about God's guidance today: *Darkness about going is light about staying.*

If your next step leads into darkness, perhaps God is instructing you to delay that step. Make your next move only as light (clarity) is given for the next step. *Darkness about going is light about staying.* We experience the peace of God as we adopt the pace of God.

What decision would you like God to shed light on? Have you asked him to clear up your confusion? Perhaps you should let him know you're willing to take the next step only as he provides the needed clarity.

Exodus 20

¹ Then God spoke all these words:

² I am the LORD your God, who brought you out of the land of Egypt, out of the place of slavery.

³ Do not have other gods besides me.

⁴ Do not make an idol for yourself, whether in the shape of anything in the heavens above or on the earth below or in the waters under the earth. ⁵ Do not bow in worship to them, and do not serve them; for I, the LORD your God, am a jealous God, punishing the children for the fathers' iniquity, to the third and fourth generations of those who hate me, ⁶ but showing faithful love to a thousand generations of those who love me and keep my commands.

⁷ Do not misuse the name of the LORD your God, because the LORD will not leave anyone unpunished who misuses his name.

⁸ Remember the Sabbath day, to keep it holy: ⁹ You are to labor six days and do all your work, ¹⁰ but the seventh day is a Sabbath to the LORD your God. You must not do any work — you, your son or daughter, your male or female servant, your livestock, or the resident alien who is within your city gates. ¹¹ For the LORD made the heavens and the earth, the sea, and everything in them in six days; then he rested on the seventh day. Therefore the LORD blessed the Sabbath day and declared it holy.

¹² Honor your father and your mother so that you may have a long life in the land that the LORD your God is giving you.

¹³ Do not murder.

¹⁴ Do not commit adultery.

¹⁵ Do not steal.

¹⁶ Do not give false testimony against your neighbor.

¹⁷ Do not covet your neighbor's house. Do not covet your neighbor's wife, his male or female servant, his ox or donkey, or anything that belongs to your neighbor.

¹⁸ All the people witnessed the thunder and lightning, the sound of the trumpet, and the mountain surrounded by smoke. When the people saw it they trembled and stood at a distance. ¹⁹ "You speak to us, and we will listen," they said to Moses, "but don't let God speak to us, or we will die."

²⁰ Moses responded to the people, "Don't be afraid, for God has come to test you, so that you will fear him and will not sin." ²¹ And the people

remained standing at a distance as Moses approached the total darkness where God was.

²² Then the LORD told Moses, "This is what you are to say to the Israelites: You have seen that I have spoken to you from heaven. ²³ Do not make gods of silver to rival me; do not make gods of gold for yourselves.

²⁴ "Make an earthen altar for me, and sacrifice on it your burnt offerings and fellowship offerings, your flocks and herds. I will come to you and bless you in every place where I cause my name to be remembered. ²⁵ If you make a stone altar for me, do not build it out of cut stones. If you use your chisel on it, you will defile it. ²⁶ Do not go up to my altar on steps, so that your nakedness is not exposed on it."

8

Ten Keys You Can't Live Without
Exodus 20

When I was a young father, with my children still in diapers, I would walk through the doorway after a long day of work and announce, "I'm home!" In a flash all my children would run to me and tackle me. Today my children are older. When I arrive home and announce my presence, I'm fortunate if I receive a grunt of recognition.

Every stage of parenthood is different. Yet my parenting is unchanged in at least one aspect: rules. As children grow, the specific rules may change, but the need for rules themselves doesn't.

God is our heavenly father. We're his children. His decision to give us certain rules to live by is a gift. How so? Because pleasing him is no longer a matter of guesswork. If parents are forever changing the rules, their children will become confused and frustrated. God, as our heavenly parent, has been clear and consistent about the behavior he expects from us, his children. In the Older Testament, God's ultimate rule-revealing moment came with the Ten Commandments.

Why ten commandments? Why not seven or twelve? A glimpse at the ancient Hebrew mind-set gives insight into the significance of this exact number. The number ten represented completeness, an ideal sum. Even today, ten fingers and ten toes are synonymous with a healthy newborn baby. Likewise, the total of ten commandments was meant to represent what full and free, helpful and healthy obedience to God looks like. Simply put, the Ten Commandments are keys we can't live without. While we are not redeemed by the law, we are rescued from many bad consequences when we follow God's guidelines.

Two of the most commonly held views of the Ten Commandments deprive them of their full impact and correct application. I stop short of calling these views misinterpretations, but they tell only part of the story, which is a shame.

First, we could view the commandments as nothing more than restrictions. This makes God, in essence, an eternal killjoy. With these rules, God sucks all the fun and adventure out of our lives for no other reason than he can.

Instead, try to see these commands as expressions of God's wisdom and love. Consider the concept of parenthood again. A mother isn't being cruel when she chides her child for trying to touch the attractive flames of the burner on the stove. In fact, not issuing the warning would be a greater cruelty. The parent, with wisdom gained from experience and education, offers instruction as a sign of compassion. Through his instructions, God is saying, "I don't want you to get burned! Live life within boundaries! If you don't, you'll unleash destructive forces on yourself and those around you." To put it simply, these commands aren't narrow legalism but rather great love.

A second view of the Ten Commandments is seeing them as an insurmountable moral high bar. Our reaction may be: *How can anyone reach this level of integrity and purity? Why would anyone bother to try?* Consider another view. The Ten Commandments aren't a pole-vault bar; instead, they're a limbo bar. God doesn't ask us to jump over these commands. Instead, he asks only that we avoid stooping below these minimal requirements. God doesn't ask for a moral leap; rather, he desires that we not sink below our true worth. He wants us to beware of degrading, debasing, and dehumanizing ourselves.

In 1631, King Charles I of Britain commissioned a printing of one thousand copies of the Bible translated into English. The commandment that should have read "Thou shalt not commit adultery" was misprinted, omitting the word *not*. This edition of the Bible became known as the Wicked Bible, which became so popular that the king ordered a recall and burned every copy that could be found. Only a handful of these Bibles remain today.

The Ten Commandments challenge to us to live beyond what *feels* good to what God has *revealed* as good. While none of the commandments are convenient, they're all critical for life to work as God intended.

The Ten Commandments are found in two places in the Bible. They make their first appearance in Exodus 20, and they're repeated in Deuteronomy 5. In a meaningful way, they offer a snapshot of the entire Bible.

The first four commandments focus on giving God all he deserves. God wants (and merits) nothing less than our worship—our full attention and complete affection. No other gods (the first commandment) and no other objects in creation (the second commandment) are to take his place of priority. God makes it clear: he wants first place in our lives, or he will have no place at all.

The third commandment concentrates on respecting God's name. We wrongly assume that this command condemns using God's name in flippant language. However, the original intent is for the follower of God not to be a follower in name only. When we as Christ followers soil our character, we also dirty the reputation of God. Lifestyle, not language, is the heart of this command.

Rounding out the first four commands is "Remember the Sabbath day" (Exod. 20:8). The word *Sabbath* comes from a Hebrew word meaning "to rest." Life is meant to have a rhythm of work and rest. The fourth commandment is especially necessary in our stress- and speed-addicted society. Guilt-free rest is not only possible; it's also a command! If we believe the world cannot survive one day without our labors, we run the risk of committing idolatry by worshipping the false sense of our own importance.

Between commands four and five, there is a clean break. The commands shift in focus from how to reverence God to how to respect other people. The unifying theme of these final six commands is the value of giving instead of taking.

- "Honor your father and your mother" (v. 12).
  Give respect where respect is due. The home

is the school of relationships. If we fail in our relationships at home, we'll surely fail in other important relationships in life.

- "Do not murder" (v. 13). Don't take someone's life.
- "Do not commit adultery" (v. 14). Don't take someone's spouse.
- "Do not steal" (v. 15). Don't take someone's possessions.
- "Do not give false testimony" (v. 16). Do not lie. Don't twist the truth for your own purposes.
- "Do not covet" (v. 17). Don't allow the attitude of taking to dominate your thinking and personality. It isn't enough to keep your hand from doing evil. You must also protect your heart from entertaining evil.

Any external application of these commands begins with the internal decision and desire to live to the core a life that fully honors God.

As a whole, these commands communicate an important truth: life is about relationships. The first four commands focus on loving God, while the final six detail what love for other people should look like. The Ten Commandments are commentary to the greatest commands to love God and love others, which Moses gave and Jesus endorsed (we'll discuss these later). A life well lived keeps these two relationships in proper working order. The Ten

Commandments are a tangible guide. When we live only for ourselves, we miss the point of life and mistreat the relationships for
which God created us.

After reading the Ten Commandments, it's appropriate to ask
this question: What is the most frequently repeated command in the
Bible? Remember, it's this: *"Do not fear. Do not be afraid. Fear not."*
This command isn't a prohibition but a permission. God's intent
for life is freedom, not fear. This truth is a key to appreciating all of
God's commands, especially the Ten Commandments. God offers
us liberty. We don't have to live as idolaters or adulterers or as over-
committed or untruthful people. We can experience freedom from
sin in our lives under the life-giving guidance of a loving Father.

FOR REFLECTION

John 1:17 says, "The law was given through Moses; grace and truth
came through Jesus Christ." Jesus didn't discard the law contained
in the Older Testament. In fact, Jesus fulfilled the law (see Matt.
5:17). We aren't asked to obey a set of impersonal rules. Instead, we
see obedience as an opportunity to imitate and please Jesus Christ.

Read through the Ten Commandments again (Exod. 20:1–17).
Which command do you tend to ignore in your own life? Most
of God's commands are simple and direct. What we typically
lack is not the ability to understand but the willingness to obey.
Regarding the command you're inclined to neglect, ask God for
the needed strength to change.

Judges 16

¹ Samson went to Gaza, where he saw a prostitute and went to bed with her. ² When the Gazites heard that Samson was there, they surrounded the place and waited in ambush for him all that night at the city gate. They kept quiet all night, saying, "Let's wait until dawn; then we will kill him." ³ But Samson stayed in bed only until midnight. Then he got up, took hold of the doors of the city gate along with the two gateposts, and pulled them out, bar and all. He put them on his shoulders and took them to the top of the mountain overlooking Hebron.

⁴ Some time later, he fell in love with a woman named Delilah, who lived in the Sorek Valley. ⁵ The Philistine leaders went to her and said, "Persuade him to tell you where his great strength comes from, so we can overpower him, tie him up, and make him helpless. Each of us will then give you 1,100 pieces of silver."

⁶ So Delilah said to Samson, "Please tell me, where does your great strength come from? How could someone tie you up and make you helpless?"

⁷ Samson told her, "If they tie me up with seven fresh bowstrings that have not been dried, I will become weak and be like any other man."

⁸ The Philistine leaders brought her seven fresh bowstrings that had not been dried, and she tied him up with them. ⁹ While the men in ambush were waiting in her room, she called out to him, "Samson, the Philistines are here!" But he snapped the bowstrings as a strand of yarn snaps when it touches fire. The secret of his strength remained unknown.

¹⁰ Then Delilah said to Samson, "You have mocked me and told me lies! Won't you please tell me how you can be tied up?"

¹¹ He told her, "If they tie me up with new ropes that have never been used, I will become weak and be like any other man."

¹² Delilah took new ropes, tied him up with them, and shouted, "Samson, the Philistines are here!" But while the men in ambush were waiting in her room, he snapped the ropes off his arms like a thread.

¹³ Then Delilah said to Samson, "You have mocked me all along and told me lies! Tell me how you can be tied up."

He told her, "If you weave the seven braids on my head into the fabric on a loom —"

¹⁴ She fastened the braids with a pin and called to him, "Samson, the Philistines are here!" He awoke from his sleep and pulled out the pin, with the loom and the web.

¹⁵ "How can you say, 'I love you,'" she told him, "when your heart is not with me? This is the third time you have mocked me and not told me what makes your strength so great!"

¹⁶ Because she nagged him day after day and pleaded with him until she wore him out, ¹⁷ he told her the whole truth and said to her, "My hair has never been cut, because I am a Nazirite to God from birth. If I am shaved, my strength will leave me, and I will become weak and be like any other man."

¹⁸ When Delilah realized that he had told her the whole truth, she sent this message to the Philistine leaders: "Come one more time, for he has told me the whole truth." The Philistine leaders came to her and brought the silver with them.

¹⁹ Then she let him fall asleep on her lap and called a man to shave off the seven braids on his head. In this way, she made him helpless, and his strength left him. ²⁰ Then she cried, "Samson, the Philistines are here!" When he awoke from his sleep, he said, "I will escape as I did before and shake myself free." But he did not know that the Lord had left him.

²¹ The Philistines seized him and gouged out his eyes. They brought him down to Gaza and bound him with bronze shackles, and he was forced to grind grain in the prison. ²² But his hair began to grow back after it had been shaved.

²³ Now the Philistine leaders gathered together to offer a great sacrifice to their god Dagon. They rejoiced and said:

Our god has handed over
our enemy Samson to us.

²⁴ When the people saw him, they praised their god and said:

Our god has handed over to us
our enemy who destroyed our land
and who multiplied our dead.

²⁵ When they were in good spirits, they said, "Bring Samson here to entertain us." So they brought Samson from prison, and he entertained them. They had him stand between the pillars.

²⁶ Samson said to the young man who was leading him by the hand, "Lead me where I can feel the pillars supporting the temple, so I can lean

against them." ²⁷ The temple was full of men and women; all the leaders of the Philistines were there, and about three thousand men and women were on the roof watching Samson entertain them. ²⁸ He called out to the LORD: "Lord GOD, please remember me. Strengthen me, God, just once more. With one act of vengeance, let me pay back the Philistines for my two eyes." ²⁹ Samson took hold of the two middle pillars supporting the temple and leaned against them, one on his right hand and the other on his left. ³⁰ Samson said, "Let me die with the Philistines." He pushed with all his might, and the temple fell on the leaders and all the people in it. And those he killed at his death were more than those he had killed in his life.

³¹ Then his brothers and all his father's family came down, carried him back, and buried him between Zorah and Eshtaol in the tomb of his father Manoah. So he judged Israel twenty years.

9

God Can Use Even Your Failures
Judges 16

The Israelites were finally free! No longer were they required to work for their Egyptian overlords. They were now living for themselves, and God. In these first days of freedom, the Israelites were privileged to experience the leadership of two great men: Moses and Joshua. Moses led Israel out of Egypt; Joshua led the people into the Promised Land. Moses delivered God's Ten Commandments, and Joshua provided an example of living in intimacy with the Lord and integrity with others (Josh. 24:15). Moses and Joshua were good leaders of people because they were great followers of God.

Then Joshua died. It was obvious to every Israelite that no one leader had the competence to fill his shoes. A new era for Israel had begun, and it wouldn't be a pleasant one. This era of Older Testament history—spanning about three hundred years—is called the period of the judges, which is recorded in a book titled (creatively enough) Judges. An era that began not long after the death of Joshua concluded with the appointment of the first king of Israel, Saul. Twice in the book of Judges a statement is used to sum up the ethos of the age: "In those days there was no king in Israel; everyone did whatever seemed right to him" (Judg. 17:6; 21:25). In other words, national chaos characterized this era of Israel's history.

A five-step cycle repeats itself throughout the pages of Judges. First, the people would abandon or neglect their commitment to the Lord. Next, God would attempt to get his people's attention by permitting a crisis to erupt, typically an attack or oppression from a neighboring nation. Then, in desperation, the Israelites would call out to the Lord for deliverance. Next, God would appoint a "judge" to take immediate action. A judge embodied the skills of military leadership, political prowess, and spiritual authority. To put it in terms we understand, the judges were the ancient equivalent of action heroes. Finally, with the situation resolved, a temporary season of peace would ensue. This cycle of insanity repeated itself time after time in Judges. And if you take careful note, you might see this same cycle repeating in your life.

The book of Judges contains the accounts of twelve leaders. Twelve is a highly significant number in the Bible. The nation of Israel itself was composed of twelve families or tribes. (In the New Testament, Jesus would choose twelve disciples.) That there were twelve judges was a numerical reminder that God cares for his people even in chaotic times.

The twelve judges God appointed were far from perfect people. While many of them were noble, they were all flawed individuals— much like leaders today. Unique among the twelve judges was a woman named Deborah. Not only did she demonstrate capable leadership in a male-dominated society, but her contribution to the Bible is also unmistakable. Deborah's song, recorded in Judges 5, is believed to be one of the earliest poems in the Bible. What qualified Deborah for leadership wasn't her gender but her relationship with the Lord. God uses anyone he chooses—man or woman—in any way he pleases.

And then there was Samson, who was last in the line of the twelve judges. Samson embodied the best and worst of the judges. He epitomized the extremes of his era—the honor and the horror of a time when Israel lacked true leadership from the top. As we see from his story, Samson was a man of supernatural strength and natural weakness.

Understanding Samson requires that we recognize a special commitment he made to God called a Nazirite vow. This voluntary vow prohibited a person from three things: touching a dead body, drinking wine, and cutting his hair. An oversimplification of Samson's story suggests that his strength was in the length of his hair. A better understanding suggests that Samson's strength originated from his vows to God. Our lives are filled with power as we keep our commitments to God. The formula for weakness is compromise.

Little by little, Samson's commitment to God eroded. Judges 16 details Samson's last and greatest compromise. With this, Samson had no real integrity left.

The first words of the chapter give us a clue to Samson's spiritual state: "Samson went to Gaza, where he saw a prostitute and went to bed with her" (v. 1). Samson's weakness is all too familiar—sex. In Samson's case, the misuse of sex unleashed destructive forces in his life from which he was unable to fully recover. While sex is a wonderful gift from God, its misuse can harm us in unfortunate ways. Frederick Buechner put it plainly: "Like nitroglycerin, [sex] can be used either to blow up bridges or heal hearts."[1] Administered wisely and within proper boundaries, sex is a beautiful, life-giving experience. When applied carelessly, destruction surely results.

Samson's ultimate downfall was a woman named Delilah, a name synonymous with seduction. In fact, her name means "flirtatious." Here's a glimpse: "Delilah said to Samson, 'Please tell me, where does your great strength come from? How could someone tie you up and make you helpless?'" (v. 6).

What does the life of Samson teach us? What spiritual insights might Samson offer us? Whereas many personalities in the Bible model ways we should aspire to live, Samson offers an example of what we should avoid.

First, Samson toyed with temptation. He wasn't blind to Delilah's agenda. Samson was willing to see how far he could go without experiencing failure. He thought he was clever and in control. Only too late did he realize he was neither. In the New Testament, we're clearly instructed how to respond to the reality of temptation in our lives: "Flee from youthful passions" (2 Tim. 2:22). Samson chose to flirt rather than flee. We would do well to learn from his error in judgment.

Second, Samson made the mistake of confusing his physical power for spiritual strength. The truth may be summed up like this: thinking we're strong is a weakness, but acknowledging our weakness makes us stronger.

What is your greatest temptation? It's worth the time to consider three or four of your most glaring spiritual weaknesses. Owning our biggest temptations is the surest defense against them. When I understand the sins I'm most prone to commit, I can take the necessary steps to avoid any situation that introduces temptation.

Samson did offer a redeeming quality worth admiring. He was a model for all of us who suffer from personal mistakes. This is good news! God may choose to use our weaknesses and mistakes. As the story of his life drew to a close, Samson experienced for himself the God of second chances. Judges 16:22 almost twinkles on the page when it says that "[Samson's] hair began to grow back after it had been shaved." These words describe what was happening not only to his follicles but also with his faith. In a dark prison, growth was happening. Along with the length of his hair, the depth of Samson's commitment to God began to mature. God redeems our mistakes as we renew our desire to serve him.

In his last act—not an act of desperation but of dependence on God—Samson managed one final feat for God and God's people. It's comforting to know that God never fails even those who fail him.

Ruth Bell Graham, wife of the famous evangelist Billy Graham, died in 2007. When Dr. Graham visited his wife's grave for the first time, the words she wrote for her headstone so moved him that he asked a friend to read them to him several times. The stone reads, "End of construction. Thank you for your patience."

We're meant to grow until we die. Through our seasons of compromise and commitment, God will mature our faith even when we fail. God wants our strength, but it's good to know that he will use even our weaknesses.

FOR REFLECTION

Outside the book of Judges, Samson is mentioned only one time in the Bible, among a list of the faithful in Hebrews 11. Even though he was a deeply flawed individual, subsequent generations have remembered him as a faithful person, in part because he finished his life well.

Looking at your life with the end in mind, how do you want to be remembered? What are the three or four words you want people to associate with you once your life is complete? Are you living by these qualities today?

1 Samuel 17

¹ The Philistines gathered their forces for war at Socoh in Judah and camped between Socoh and Azekah in Ephes-dammim. ² Saul and the men of Israel gathered and camped in the Valley of Elah; then they lined up in battle formation to face the Philistines.

³ The Philistines were standing on one hill, and the Israelites were standing on another hill with a ravine between them. ⁴ Then a champion named Goliath, from Gath, came out from the Philistine camp. He was nine feet, nine inches tall ⁵ and wore a bronze helmet and bronze scale armor that weighed one hundred twenty-five pounds. ⁶ There was bronze armor on his shins, and a bronze javelin was slung between his shoulders. ⁷ His spear shaft was like a weaver's beam, and the iron point of his spear weighed fifteen pounds. In addition, a shield-bearer was walking in front of him.

⁸ He stood and shouted to the Israelite battle formations: "Why do you come out to line up in battle formation?" He asked them, "Am I not a Philistine and are you not servants of Saul? Choose one of your men and have him come down against me. ⁹ If he wins in a fight against me and kills me, we will be your servants. But if I win against him and kill him, then you will be our servants and serve us." ¹⁰ Then the Philistine said, "I defy the ranks of Israel today. Send me a man so we can fight each other!" ¹¹ When Saul and all Israel heard these words from the Philistine, they lost their courage and were terrified.

¹² Now David was the son of the Ephrathite from Bethlehem of Judah named Jesse. Jesse had eight sons and during Saul's reign was already an old man. ¹³ Jesse's three oldest sons had followed Saul to the war, and their names were Eliab, the firstborn, Abinadab, the next, and Shammah, the third, ¹⁴ and David was the youngest. The three oldest had followed Saul, ¹⁵ but David kept going back and forth from Saul to tend his father's flock in Bethlehem.

¹⁶ Every morning and evening for forty days the Philistine came forward and took his stand. ¹⁷ One day Jesse had told his son David: "Take this half-bushel of roasted grain along with these ten loaves of bread for your brothers and hurry to their camp. ¹⁸ Also take these ten portions of cheese to the field commander. Check on the well-being of your brothers and bring a confirmation from them. ¹⁹ They are with Saul and all the men of Israel in the Valley of Elah fighting with the Philistines."

²⁰ So David got up early in the morning, left the flock with someone to keep it, loaded up, and set out as Jesse had charged him.

He arrived at the perimeter of the camp as the army was marching out to its battle formation shouting their battle cry. ²¹ Israel and the Philistines lined up in battle formation facing each other. ²² David left his supplies in the care of the quartermaster and ran to the battle line. When he arrived, he asked his brothers how they were. ²³ While he was speaking with them, suddenly the champion named Goliath, the Philistine from Gath, came forward from the Philistine battle line and shouted his usual words, which David heard. ²⁴ When all the Israelite men saw Goliath, they retreated from him terrified.

²⁵ Previously, an Israelite man had declared: "Do you see this man who keeps coming out? He comes to defy Israel. The king will make the man who kills him very rich and will give him his daughter. The king will also make the family of that man's father exempt from paying taxes in Israel."

²⁶ David spoke to the men who were standing with him: "What will be done for the man who kills that Philistine and removes this disgrace from Israel? Just who is this uncircumcised Philistine that he should defy the armies of the living God?"

²⁷ The troops told him about the offer, concluding, "That is what will be done for the man who kills him."

²⁸ David's oldest brother Eliab listened as he spoke to the men, and he became angry with him. "Why did you come down here?" he asked. "Who did you leave those few sheep with in the wilderness? I know your arrogance and your evil heart — you came down to see the battle!"

²⁹ "What have I done now?" protested David. "It was just a question." ³⁰ Then he turned from those beside him to others in front of him and asked about the offer. The people gave him the same answer as before.

³¹ What David said was overheard and reported to Saul, so he had David brought to him. ³² David said to Saul, "Don't let anyone be discouraged by him; your servant will go and fight this Philistine!"

³³ But Saul replied, "You can't go fight this Philistine. You're just a youth, and he's been a warrior since he was young."

³⁴ David answered Saul: "Your servant has been tending his father's sheep. Whenever a lion or a bear came and carried off a lamb from the flock, ³⁵ I went after it, struck it down, and rescued the lamb from its mouth. If it reared up against me, I would grab it by its fur, strike it down, and kill it. ³⁶ Your servant has killed lions and bears; this uncircumcised Philistine will be like one of them, for he has defied the armies of the

living God." ³⁷ Then David said, "The LORD who rescued me from the paw of the lion and the paw of the bear will rescue me from the hand of this Philistine."

Saul said to David, "Go, and may the LORD be with you."

³⁸ Then Saul had his own military clothes put on David. He put a bronze helmet on David's head and had him put on armor. ³⁹ David strapped his sword on over the military clothes and tried to walk, but he was not used to them. "I can't walk in these," David said to Saul, "I'm not used to them." So David took them off. ⁴⁰ Instead, he took his staff in his hand and chose five smooth stones from the wadi and put them in the pouch, in his shepherd's bag. Then, with his sling in his hand, he approached the Philistine.

⁴¹ The Philistine came closer and closer to David, with the shield-bearer in front of him. ⁴² When the Philistine looked and saw David, he despised him because he was just a youth, healthy and handsome. ⁴³ He said to David, "Am I a dog that you come against me with sticks?" Then he cursed David by his gods. ⁴⁴ "Come here," the Philistine called to David, "and I'll give your flesh to the birds of the sky and the wild beasts!"

⁴⁵ David said to the Philistine: "You come against me with a sword, spear, and javelin, but I come against you in the name of the LORD of Armies, the God of the ranks of Israel — you have defied him. ⁴⁶ Today, the LORD will hand you over to me. Today, I'll strike you down, remove your head, and give the corpses of the Philistine camp to the birds of the sky and the wild creatures of the earth. Then all the world will know that Israel has a God, ⁴⁷ and this whole assembly will know that it is not by sword or by spear that the LORD saves, for the battle is the LORD's. He will hand you over to us."

⁴⁸ When the Philistine started forward to attack him, David ran quickly to the battle line to meet the Philistine. ⁴⁹ David put his hand in the bag, took out a stone, slung it, and hit the Philistine on his forehead. The stone sank into his forehead, and he fell facedown to the ground. ⁵⁰ David defeated the Philistine with a sling and a stone. David over-powered the Philistine and killed him without having a sword. ⁵¹ David ran and stood over him. He grabbed the Philistine's sword, pulled it from its sheath, and used it to kill him. Then he cut off his head. When the Philistines saw that their hero was dead, they fled. ⁵² The men of Israel and Judah rallied, shouting their battle cry, and chased the Philistines to the entrance of the valley and to the gates of Ekron. Philistine bodies were strewn all along the Shaaraim road to Gath and Ekron.

⁵³ When the Israelites returned from the pursuit of the Philistines, they plundered their camps. ⁵⁴ David took Goliath's head and brought it to Jerusalem, but he put Goliath's weapons in his own tent.

⁵⁵ When Saul had seen David going out to confront the Philistine, he asked Abner the commander of the army, "Whose son is this youth, Abner?"

"Your Majesty, as surely as you live, I don't know," Abner replied.

⁵⁶ The king said, "Find out whose son this young man is!"

⁵⁷ When David returned from killing the Philistine, Abner took him and brought him before Saul with the Philistine's head still in his hand. ⁵⁸ Saul said to him, "Whose son are you, young man?"

"The son of your servant Jesse of Bethlehem," David answered.

10

Why Hard Times Help
1 Samuel 17

We all face hard times—it's as simple as that.

Researchers at the University of California at Berkeley conducted an experiment using an amoeba. It was given the perfect amount of light, moisture, and food to support its single-celled life. The amoeba was required to expend no energy or effort. Everything it needed was provided. This was an amoeba paradise with only one small problem. The amoeba promptly died. Researchers concluded from this experiment that every living thing requires a challenge to survive and thrive.[1]

A famous challenge is detailed in 1 Samuel 17. This account offers guidance for facing our own difficulties when they present themselves.

When the people of Israel emerged from the period of the judges, they were united under their first king, Saul. Threatened once again by their mortal enemies the Philistines, the Israelites faced off across battle lines. The Philistines' champion fighter—a nine-foot-plus giant of a man named Goliath—proposed an alternative to outright battle. Instead of the armies fighting to the finish, one fighter from each camp would face the other, winner take all.

First Samuel 17:4–7 gives the most detailed physical description of any person in the Bible. Goliath was a picture of intimidation. Obviously this is why a volunteer from the men of Israel was slow to emerge. No one felt up to the task of facing the oversize adversary. No one, that is, except David.

Consider the difference between a celebrity and a hero. A celebrity is someone known for being known. A hero is someone who knows how to take action. A celebrity is a big name; a hero is a big person. A celebrity makes headlines, but a hero makes history. David was destined to become the greatest hero-king in Jewish history. The Bible spends sixty-six chapters telling the life story of David—more chapters than anyone else except for Jesus himself. David's first step on the rise to renown is chronicled in 1 Samuel 17. As he faced Goliath, he exhibited character qualities essential not only for an ancient king but also for an active Jesus follower today.

David had confidence in God. David declared, "The LORD who rescued me from the paw of the lion and the paw of the bear will rescue me from the hand of this Philistine" (v. 37). David's life was no tame existence. As a shepherd, he had dealt with his fair share of hungry lions and charging bears. He was no stranger to conflict. He had learned from stress-filled days and lonely nights the sufficiency of the Lord's strength. God had preserved David's life on more than one occasion, and David trusted he would do it again.

David was not only confident in God, but *he was also confident in himself.* "Your servant has killed lions and bears; this uncircumcised Philistine will be like one of them" (v. 36). David acknowledged a simple truth: past experiences prepare us for present and future challenges. Guarding sheep, a potential food source for predators, was no easy occupation. Each encounter David had with a bear or a lion prepared him for this encounter with Goliath. David's muscles and mental powers had been refined into steel. God has a way of using our unique experiences to prepare us for our eventual destinies.

My first job was in fast food. At the time I viewed the job simply as a means to earn money for college. Looking back, with the perspective of twenty-five years, I see a much different purpose. No job proved as valuable in my preparation for pastoring a church. My first job was more than scooping fries and serving burgers. It was an undergraduate equivalent of managing the expectations of hurried people.

I no longer serve physical food. Instead, I provide spiritual sustenance to busy people, many of whom live too fast for their own good. From time to time, I deal with people's unrealistic expectations. But I've come to understand that their hasty opinions and unpredictable emotions say more about who they are than who I am. It was true for David, and it's true for you and me: the past prepares us for the future.

The balance of David's confidence in God and confidence in himself was exactly that—*a balance*. Confidence in God without confidence in self translates into foolishness. We can't expect God to regularly rescue us from our lack of experience. A failure to learn and prepare can lead to our ultimate undoing. On the other hand, confidence in self with no confidence in God is arrogance. Our own strength has its limits. God's strength knows no boundaries.

In contrast to David's confidence in the Lord and in himself was the obvious lack of confidence expressed by those around him. Everyone, it seems, had an opinion of this unknown shepherd boy. His brother accused him of selfish motives (v. 28). Saul attempted to persuade David to fight the giant the way he would have done so (vv. 38–39). Goliath insulted David's underdeveloped appearance (vv. 42–44).

Anytime one assumes leadership, others will offer their opinions, usually in the form of criticism. In fact, the word *leader* comes from the Indo-European word *leit*. The *leit* was the person who carried the flag at the front of an advancing army. In other words, the *leit* was the first person to be shot at!

What was David's secret to overcoming all these differing and disconcerting opinions? Volleys from both sides of the battle line could have paralyzed him. David's greatest strength was this: he had nothing to prove and nothing to lose. What a way to live! What a perfect means to meet the struggles and battles of life.

David used the weapons customary to shepherds—a sling and stones. These ordinary tools became the means of God to achieve victory. God still uses simple tools and simple people today. One shot from a destiny-appointed person can bring down the most formidable of foes.

Don't go looking for adversity; it will find you. Hard times may come in the form of difficult people, unpredictable circumstances, or fears that seem beyond your control. While none of these Goliaths feel glorious at the moment, their purpose is to form in us the character of Christ.

When David walked away from the battlefield, he carried with him Goliath's sword as a souvenir of his conquest. Years later David would use Goliath's sword to fight on other battlefields. The sword that once threatened his life became the very tool used to protect his life. The simple truth is this: today's greatest threats can become tomorrow's most reliable resources.

We all face hard times; it's as simple as that. As important as knowing how to face those challenges is remembering who faces the challenges of life with us. God's presence is our greatest source of confidence and courage.

FOR REFLECTION

Consider a quote from an early twentieth-century pastor, Smith Wigglesworth: "Great faith is the product of great fights. Great testimonies are the outcome of great tests. Great triumphs can only come out of great trials." Hard times help us by producing a stronger faith based on real-life experience with our reliable God.

What great fight do you face today? Ask God not only for a good outcome; ask him to also produce a more confident character in you through that experience.

GOD IS BIG

Job 1

¹ There was a man in the country of Uz named Job. He was a man of complete integrity, who feared God and turned away from evil. ² He had seven sons and three daughters. ³ His estate included seven thousand sheep and goats, three thousand camels, five hundred yoke of oxen, five hundred female donkeys, and a very large number of servants. Job was the greatest man among all the people of the east.

⁴ His sons used to take turns having banquets at their homes. They would send an invitation to their three sisters to eat and drink with them. ⁵ Whenever a round of banqueting was over, Job would send for his children and purify them, rising early in the morning to offer burnt offerings for all of them. For Job thought, "Perhaps my children have sinned, having cursed God in their hearts." This was Job's regular practice.

⁶ One day the sons of God came to present themselves before the LORD, and Satan also came with them. ⁷ The LORD asked Satan, "Where have you come from?"

"From roaming through the earth," Satan answered him, "and walking around on it."

⁸ Then the LORD said to Satan, "Have you considered my servant Job? No one else on earth is like him, a man of perfect integrity, who fears God and turns away from evil."

⁹ Satan answered the LORD, "Does Job fear God for nothing? ¹⁰ Haven't you placed a hedge around him, his household, and everything he owns? You have blessed the work of his hands, and his possessions have increased in the land. ¹¹ But stretch out your hand and strike everything he owns, and he will surely curse you to your face."

¹² "Very well," the LORD told Satan, "everything he owns is in your power. However, do not lay a hand on Job himself." So Satan left the LORD's presence.

¹³ One day when Job's sons and daughters were eating and drinking wine in their oldest brother's house, ¹⁴ a messenger came to Job and reported: "While the oxen were plowing and the donkeys grazing nearby, ¹⁵ the Sabeans swooped down and took them away. They struck down the servants with the sword, and I alone have escaped to tell you!"

¹⁶ He was still speaking when another messenger came and reported: "God's fire fell from heaven. It burned the sheep and the servants and devoured them, and I alone have escaped to tell you!"

¹⁷ That messenger was still speaking when yet another came and reported: "The Chaldeans formed three bands, made a raid on the camels, and took them away. They struck down the servants with the sword, and I alone have escaped to tell you!"

¹⁸ He was still speaking when another messenger came and reported: "Your sons and daughters were eating and drinking wine in their oldest brother's house. ¹⁹ Suddenly a powerful wind swept in from the desert and struck the four corners of the house. It collapsed on the young people so that they died, and I alone have escaped to tell you!"

²⁰ Then Job stood up, tore his robe, and shaved his head. He fell to the ground and worshiped, ²¹ saying:

Naked I came from my mother's womb,
and naked I will leave this life.
The LORD gives, and the LORD takes away.
Blessed be the name of the LORD.

²² Throughout all this Job did not sin or blame God for anything.

11

Making Sense of Your Suffering
Job 1

Why do we suffer? Why must we endure pain?

Sometimes the suffering we experience is physical. I have a friend whose son was born with a rare genetic disorder. For this young man, life has been about suffering from the get-go.

At other times the suffering we feel is primarily mental or emotional. Suffering becomes particularly hard to bear whenever it seems endless. Try holding a bottle of water in your outstretched arm. It's not that hard. But if you hold it for an hour, your arm will become uncomfortably numb. Attempt to hold the bottle for an entire day, and a visit to the hospital will be required for the damage inflicted on your muscles. The fact of physics is this: the longer you hold something, the heavier it feels. For many the emotional weight of life has created damage seemingly beyond repair. Psyches are strained and torn under the massive weight of fear, anxiety, and guilt. These emotions, held for so long, cause life to buckle and give way.

For still others, the cause of suffering is external. The number of people worldwide living on only a dollar or two a day is staggering. Suffering indeed.

Does the Bible offer an answer? Or at least some advice? In the wake of the 9/11 terror attacks, Bible sales jumped 25 percent. Instinctively we believe there is something in Scripture to help us make sense of suffering.

Enter Job. His is the one name in the Bible most associated with travail. Some scholars believe that the book of Job was written down before any other book in the Older Testament. That would make suffering the oldest theme in Scripture. Job quite possibly lived during the time of Abraham, meaning his story took place some two thousand years before Jesus. But more important than *when* Job lived is *how* he lived.

The Bible depicts Job as an innocent man, saying, "He was a man of complete integrity, who feared God and turned away from evil" (Job 1:1). By the time we meet him, Job had already made the important decisions of life. He had chosen what was good and rejected what was wicked.

And Job was rewarded. Note how often the number ten can be calculated in this chapter, a number that in the Hebrew mind symbolizes completion and perfection. (Remember the Ten Commandments?) Job had seven sons and three daughters, thus ten children in all. With seven thousand sheep and goats, and three thousand camels, his herds numbered a total of ten thousand. Five hundred yoke of oxen and five hundred donkeys provided an animal workforce of one thousand (ten times ten times ten).

Job was a perfect ten! In every measurable sense, his life was as near perfect as could be expected or experienced. But then came suffering, and everything fell apart.

At the center of Job's suffering—according to the first chapter of his story—was Satan. The word *Satan* is used several times in Job 1. It's a word that means "adversary" or "opponent." Because Satan is averse to anything and anyone associated with God, he is opposed to you, especially if you choose to follow Jesus. Fortunately, Satan isn't on par with God. Notice how he had to ask God's permission to even attack Job.

So Job lost everything—his cattle, donkeys, sheep, servants, and children. While the details seem fantastic and fanciful, they're as realistic as any daily news report. Loss and suffering always make the headlines. Given this reality, how are we to cope?

John Kavanaugh was one of many who went to work with Mother Teresa at her mission in Calcutta, India. At their first meeting, John encountered Mother Teresa after Mass at dawn. She asked what she could do for him, and John requested that she pray for him.

"What do you want me to pray for?" she inquired.

He had thought about it for a long time, so he was prepared to say, "Pray that I have clarity."

John recalls Mother Teresa's response: "She said no. That was that. When I asked why, she announced that clarity was the last thing I was clinging to and had to let go of. When I commented that she herself had always seemed to have the clarity I longed for, she laughed: 'I have never had clarity; what I've always had is trust. So I will pray that you trust.'"[1]

Trust is the most powerful response to suffering there is. Remember that Job wasn't privy to the conversation about him that took place in heaven. Neither are we privy to heavenly conversations about us. Not knowing what God is doing behind the scenes, we must trust that he is in control even when we can't sense his presence. We trust that he has our best interests in mind even when the worst is happening around us.

Job's response is summed up in verse 21: "The LORD gives, and the LORD takes away. Blessed be the name of the LORD." Job's trust was bold, though not blind. Satan's worst brought out Job's best.

Throughout the book, Job pondered the question we started with: Why do we suffer? In our day we might ask the same question in a slightly different way: Why do bad things happen to good people? Job asked this question as many as twenty-seven times throughout the course of the book. Yet God never once answered it.

As the story progresses, Job learned to exchange the wrong question for the right one. He stopped asking, *Why am I suffering? Why me? Why now?* and he started asking, *Who are you, God? Who will accompany me through this crisis?*

From Job we learn that God was more interested in revealing himself than resolving Job's problems. When we suffer, we're also inclined to look for answers. But what if we don't need answers as much as we need love? What if we don't need solutions as much as we need a savior? If there is one truth from Job's life worth holding on to, it is this: Job learned to trust the Almighty rather than the answers. May we learn the same.

When my father was in the hospital, dangerously close to death, I told him how the whole family was gathered around him. "Mom is here. I'm here. Wayne, Dee Ann, Ed, Paula—we're all here."

Through the delirium of pneumonia and antibiotics, my father grabbed hold of this one thought. At several critical times during his recovery, he would say, "Tell me again how the whole family is here." Even now, years later, he still fondly recounts that in his suffering he was surrounded by those most dear to him.

Presence is powerful, more powerful than any answer. In the end Job had one of the deepest, richest relationships with God of anyone in the Bible. Great suffering produces strong faith.

FOR REFLECTION

Travail is another word for suffering. *Travail* is also the root word for the term *travel*. Before high-speed transportation, five-star accommodations, and fast food at every fork in the road, traveling was a challenge, to say the least.

We're all travelers as we follow Christ. In your travels to date, what has been your most challenging travail? Can you join with Job in saying, "The LORD gives, and the LORD takes away. Blessed be the name of the LORD" (1:21)?

Psalm 23

A psalm of David.

¹ The LORD is my shepherd;
I have what I need.
² He lets me lie down in green pastures;
he leads me beside quiet waters.
³ He renews my life;
he leads me along the right paths
for his name's sake.
⁴ Even when I go through the darkest valley,
I fear no danger,
for you are with me;
your rod and your staff — they comfort me.

⁵ You prepare a table before me
in the presence of my enemies;
you anoint my head with oil;
my cup overflows.
⁶ Only goodness and faithful love will pursue me
all the days of my life,
and I will dwell in the house of the LORD
as long as I live.

12

Forget the Funeral—This Is Life!
Psalm 23

I knocked as I opened the hospital-room door. Across the room I could see the patient I was scheduled to visit, sound asleep. As I walked to his bedside, I said his name once, then twice. By the third time I called his name, I had arrived next to the man's bed. Only then was I close enough to see that he wasn't asleep but dead. I then became fully aware of my surroundings. The room was dark. The machines, typically buzzing and beeping, were silent. The man had died just moments before.

It was an unsettling encounter. Death always is.

Psalm 23 is often recited at funerals. We pair this psalm with passing away. During my hospital visit, I expected to find life and was greeted by death. Psalm 23 is just the opposite. We assume this psalm is about death, but instead life welcomes us—pure, joyful, boundless life.

Two questions must be addressed before we look carefully at this famous chapter in the Bible.

First, what is a psalm? With so many psalms in the Bible—150 in the book of Psalms—what role do they serve? A psalm is a prayer originally accompanied by music. Historically, the book of Psalms served as the prayer book and songbook for God's people. For both ancient Jews and early Christians, the Psalms provided words for every emotion and experience. Psalms capture a praying person's highest thoughts and deepest feelings. This book subtly instructs us that we need hide no emotion from the Almighty.

A second question: Who wrote Psalm 23? The best evidence points to David as the author of this well-known poem-prayer. If anyone qualifies as the Renaissance man of the Bible, it is David. David started life as a shepherd. But he was destined to become an accomplished politician, soldier, administrator, architect, and poet. David's experience as a shepherd and his expertise as a poet were combined to create this skillful psalm.

"The LORD is my shepherd" (v. 1). We can imagine that on one long day in some nondescript desert, David made a mental leap, connecting his occupation to the care of God. Just as David served as protector of his sheep, God serves as the provider of care and compassion for his people. Sheep are unable to provide for themselves. Using this picture of utter helplessness, Psalm 23 gives particulars on how God provides for his people.

God provides resources. "I have what I need" (v. 1). God is the giver of all good things—emotionally, physically, spiritually, mentally, and relationally. The apostle Peter agreed when he wrote, "His divine power has given us everything required for life and godliness" (2 Pet. 1:3). If we lack any resource, we're encouraged to ask God.

"He lets me lie down in green pastures" (Ps. 23:2). In terms of giving, God doesn't give the bare minimum. "Green pastures" signifies *plenty*. God is generous in his giving. His love bears the characteristic of unrestrained lavishness.

"He leads me beside quiet waters" (v. 2). This verse expresses what experienced shepherds know. Sheep need rest. Just as much as they need water, they require unrushed moments to maintain health and well-being. How refreshing it is to know that God makes our good his priority.

God provides rescue. "Your rod and your staff—they comfort me" (v. 4). Sheep are danger prone. Cliffs and predators are two threats sheep consistently face. As sheep graze, they pay little attention to their surroundings, drifting from one tuft of grass to the next. The sheep might even wander out onto a ledge or crag of a cliff face. It isn't until the sheep wishes to return to level ground that it realizes its plight. The shepherd's staff is designed with a crook for such emergencies. With it, the shepherd can hoist the sheep to safety.

Predators pose a second great danger to the sheep. Shepherds are equipped with a club-shaped weapon called a rod to protect the sheep. In a world of predators, it seems we need the protection of God more than ever. God often provides rescue for his people, whether from circumstances of our own making or from situations that are no fault of our own.

God provides restoration. My favorite line from Psalm 23 is this: "He renews my life" (v. 3). Life is exhausting. Life promotes weariness. Whether it's the difficulties of our jobs, the challenge of raising teenagers, or a critic who is never satisfied with our best efforts, life has a way of wearing us down and whittling at our resolve. No matter how much life dings or damages us, we're never beyond God's restorative reach.

God provides righteousness. "He leads me along the right paths [paths of righteousness] for his name's sake" (v. 3). *Righteousness*, while a difficult-sounding word, is easy to understand. Not only is this word important in understanding Psalm 23, but it's also indispensable to understanding the entire Bible.

In simplest terms, the word *righteousness* means "to be in a right relationship" with another person. As a husband, I understand what is required to remain in a right relationship with my wife. It involves significant commitments, such as sexual fidelity and honest communication. A right relationship also involves more subtle obligations, such as taking out the trash and putting Christmas lights on the house each year. Every relationship develops spoken and unspoken expectations of a right relationship. For any relationship to work, these requirements must be consistent and respected by both parties.

How do we remain in a right relationship with God? One thing is sure: we don't have to guess. God guides. "He leads me along the right paths for his name's sake" (v. 3). Ultimately, God the Father leads us to his Son, Jesus. It is Jesus who equips us—through his death, burial, and resurrection—to relate rightly to God. God himself provides the righteousness—the right relationship with himself through Jesus.

A story has been told about a fire that raged through a national park. After the fire had burned out, rangers trekked high into the mountains to survey the damage. One ranger discovered the scorched remains of a bird. Underneath its wings were three living baby chicks. Apparently, as the fire approached, the mother bird had chosen to stay even though she could have flown to safety. Under the security of her wings, she provided her chicks with protection. In the same way, God provides all we need for life and eternity under his protective care.

FOR REFLECTION

Isaiah 53:6 captures the shepherd-sheep relationship when it says, "We all went astray like sheep; we all have turned to our own way; and the LORD has punished him for the iniquity of us all." God's ultimate provision for our sinful straying is the sacrifice of Jesus Christ. Jesus himself is our resource, rescue, restoration, and righteousness.

Have you allowed Jesus to bring you into a restored, right relationship with God, or are you still trying to do it all on your own? What evidence can you provide to support your answer? Righteousness in Jesus comes when we stop trying and begin trusting.

it's not about what we do.

Psalm 51

For the choir director. A psalm of David, when the prophet Nathan came to him after he had gone to Bathsheba.

[1] Be gracious to me, God,
according to your faithful love;
according to your abundant compassion,
blot out my rebellion.
[2] Completely wash away my guilt
and cleanse me from my sin.
[3] For I am conscious of my rebellion,
and my sin is always before me.
[4] Against you — you alone — I have sinned
and done this evil in your sight.
So you are right when you pass sentence;
you are blameless when you judge.
[5] Indeed, I was guilty when I was born;
I was sinful when my mother conceived me.

[6] Surely you desire integrity in the inner self,
and you teach me wisdom deep within.
[7] Purify me with hyssop, and I will be clean;
wash me, and I will be whiter than snow.
[8] Let me hear joy and gladness;
let the bones you have crushed rejoice.
[9] Turn your face away from my sins
and blot out all my guilt.

[10] God, create a clean heart for me
and renew a steadfast spirit within me.
[11] Do not banish me from your presence
or take your Holy Spirit from me.
[12] Restore the joy of your salvation to me,
and sustain me by giving me a willing spirit.
[13] Then I will teach the rebellious your ways,
and sinners will return to you.

[14] Save me from the guilt of bloodshed, God —
God of my salvation —

and my tongue will sing of your righteousness.
¹⁵ Lord, open my lips,
and my mouth will declare your praise.
¹⁶ You do not want a sacrifice, or I would give it;
you are not pleased with a burnt offering.
¹⁷ The sacrifice pleasing to God is a broken spirit.
You will not despise a broken and humbled heart, God.

¹⁸ In your good pleasure, cause Zion to prosper;
build the walls of Jerusalem.
¹⁹ Then you will delight in righteous sacrifices,
whole burnt offerings;
then bulls will be offered on your altar.

13

Guilty but at Peace
Psalm 51

The British fox is both beautiful and crafty. It has devised an imaginative—make that *ingenious*—method to rid itself of fleas. First, the fox will find and collect small bits of wool. Holding this wool in its mouth, the fox gradually submerges its body in a slow-moving stream. The fleas, desperate to escape the rising water, migrate north on the fox's body. Soon only the fox's snout remains above water. Given no alternative, the parasites abandon ship and jump aboard the small lifeboat of wool held in the animal's mouth. When the fox releases the fur, the pests float away. As it emerges from the water, the fox is free of fleas.[1]

What a picture of cleansing! Similarly, Psalm 51 is one of the most compelling pictures of personal purification found in the Bible. David was covered with sin, like fleas on a British fox. But as David stepped into the flow of God's grace, he experienced a depth of cleansing more complete than he could ever have dreamed.

The full account of David's failure is recorded in 2 Samuel 11–12. He was no longer the shepherd we found in Psalm 23. He was now the king of Israel. Yet although he had become a powerful ruler, he was still subject to his sinful tendencies. To put it plainly, David committed the act of adultery. On impulse he slept with a woman he knew to be married. In fact, she was married to one of David's most trusted soldiers. Once David learned she was pregnant, he conspired to have the woman's husband killed, even managing to make the man's death appear to be a casualty of war.

As we read the account, it's obvious that David was thinking only of himself. His decisions were driven by the desire to protect his reputation, regardless of the cost to others. Ultimately, David's guilt was exposed and his sin uncovered for all to see.

It's essential we learn to recognize the sin in our lives. Of equal importance is the practice of repentance. *Repentance* is one of the most essential words in a Jesus follower's vocabulary. Mark Buchanan put it well: "Repentance means you can change. It means you're not stuck. It means what has been does not control what will be: your past need not derange, deform, hold ransom your future. It means that the difference between brokenness and wholeness, dirtiness and cleanness, folly and wisdom, is one door—the door of repentance."[2] Psalm 51 gives us front-row seats to David's act of repentance and his experience with the forgiveness of God.

David opened Psalm 51 using three words to describe his moral failure: *rebellion*, *guilt*, and *sin* (vv. 1–2). He admitted that his disobedience had been nothing less than deliberate. He did wrong with full awareness that he was doing wrong.

As a six-year-old, I had a best friend named Dan. We lived directly across the street from each other. We could talk—or more accurately, *yell*—from our respective curbs. Our parents had given us a single command: *Don't cross the street.* Yet one morning I stood with my arms around Dan's shoulders on his side of the street. I had walked to the far side and lived to tell about it.

To this day I remember the look on my mother's face. I remember awaiting the final judgment when my father arrived home from work that evening. While I don't recall my punishment, I can say with certainty that I never dared cross the street unsupervised again! This simple childhood memory reveals a pattern of behavior I've repeated many times since—deliberate disobedience. I knew what I did was wrong. I knew what I was doing. I felt I could get away with it. I am sure you know exactly what I am talking about.

Just as David's deliberate disobedience was expressed in three words, so also God's response was expressed with a trinity of terms: *graciousness, faithful love,* and *abundant compassion* (v. 1).

Theologian Walter Brueggemann has divided the book of Psalms into three groupings. The first group is the "psalms of orientation." The psalmist experienced intimacy with God and enjoyed all the good the world has to offer. These are the psalms, like Psalm 23, that are a pleasure to read because they capture the pleasure of life. Second, there are the "psalms of disorientation." The psalmist felt disconnected from God and his goodness. Be it sin of his own doing or circumstances beyond his control, the psalmist failed to sense God and his love. The final group includes the "psalms of new orientation." God stepped into a desperate moment, bringing his presence and his peace.[3] Graciousness, faithful love, and abundant compassion are God's tools of reorientation. The psalmist suddenly realized that nothing of real value was missing when God was present.

The reality of our rebellion, guilt, and sin and the realization of God's graciousness, love, and compassion create the possibility that we can be in the wrong given God's high standards, and yet God's boundless love can make us right. It is this guilty-but-at-peace possibility that permeates the remainder of Psalm 51. Three verses in particular openly acknowledge remorse while at the same time conveying overtones of God's restoration. These verses also lay a solid foundation for a biblical understanding of sin.

"Against you—you alone—I have sinned and done this evil in your sight" (v. 4). Sin indeed damages us and the people around us. If I lie to my wife and she discovers my deception, I damage my credibility as well as her ability to trust me. I've harmed both myself and her. But sin's ultimate destructive power is experienced in the damage done to our intimacy with God.

David confessed, "Indeed, I was guilty when I was born; I was sinful when my mother conceived me" (v. 5). Sin, while an act, is also part of our identity. Sin is more than what we do; sin is embedded in our human nature.

Michel Lotito was born with a little-known mental disorder called pica. A person with this disorder is compelled to eat non-food items. Most sufferers crave dirt or plastics; Michel preferred metals. Over the course of his lifetime, Michel consumed two beds, six chandeliers, seven televisions, fifteen shopping carts, eighteen bicycles, and one Cessna airplane. And this is just a partial list.[4]

While this account is strange, it also illustrates sin as something imprinted on our identities. We're somehow compelled to consume things harmful to us. While sin is unexplainable and irrational, we simply can't bring ourselves to stop. And the more we wrestle with sin, the more we discover we're fighting with ourselves.

"God, create a clean heart for me and renew a steadfast spirit within me" (v. 10). God is in the character-transforming business. This is good news! Character change is possible for those in a relationship with God through Jesus Christ. Your past behavior may include lying, but in Christ your identity is no longer that of a liar. Perhaps your past involved stealing from others. But with God's restoring power, your character transcends such petty behaviors. And here is a momentous thought: you may have lost, but you're no longer a loser. God's power to forgive is stronger than your past. God's forgiveness not only removes guilt but also transforms your flaws into examples of his faithfulness. Here are words of hope for those of us covered with sin: "Wash me, and I will be whiter than snow" (v. 7).

Despite his profound public failure, David is referred to in the New Testament as "a man after [God's] own heart" (Acts 13:22). No sin can completely destroy your usefulness to God. He isn't in the habit of throwing lives away. Certainly, if God can restore David through repentance, he can do the same with you.

FOR REFLECTION

The book of Psalms contains seven "penitential psalms" that focus on asking for God's forgiveness. These are Psalms 6, 32, 38, 51, 102, 130, and 143. The repeated calls for forgiveness remind us that repentance is an ongoing habit in the life of a Jesus follower.

What do you need to ask God's forgiveness for today? Hold nothing back. He already knows all. God is waiting for you to come clean so that his forgiving power can be released to flow through your life. Even though you're guilty, you can be at peace.

Psalm 139

For the choir director. A psalm of David.

¹ LORD, you have searched me and known me.
² You know when I sit down and when I stand up;
you understand my thoughts from far away.
³ You observe my travels and my rest;
you are aware of all my ways.
⁴ Before a word is on my tongue,
you know all about it, LORD.
⁵ You have encircled me;
you have placed your hand on me.
⁶ This wondrous knowledge is beyond me.
It is lofty; I am unable to reach it.

⁷ Where can I go to escape your Spirit?
Where can I flee from your presence?
⁸ If I go up to heaven, you are there;
if I make my bed in Sheol, you are there.
⁹ If I live at the eastern horizon
or settle at the western limits,
¹⁰ even there your hand will lead me;
your right hand will hold on to me.
¹¹ If I say, "Surely the darkness will hide me,
and the light around me will be night" —
¹² even the darkness is not dark to you.
The night shines like the day;
darkness and light are alike to you.

¹³ For it was you who created my inward parts;
you knit me together in my mother's womb.
¹⁴ I will praise you
because I have been remarkably and wondrously made.
Your works are wondrous,
and I know this very well.
¹⁵ My bones were not hidden from you
when I was made in secret,
when I was formed in the depths of the earth.

[16] Your eyes saw me when I was formless;
all my days were written in your book and planned
before a single one of them began.

[17] God, how precious your thoughts are
to me;
how vast their sum is!
[18] If I counted them,
they would outnumber the grains of sand;
when I wake up, I am still with you.

[19] God, if only you would kill the wicked —
you bloodthirsty men, stay away from me —
[20] who invoke you deceitfully.
Your enemies swear by you falsely.
[21] LORD, don't I hate those who hate you,
and detest those who rebel against you?
[22] I hate them with extreme hatred;
I consider them my enemies.

[23] Search me, God, and know my heart;
test me and know my concerns.
[24] See if there is any offensive way in me;
lead me in the everlasting way.

14

God Is Closer Than You Think
Psalm 139

Dr. Paul Brand devoted his life to the practice of medicine. Specifically, he pioneered surgical-reconstruction techniques for those whose bodies had been damaged by Hansen's disease, commonly called leprosy. Near the end of his career, he coauthored a book with Philip Yancey called *Fearfully and Wonderfully Made*, a title he borrowed from Psalm 139.

Brand's book reveals the intricacy and majesty of the human body. As an example, consider your DNA. The DNA in your body contains the multitudinous and minuscule specifications that determine your appearance, height, eye color, and a thousand other unique qualities that make you *you*. Your full genetic code would fill one thousand six-hundred-page volumes. Even more remarkable is the fact that this same DNA "is so narrow and compacted that all the genes in all [the] body's cells would fit into an ice cube; yet if the DNA were unwound and joined together end to end, the strand could stretch from the earth to the sun and back more than four hundred times."[1]

Fearfully and wonderfully made indeed!

Psalm 139 examines not only the miracle of the human body but also the majesty of God's love for humanity. Love, as we all know, brings out the best parts of our personalities. As Psalm 139 unveils God's love for us, the richest regions of his character are also revealed.

God is all knowing (vv. 1–6). "LORD, you have searched me and known me" (v. 1). We fear that knowing someone completely may lead to boredom. But God assures us that his full knowledge of us isn't only an expression of his love but also results in an ever-deepening affection.

I adore books, especially old ones. The feel and smell of a vintage hardback is one of life's true satisfactions. One book in particular holds a special place in my library, and I read it in its entirety twice every year. It was written by my old professor and mentor, Calvin Miller. Many times I told him it was his best book. He disagreed. But something about *The Table of Inwardness* resonates with my desire for an intimate relationship with God. I know this book well, yet my appreciation for its author and content hasn't diminished with my many readings. In fact, I value it more every time I read it.

God can read you like a book, a good book.

It's worth recognizing that God's intimate awareness of our identity and actions doesn't negate our freedom of choice. At the same time, our freedom to choose doesn't diminish God's perfect knowledge of who we are. He is all knowing yet ever allows us to determine the direction and decisions of our lives.

God is ever present (vv. 7–12). "Where can I go to escape your Spirit? Where can I flee from your presence?" (v. 7). Psalm 139 leads us to the inescapable conclusion that God himself is inescapable. At times we're unable to sense his presence. This failure to feel his nearness may result from circumstances beyond our own control. The death of a loved one comes to mind. In this dark time, God's presence may be difficult to sense.

Deliberate disobedience to God also results in feelings of distance between us and him. For the most part, feelings of estrangement from the Almighty are just that—feelings. The promise of Scripture is grounded in the fact that God is ever present.

Saint Patrick was a follower of Jesus in the fifth century. Born on the British Isles, he was kidnapped at an early age and held by the Irish as a slave. Having gained his freedom, he chose to return to Ireland in his adult years to share Christ with his former captors. Patrick was a man well acquainted with helplessness and hopelessness. No wonder the prayer attributed to him is reminiscent of Psalm 139:

> Be Christ, this day, my strong protector: ...
> Christ beside me, Christ before me;
> Christ behind me, Christ within me;
> Christ beneath me, Christ above me;
> Christ to right of me, Christ to left of me;
> Christ in my lying, my sitting, my rising.[2]

God is all seeing (vv. 13–18). "My bones were not hidden from you when I was made in secret.... Your eyes saw me when I was formless; all my days were written in your book and planned before a single one of them began" (vv. 15–16). Two concerns come to mind as we consider God's all-seeing ability. First, by virtue of our nature, we're limited to being in one place at one time. It's difficult, therefore, to comprehend *how* God could manage to be all seeing. Second, even if we could accept God's all-observing nature, we would be instantly suspicious as to *why* he watches us so closely.

Years ago, I heard a simple story that for some reason has stayed with me. At a small Christian elementary school, the children lined up for lunch. Near the front of the food line was a delicious pile of apples. One of the teachers had placed a sign beside the apples that read, "Take only one apple. God is watching." At the end of the food line was a plate of cookies. A student felt the freedom to improvise her own sign that read, "Take all the cookies you want. God is watching the apples."

Psalm 139 doesn't address the *how* of God's all-seeing nature. The psalm assumes this reality. But it does speak openly about the *why* of God's constant observation. If we assume God loathes us, then the words "God is watching" carry the overtone of a threat. But when we consider how God loves us, his watching takes on an entirely different and more comforting meaning.

Until my children learned to swim, I vigilantly watched anytime our family was near a pool, lake, or river. My wife would tell you I was downright tense. Having nearly drowned as a child, I feared for my own children's safety. One day I stopped by after work to see my daughter take swim lessons. Even though the instructor was a lifeguard, I was on high alert. I couldn't believe what I witnessed as the lifeguard turned his back to my daughter. Kira lost her grip on the side of the pool and slipped beneath the surface of the water without her instructor noticing. I leaped into action and pulled her to safety. When the same series of events happened a second time, I pulled my daughter from the water and fired the instructor. He wasn't watchful or qualified to care for my child. This memorable experience reinforced what I already knew: no one can care for my children the way I can.

In the same way, your heavenly Father's watchfulness is an expression of intense love. His love is intimate and infinite. His care is deeper than you can imagine and larger than you'll ever know. No one cares for you as he does. No one can and no one will. *No one.*

Psalm 139 concludes with the beautiful prayer acknowledging God's never-ending desire for our development: "Search me, God, and know my heart; test me and know my concerns. See if there is any offensive way in me; lead me in the everlasting way" (vv. 23–24).

FOR REFLECTION

The book of Psalms contains 150 different prayers. For centuries, monks have gathered in their communities for morning prayer. Tradition holds that the first prayer of the day is Psalm 70:1: "God, hurry to rescue me. LORD, hurry to help me!" What a wonderful prayer with which to meet each morning!

In what area of your life—perhaps a relationship, your job, or financial stress—do you need God's help? Name it before him today. Ask for relief. Ask God to provide you with refuge—the safety that comes from knowing that you're never out of his loving sight or separated from his watchful protection.

Proverbs 1

¹ The proverbs of Solomon son of David, king of Israel:
² For learning wisdom and discipline;
for understanding insightful sayings;
³ for receiving prudent instruction
in righteousness, justice, and integrity;
⁴ for teaching shrewdness to the inexperienced,
knowledge and discretion to a young man —
⁵ let a wise person listen and increase learning,
and let a discerning person obtain guidance —
⁶ for understanding a proverb or a parable,
the words of the wise, and their riddles.

⁷ The fear of the LORD
is the beginning of knowledge;
fools despise wisdom and discipline.

⁸ Listen, my son, to your father's instruction,
and don't reject your mother's teaching,
⁹ for they will be a garland of favor on your head
and pendants around your neck.
¹⁰ My son, if sinners entice you,
don't be persuaded.
¹¹ If they say — "Come with us!
Let's set an ambush and kill someone.
Let's attack some innocent person just for fun!
¹² Let's swallow them alive, like Sheol,
whole, like those who go down to the Pit.
¹³ We'll find all kinds of valuable property
and fill our houses with plunder.
¹⁴ Throw in your lot with us,
and we'll all share the loot" —
¹⁵ my son, don't travel that road with them
or set foot on their path,
¹⁶ because their feet run toward evil
and they hurry to shed blood.
¹⁷ It is useless to spread a net
where any bird can see it,

¹⁸ but they set an ambush to kill themselves;
they attack their own lives.
¹⁹ Such are the paths of all who make profit dishonestly;
it takes the lives of those who receive it.

²⁰ Wisdom calls out in the street;
she makes her voice heard in the public squares.
²¹ She cries out above the commotion;
she speaks at the entrance of the city gates:
²² "How long, inexperienced ones, will you love ignorance?
How long will you mockers enjoy mocking
and you fools hate knowledge?
²³ If you respond to my warning,
then I will pour out my spirit on you
and teach you my words.
²⁴ Since I called out and you refused,
extended my hand and no one paid attention,
²⁵ since you neglected all my counsel
and did not accept my correction,
²⁶ I, in turn, will laugh at your calamity.
I will mock when terror strikes you,
²⁷ when terror strikes you like a storm
and your calamity comes like a whirlwind,
when trouble and stress overcome you.
²⁸ Then they will call me, but I won't answer;
they will search for me, but won't find me.
²⁹ Because they hated knowledge,
didn't choose to fear the LORD,
³⁰ were not interested in my counsel,
and rejected all my correction,
³¹ they will eat the fruit of their way
and be glutted with their own schemes.
³² For the apostasy of the inexperienced will kill them,
and the complacency of fools will destroy them.
³³ But whoever listens to me will live securely
and be undisturbed by the dread of danger."

15

Words of Wisdom
Proverbs 1

Stephen Covey, author of *The 7 Habits of Highly Effective People*, suggested conducting an experiment with high-level executives: gather a dozen or so of these leaders into a boardroom, and invite them to close their eyes and confidently point north. All of the executives will probably point in different directions. The lesson is simple: intuition isn't always accurate.[1]

One of the great lessons of life is learning the difference between what *feels* right and what *is* right. The book of Proverbs, like the rest of the Bible, points us in the correct direction. Proverbs helps us understand and apply God's will, which is true north for followers of Jesus.

The book of Proverbs contains a total of thirty-one chapters. It's a popular practice to read one chapter each day, thereby completing the entire book within a month. (Perhaps you would consider this idea after finishing this study.) Repetition is a key to learning. By marinating our minds in the book of Proverbs, we close the gap between our intuition and God's instruction.

One word summarizes the book of Proverbs: *wisdom*. Consider the book's opening words: "The proverbs of Solomon son of David, king of Israel: For learning wisdom and discipline; for understanding insightful sayings; for receiving prudent instruction in righteousness, justice, and integrity" (1:1–3).

So what is wisdom? It's doing the right thing at the right time for the right reasons.[2] On its face, this definition may appear to be an oversimplification. However, anyone with experience in life will appreciate the difficulty of accomplishing the right action, the right attitude, and the right agenda all at the right moment.

The word *wisdom* occurs more than two hundred times throughout the Bible, fifty-one times in the book of Proverbs alone. Proverbs covers the wisdom necessary for nearly every conceivable issue of day-to-day life. Work, sexuality, speaking, silence, thoughts, economics, emotions, and the primacy of a relationship with God are all addressed.

Oscar Wilde once said, "Experience is the name everyone gives to their mistakes." So the choice before us is an obvious one. We can learn from our own mistakes, or we can choose to learn from the mistakes of others. The difference between these two options is that of personal cost. We pay for our own mistakes with the pain of embarrassment and regret. But we can learn from the mistakes of others for free. Great people from the past who made magnificent mistakes willingly share their wisdom with us. We must now receive it. Their scars can be our instructors. Examining their wounds and the lessons they learned may well spare us the indignity of personal injury. By benefiting from their wounds, we avoid wounds of the self-inflicted variety.

In addition to *wisdom*, two other words from this chapter deserve our attention: *discipline* and *insight*.

Discipline is backing up great plans with daily decisions. For instance, I've made the long-term plan to stay healthy. But I must implement this grand plan with day-to-day choices. I choose the running track over the easy chair, the granola instead of the gravy. The purpose of Proverbs is to help us learn discipline. Everyday decisions have a cumulative power to produce a life of wisdom.

Insight is the ability to see reality with accuracy. It's the trained eye of experience. I can't read an X-ray, but my doctor can take one look at the black-and-white image and notice its subtle features. I would see only a blur, whereas he would discern a broken bone. My doctor and I may be looking at the same object, but only one of us has insight. Proverbs trains our eyes to separate the important from the inconsequential, the significant from the background static of life.

At the conclusion of the Trojan War, the Greek hero Odysseus faced a long journey home. His trek became known as his odyssey. Before Odysseus had left home for the battlefield, he placed his son, Telemachus, under the tutelage of an older, wiser man. This man, whose name was Mentor, was responsible for teaching young Telemachus much-needed street smarts in the absence of his father.[3] Even today we speak of mentors as those who teach invaluable truths at opportune times.

The book of Proverbs serves as a reliable and readable mentor. Though not a living, breathing person, Proverbs preserves the best thinking and the highest learning of great leaders. (Solomon, renowned for his wisdom, did the heavy lifting in this volume.) In addition to street smarts, the book of Proverbs provides Jesus followers with "soul smarts."

Proverbs 1:7, a well-known line, is the source of some confusion. It says, "The fear of the LORD is the beginning of knowledge; fools despise wisdom and discipline." We must take great care in understanding the phrase "the fear of the LORD." On the surface it seems to suggest that we should be afraid of God. However, emotionally speaking, we know that fear has a way of limiting instead of unleashing. Fear holds us captive instead of setting us free. It's impossible to completely love someone we consciously fear.

🕊 In the Hebrew sense of the word, *fear* is best understood as a "reverent awe" or "ultimate respect." God doesn't desire that we dread him; he asks that we have greater respect for him than anything else in our lives. Proverbs 1:7 teaches that only as we hold God and his commands in high regard do we see the great importance of our decisions. Life is a gift from our Creator to be handled with great care. This caliber of relationship with God is the starting place for wise and smart living.

In 1954, the University of Illinois Institute of Aviation recorded the efforts of twenty pilots with limited experience flying small, single-engine aircraft. These pilots were untrained in reading aircraft instrument panels. Instruments aren't needed when the weather is ideal and the horizon is visible. But they're indispensable when weather is poor and a pilot has no visual reference points to guide his or her course.

One at a time, these twenty pilots took their turn in the flight simulator. The simulator produced the effect of thick, dark clouds. On average, each pilot lost control of his aircraft within 178 seconds. With no visual reference points, flying by intuition alone, these pilots found themselves on the verge of self-destruction within minutes.[4]

We appreciate the power of intuition when life is calm and skies are clear. Well and good. But when the weather of life turns foul, when turbulence takes hold, we no longer have the luxury of operating by feelings. We require wisdom. For the Jesus follower, the book of Proverbs can serve as a reliable instrument panel. And learn to read it, we must! The wisdom of God in its pages can be relied on for necessary course corrections in life.

FOR REFLECTION

The most popular passage in Proverbs is "Trust in the LORD with all your heart, and do not rely on your own understanding; in all your ways know him, and he will make your paths straight" (3:5–6). This verse is displayed prominently in my study, a reminder of my need for God's wisdom, given my inability to navigate life on feelings alone.

In what area of your life do you need wisdom? At work? At home? In traffic? Write Proverbs 3:5–6 on a card, and display it in a strategic place as a reminder of your need for God's guidance.

TOUGH LOVE, TROUBLED TIMES

Isaiah 53

¹ Who has believed what we have heard?
And to whom has the arm of the LORD been revealed?
² He grew up before him like a young plant
and like a root out of dry ground.
He didn't have an impressive form
or majesty that we should look at him,
no appearance that we should desire him.
³ He was despised and rejected by men,
a man of suffering who knew what sickness was.
He was like someone people turned away from;
he was despised, and we didn't value him.

⁴ Yet he himself bore our sicknesses,
and he carried our pains;
but we in turn regarded him stricken,
struck down by God, and afflicted.
⁵ But he was pierced because of our rebellion,
crushed because of our iniquities;
punishment for our peace was on him,
and we are healed by his wounds.
⁶ We all went astray like sheep;
we all have turned to our own way;
and the LORD has punished him
for the iniquity of us all.

⁷ He was oppressed and afflicted,
yet he did not open his mouth.
Like a lamb led to the slaughter
and like a sheep silent before her shearers,
he did not open his mouth.
⁸ He was taken away because of oppression and judgment;
and who considered his fate?
For he was cut off from the land of the living;
he was struck because of my people's rebellion.
⁹ He was assigned a grave with the wicked,
but he was with a rich man at his death,
because he had done no violence
and had not spoken deceitfully.

[10] Yet the LORD was pleased to crush him severely.
When you make him a guilt offering,
he will see his seed, he will prolong his days,
and by his hand, the LORD's pleasure will be accomplished.
[11] After his anguish,
he will see light and be satisfied.
By his knowledge,
my righteous servant will justify many,
and he will carry their iniquities.
[12] Therefore I will give him the many as a portion,
and he will receive the mighty as spoil,
because he willingly submitted to death,
and was counted among the rebels;
yet he bore the sin of many
and interceded for the rebels.

16

The Real Face of Jesus
Isaiah 53

Several years ago, *Popular Mechanics* magazine featured a story about archaeologists and anthropologists who were on a quest to discover "The Real Face of Jesus."[1] To accurately depict how Jesus might have looked, researchers factored in the average height of men in Jesus's day and used skeletal remains from the era to reconstruct common facial features. They concluded that Jesus had a dark complexion, stood no more than five feet one inch in height, and weighed around 110 pounds.

Whatever you might think about the face that peers out from the cover of the magazine, one thing is sure: Jesus didn't look at all like many people have come to imagine him—the idealized image of Anglo attractiveness.

The Bible itself never bothers to address Jesus's appearance. Scripture offers not even a hint of his eye color, hair length, or height. I find this lack of detail refreshing, a stark contrast to our own culture's obsession with appearance over substance.

The closest thing to a physical description of Jesus in the Bible can be found in Isaiah 53. Remarkably, this description was rendered some seven hundred years before Jesus's birth. Isaiah painted Jesus with broad strokes, saying, "He didn't have an impressive form or majesty that we should look at him, no appearance that we should desire him.... He was like someone people turned away from; he was despised, and we didn't value him" (vv. 2–3). Perhaps the rendering on the cover of *Popular Mechanics* wasn't so far from the truth after all.

According to Isaiah, Jesus's appearance was that of an ordinary man. Nothing about the way he looked would have caught our eye. But if life teaches us one thing about people, it's this: there's often more to a person than meets the eye. Isaiah gives us a second look at the Son of God.

But first, who was Isaiah? And what qualified him to describe with such certainty the still-future Jesus?

The book Isaiah wrote is one of sixteen books of prophecy in the Older Testament. Roughly speaking, the final third of the Older Testament consists of writings collectively called the Prophets. The four largest books of this group—Isaiah, Jeremiah, Ezekiel, and Daniel—are commonly referred to as the Major Prophets. The twelve shorter writings are labeled the Minor Prophets. This distinction between major and minor is superficial, based solely on the length of the book. The Major Prophets have a larger word count than their minor counterparts. The length of the book notwithstanding, the messages of the Major and Minor Prophets carry equal weight and importance.

Convention often assumes a prophet is someone who predicts future events. To be sure, there are several instances throughout the prophetic writings when the future comes into play. Isaiah 53 is a shining example. A prophet may indeed tell the future, but more often a prophet simply tells it like it is.

When, as a young man, I began an earnest search for God, Isaiah 53 was the first chapter I turned to. To this day I don't know why. Yet I vividly remember being attracted to Isaiah's tone of certainty as I sat reading on my bedroom floor in my boyhood home. Even with my limited understanding of God and the Bible, I could see the silhouette of Jesus in Isaiah's words.

Isaiah, even from the distance of seven hundred years pre-Jesus, spoke with amazing detail about Jesus's true identity and lasting impact. Prophets like Isaiah remind us that God isn't making up history as he goes. The simple fact that Isaiah would see God's actions from a seven-hundred-year horizon says something about God's forethought. History isn't ad-lib; God designed it with an intricacy that could only originate from his eternal mind.

In this chapter Isaiah moved from a near-physical description of Jesus to another and perhaps better way to look at him. Instead of being content with a description of his appearance, we're invited to observe his actions.

As we read Isaiah 53:3–5, images from Jesus's crucifixion flash before our eyes. Verses 9–10 are reminiscent of Jesus's burial, and verses 11–12 are an advance echo of the resurrection. Taking each image in turn, we get a fuller picture of Jesus.

Crucifixion. "He was pierced because of our rebellion, crushed because of our iniquities; punishment for our peace was on him, and we are healed by his wounds" (v. 5). On bridges and boxcars everywhere, adolescents have scrawled their love in paint. "Liam loves Lauren" is written for the entire world to see. Likewise, God's love for humanity was written on the body of Christ. Isaiah helps us see the indelible wounds on the hands, feet, and side of Jesus as true marks of sacrificial love.

Burial. "He was assigned a grave with the wicked" (v. 9). I've already purchased my grave plot. My desire is to be buried in the western reaches of Texas where I'm from. I like the idea of a beautiful bookending to life—being buried where I was born, entombed where I first entered the world. Recently on a visit home, I stopped by the cemetery where I'll end up. Far from being creepy, the experience inspired me to live every day to the fullest.

Jesus owned no grave. In fact, the New Testament tells of a man who allowed Jesus to be buried in a tomb he had recently carved out for himself. So sudden was Jesus's death that no plans had been considered.

Resurrection. "After his anguish, he will see light and be satisfied" (v. 11). Each of the four New Testament accounts of Jesus's life ends with a record of the resurrection. Jesus isn't only a memory; his presence is a reality even today.

The Russian priest Alexander Schmemann was riding a subway while visiting Paris with his fiancée. An elderly woman wearing a Salvation Army uniform boarded the train and sat next to him. He spoke openly to his fiancée about the appearance of the old woman, certain that no one would understand his Russian dialect. To him she appeared ugly and repulsive. After a few stops, the woman rose from her seat to depart the train. Before exiting, she paused directly in front of Schmemann and in flawless Russian said, "I wasn't always ugly." Then she turned and left the train.[2]

Schmemann, who would go on to be a reformer in his faith community, considered this event a transformative moment in his life. He learned to look beneath the surface to discover the value of a person.

Similarly, Jesus's actions, not his appearance, are what make him truly beautiful.

FOR REFLECTION

Isaiah 53:6 is the most familiar verse in this important chapter: "We all went astray like sheep; we all have turned to our own way; and the LORD has punished him [Jesus] for the iniquity of us all." In the original Hebrew, Isaiah 53:6 begins and ends with the same word—meaning essentially "all of us." *All of us* have wandered away from God. *All of us* are eligible for forgiveness. *All of us.*

What are some specific ways you've strayed from a right relationship with God? Take a few moments to allow Isaiah 53:6 to become personal. Practice the essential but often overlooked spiritual act of confessing your sins to God.

Jeremiah 1

¹ The words of Jeremiah, the son of Hilkiah, one of the priests living in Anathoth in the territory of Benjamin. ² The word of the LORD came to him in the thirteenth year of the reign of Josiah son of Amon, king of Judah. ³ It also came throughout the days of Jehoiakim son of Josiah, king of Judah, until the fifth month of the eleventh year of Zedekiah son of Josiah, king of Judah, when the people of Jerusalem went into exile.

⁴ The word of the LORD came to me:

⁵ I chose you before I formed you in the womb;
I set you apart before you were born.
I appointed you a prophet to the nations.

⁶ But I protested, "Oh no, Lord GOD! Look, I don't know how to speak since I am only a youth."
⁷ Then the LORD said to me:

Do not say, "I am only a youth,"
for you will go to everyone I send you to
and speak whatever I tell you.
⁸ Do not be afraid of anyone,
for I will be with you to rescue you.
This is the LORD's declaration.

⁹ Then the LORD reached out his hand, touched my mouth, and told me:

I have now filled your mouth with my words.
¹⁰ See, I have appointed you today
over nations and kingdoms
to uproot and tear down,
to destroy and demolish,
to build and plant.

¹¹ Then the word of the LORD came to me, asking, "What do you see, Jeremiah?"
I replied, "I see a branch of an almond tree."

¹² The LORD said to me, "You have seen correctly, for I watch over my word to accomplish it." ¹³ Again the word of the LORD came to me asking, "What do you see?"

And I replied, "I see a boiling pot, its lip tilted from the north to the south."

¹⁴ Then the LORD said to me, "Disaster will be poured out from the north on all who live in the land. ¹⁵ Indeed, I am about to summon all the clans and kingdoms of the north."

This is the LORD's declaration.

They will come, and each king will set up his throne
at the entrance to Jerusalem's gates.
They will attack all her surrounding walls
and all the other cities of Judah.

¹⁶ "I will pronounce my judgments against them for all the evil they did when they abandoned me to burn incense to other gods and to worship the works of their own hands.

¹⁷ "Now, get ready. Stand up and tell them everything that I command you. Do not be intimidated by them or I will cause you to cower before them. ¹⁸ Today, I am the one who has made you a fortified city, an iron pillar, and bronze walls against the whole land — against the kings of Judah, its officials, its priests, and the population. ¹⁹ They will fight against you but never prevail over you, since I am with you to rescue you."

This is the LORD's declaration.

17

Inferiority and Obedience
Jeremiah 1

I live with a mystery. Summers in Oklahoma are nothing short of brutally hot. I'm diligent to water my lawn during these sweltering months, but by midsummer no amount of moisture will prevent the grass from turning a crispy brown.

Here's a mystery: How can there be large swaths of dead grass in my yard while sprigs of green grass grow in the cracks of my driveway? I saturate my yard, and it turns brown. I don't put a drop of water on my driveway, and the grass in the crevices remains a verdant green.

Whatever the explanation, this mystery reveals a spiritual reality: Life grows in the cracks. Life survives in spaces we wouldn't expect. Life thrives best in the hard and difficult places.

One of my dearest friends grew up in a home with an abusive, alcoholic father. Despite being born and brought up in a hard place, he went to college, established a career, and raised a family. I often hear people blame the outcome of their lives on their parents; my friend isn't among them. He made the decision to grow in the hard place.

Whenever I drive past churches in suburbia, I notice the sprawling campuses and all the smiling people. By contrast, I serve a church in an urban setting. We serve a clientele who live on the precipice of poverty. Smiles are harder to come by. Daily I live with the reality that my church is planted in a place as hard as the concrete that surrounds our campus. Yet our church thrives in our crack of downtown asphalt.

Jeremiah was an Older Testament figure who personified this crack-in-the-slab existence. We know more personal details about Jeremiah than any other Older Testament prophet—most of which Jeremiah revealed himself. Though I hesitate to mention dates and events, to appreciate Jeremiah we must understand the hard place in history in which he served God.

God's chosen people, the Israelites, lived as a unified nation under the strong leadership of three kings—Saul, David, and Solomon. After the death of Solomon, civil war tore the nation apart. This conflict, not unlike the American Civil War, divided the Jewish nation in two—north and south. The northern tribes became known as Israel, while the southern tribes were collectively called Judah. Israel and Judah coexisted under a tense truce for more than two centuries.

Assyria, the world's first superpower, emerged during this period. Its foreign-relations strategy could be summed up in one word: *conquest*. Assyria was bent on assimilating every nation within its reach of power. In 721 BC, Assyria conquered Israel.

Some of the Jewish survivors were deported to the Assyrian home-land. The survivors who remained in Israel eventually intermarried with their Assyrian conquerors, creating the Samaritan race. The northern kingdom of Israel was essentially obliterated. Only Judah remained. But for how long?

More than a century after the conquest of Israel, Assyria itself was swallowed up by a new big kid on the block, a nation named Babylon. Like Assyria, Babylon had visions of an ever-expanding empire. With Israel out of the way, the Babylonians licked their chops at the prospect of consuming the southern kingdom of Judah.

Jeremiah was born in this craggy place in history. Babylon was threatening Judah from the outside. Political strife and religious corruption were destroying it from within. Yet the very events Jeremiah might have interpreted as inconvenient were, in fact, the makings of his destiny. During this chaotic time, God was not silent. "The word of the LORD came to [Jeremiah]: I chose you before I formed you in the womb; I set you apart before you were born. I appointed you a prophet to the nations" (Jer. 1:4–5).

Jeremiah's reaction to the voice of God was like that of many great leaders in the Bible—he was overwhelmed! We see a similar response from the likes of Abraham (Gen. 15:2), Moses (Exod. 3:11), and Mary (Luke 1:34). Jeremiah attempted to excuse himself from the service of God, citing his lack of maturity and experience: "I am only a youth" (Jer. 1:6). While we can't say for sure, many scholars believe that Jeremiah may have been about twenty years of age.

When I was asked to lead a sizable church at the age of twenty-nine, I found myself paying careful attention to Jeremiah. It became a personal resource during my early days of ministry. I distinctly remember sitting on a flight between Atlanta, Georgia, and Tulsa, Oklahoma, reading the first chapter of Jeremiah repeatedly. This convinced me to embrace any opportunity God saw fit to send my way, despite my lack of know-how.

Jeremiah offers a vital lesson to those who feel underqualified to serve God. The lesson is this: you *are* underqualified to serve God. But lack of experience takes a backseat to obeying him. His commands, not your personal qualifications, determine how life is to be spent in his service.

I carry a 1965 British crown coin in my pocket. I carry this coin for two reasons. First, I'm an admirer of Winston Churchill and regard him as the greatest leader of the twentieth century. Second, this coin represents a first in the history of British coinage. In 1965, the year Churchill died, the British Royal Mint issued a coin bearing his image in honor of his life and contributions. For as long as coins have been minted on the British Isles—back to the era of the Romans—coins have exclusively carried the images of royalty. One must be a caesar, an emperor, a king, or a queen for a portrait to earn a place on currency.

In 1965, however, Churchill became the first commoner to appear on a British coin. When an ordinary person encounters extraordinary odds, it puts him on par with royalty. Churchill became prime minister of England at the beginning of war with Germany. He understood the hard places. Facing his own set of difficulties, he said, "I felt as if I were walking with destiny, and that all my past life had been but a preparation for this hour and for this trial."[1]

Jeremiah was an ordinary individual, to be sure. But he chose to walk with destiny—and with God—in the hard places. At the command of God, he was in constant conflict with the politicians, the priests, and the other prophets of his day. On more than one occasion, Jeremiah was even in conflict with himself. He dealt with his fair share of self-doubt, but his feelings of inferiority never stopped him from obeying God's commands. Even when Jeremiah didn't *feel* strong, he *was* strong. Instead of answering to his inferior instincts, he observed the orders of the Lord.

Accompanying Jeremiah's call was his first vision and message: danger and disaster were coming from the north. Despite this, God's command to Jeremiah inspires all of us to live boldly: "Now, get ready. Stand up and tell them everything that I command you. Do not be intimidated by them or I will cause you to cower before them" (v. 17).

In the end Babylon conquered Judah in 586 BC. The nation didn't remain intact, but Jeremiah's integrity did. While Judah crumbled around him, Jeremiah remained solid in his unwavering obedience to God.

Future generations of Jews admired Jeremiah as a good man who thrived in the hard places of life. As Jews in Jesus's day tried to make sense of who he was, there were some who suggested that Jesus might be on par with Jeremiah (see Matt. 16:14). What a compliment! What an achievement it would be to live in such a way that people would confuse us with Christ. This kind of reputation results only from living obediently despite feelings of inferiority.

FOR REFLECTION

What is your greatest insecurity or deepest inferiority? We all have at least one. Talk to God about it today. Consider your inadequacy as a perfect opportunity to practice obedience. Being scared presents the ideal occasion to surrender yourself to God's will. God said to Jeremiah (and perhaps he's saying to you), "Now, get ready." (Jer. 1:17). So get moving!

Daniel 3

[1] King Nebuchadnezzar made a gold statue, ninety feet high and nine feet wide. He set it up on the plain of Dura in the province of Babylon. [2] King Nebuchadnezzar sent word to assemble the satraps, prefects, governors, advisers, treasurers, judges, magistrates, and all the rulers of the provinces to attend the dedication of the statue King Nebuchadnezzar had set up. [3] So the satraps, prefects, governors, advisers, treasurers, judges, magistrates, and all the rulers of the provinces assembled for the dedication of the statue the king had set up. Then they stood before the statue Nebuchadnezzar had set up.

[4] A herald loudly proclaimed, "People of every nation and language, you are commanded: [5] When you hear the sound of the horn, flute, zither, lyre, harp, drum, and every kind of music, you are to fall facedown and worship the gold statue that King Nebuchadnezzar has set up. [6] But whoever does not fall down and worship will immediately be thrown into a furnace of blazing fire."

[7] Therefore, when all the people heard the sound of the horn, flute, zither, lyre, harp, and every kind of music, people of every nation and language fell down and worshiped the gold statue that King Nebuchadnezzar had set up.

[8] Some Chaldeans took this occasion to come forward and maliciously accuse the Jews. [9] They said to King Nebuchadnezzar, "May the king live forever. [10] You as king have issued a decree that everyone who hears the sound of the horn, flute, zither, lyre, harp, drum, and every kind of music must fall down and worship the gold statue. [11] Whoever does not fall down and worship will be thrown into a furnace of blazing fire. [12] There are some Jews you have appointed to manage the province of Babylon: Shadrach, Meshach, and Abednego. These men have ignored you, the king; they do not serve your gods or worship the gold statue you have set up."

[13] Then in a furious rage Nebuchadnezzar gave orders to bring in Shadrach, Meshach, and Abednego. So these men were brought before the king. [14] Nebuchadnezzar asked them, "Shadrach, Meshach, and Abednego, is it true that you don't serve my gods or worship the gold statue I have set up? [15] Now if you're ready, when you hear the sound of the horn, flute, zither, lyre, harp, drum, and every kind of music, fall down and worship the statue I made. But if you don't worship it, you will immediately be thrown into a furnace of blazing fire — and who is the god who can rescue you from my power?"

¹⁶ Shadrach, Meshach, and Abednego replied to the king, "Nebuchadnezzar, we don't need to give you an answer to this question. ¹⁷ If the God we serve exists, then he can rescue us from the furnace of blazing fire, and he can rescue us from the power of you, the king. ¹⁸ But even if he does not rescue us, we want you as king to know that we will not serve your gods or worship the gold statue you set up."

¹⁹ Then Nebuchadnezzar was filled with rage, and the expression on his face changed toward Shadrach, Meshach, and Abednego. He gave orders to heat the furnace seven times more than was customary, ²⁰ and he commanded some of the best soldiers in his army to tie up Shadrach, Meshach, and Abednego and throw them into the furnace of blazing fire. ²¹ So these men, in their trousers, robes, head coverings, and other clothes, were tied up and thrown into the furnace of blazing fire. ²² Since the king's command was so urgent and the furnace extremely hot, the raging flames killed those men who carried Shadrach, Meshach, and Abednego up. ²³ And these three men, Shadrach, Meshach, and Abednego fell, bound, into the furnace of blazing fire.

²⁴ Then King Nebuchadnezzar jumped up in alarm. He said to his advisers, "Didn't we throw three men, bound, into the fire?"

"Yes, of course, Your Majesty," they replied to the king.

²⁵ He exclaimed, "Look! I see four men, not tied, walking around in the fire unharmed; and the fourth looks like a son of the gods."

²⁶ Nebuchadnezzar then approached the door of the furnace of blazing fire and called: "Shadrach, Meshach, and Abednego, you servants of the Most High God — come out!" So Shadrach, Meshach, and Abednego came out of the fire. ²⁷ When the satraps, prefects, governors, and the king's advisers gathered around, they saw that the fire had no effect on the bodies of these men: not a hair of their heads was singed, their robes were unaffected, and there was no smell of fire on them. ²⁸ Nebuchadnezzar exclaimed, "Praise to the God of Shadrach, Meshach, and Abednego! He sent his angel and rescued his servants who trusted in him. They violated the king's command and risked their lives rather than serve or worship any god except their own God. ²⁹ Therefore I issue a decree that anyone of any people, nation, or language who says anything offensive against the God of Shadrach, Meshach, and Abednego will be torn limb from limb and his house made a garbage dump. For there is no other god who is able to deliver like this." ³⁰ Then the king rewarded Shadrach, Meshach, and Abednego in the province of Babylon.

18

Whose Side Is God On?
Daniel 3

In the middle of the nineteenth century, America was divided by civil war. Christians on both sides of the conflict prayed for the safety of their fathers, brothers, and sons as they faced the reality of war and the possibility of death. Northern pastors and Southern pastors alike implored God from their pulpits to lend success to their military endeavors. Believers on both sides of the war asked for God's blessing and ultimate victory. The question could be asked, "Whose side was God on?"

Abraham Lincoln offered a unique perspective. Lincoln believed it borderline foolish to say that God is on our side—whatever that side may be. Rather, he was most concerned about being on God's side.

The challenge is before you: never assume God is on your side. Instead, make every effort to be certain you're on God's side. Many of history's most dangerous and destructive people have been those who assumed that God supported their every action and agenda.

Wise are those who don't see themselves as infallible. Humble are those who consistently take inventory of their motives and means of success.

Three strangely named young men in the Older Testament embodied this ideal. They aspired to remain on God's side, even when they weren't guaranteed victory.

In the previous chapter's reading from the book of Jeremiah, we witnessed the Babylonians conquering the kingdom of Judah around 586 BC. While many Jews remained in the land of Judah after the conquest, the best and brightest members of the up-and-coming generation were exiled to Babylon. Their intellect was employed in the service of the conquering nation. It wasn't long before the pagan culture of Babylon collided with the pious convictions of the Jews. Given the situation, it would have been all too tempting for the Jews to assume that God was on their side.

During his reign, King Nebuchadnezzar ordered a large image to be crafted and displayed for all to see. This statue, standing close to ninety feet in height, was pure politics. The larger-than-life statue, representing the king's royal authority, reminded all Nebuchadnezzar's subjects who held ultimate authority in the realm. For the ancients, worship of the king and his god was on par with patriotic loyalty. Refusal to worship was tantamount to treason.

Three young subjects of the king—who had been given the Babylonian names Shadrach, Meshach, and Abednego—held an allegiance that ran deeper than popular loyalties. They held a conviction common to the Jewish people: idolatry was forbidden. The only person worthy of worship was the unseen but ever-present God.

This ancient account of friends, flames, and faithfulness opens a treasure trove of truths that can enrich our faith today. We'll highlight three: the importance of community, the nearness of God, and the courage necessary to face uncertainty.

1. The importance of community. We must not overlook the simple truth that these three young men benefited from one another as they faced the pressure of conformity and the possibility of death. Their boldness resulted from being banded together in their resolve. When the king issued his final ultimatum to worship the image, the band of brothers replied,

> Nebuchadnezzar, we don't need to give you an answer to this question. If the God we serve exists, then he can rescue us from the furnace of blazing fire, and he can rescue us from the power of you, the king. But even if he does not rescue us, we want you as king to know that we will not serve your gods or worship the gold statue you set up. (Dan. 3:16–18)

Notice the number of times the words *we* and *us* appear in these verses.

By ourselves we aren't as strong as we think; in community we become stronger than we imagine.

My brother-in-law, Ed, runs marathons—for fun, so he tells me. Prior to running the Boston Marathon, Ed used a black marker to write his name in large letters down the length of each arm. He had heard of spectators lining the race route, reading the runners' arms and encouraging them by name. As my brother-in-law crested Heartbreak Hill, the course's most infamous incline, the crowd's chant of "Ed! Ed! Ed!" kept him going at a time when many runners give out. Shadrach, Meshach, and Abednego were in need of courage. The power of community made for collective courageousness.

2. The nearness of God. Nebuchadnezzar was accustomed to having his way. To be told no by a group of nobodies inflamed his royal temper. The furnace's temperature reflected his white-hot rage toward these underlings.

As the friends entered the fire, Nebuchadnezzar saw something he didn't expect and couldn't fully explain. "He exclaimed, 'Look! I see four men, not tied, walking around in the fire unharmed; and the fourth looks like a son of the gods'" (v. 25). Exactly who was the fourth person in the fire? Some believe this was a pre-incarnation appearance of Jesus. Others assume the fourth person was an angelic being. While it's understandable to speculate, the fact is, we aren't told. Regardless, the appearance of the fourth person in the fire represents the unmistakable presence of God in a dire situation.

The old tale of the elephant and the flea offers an insight into this moment. A large elephant is befriended by a flea, which takes up residence inside the elephant's left ear. One day the elephant approached a ravine with a rope-suspension bridge spanning the chasm. As the elephant lumbered across the bridge, the wood creaked and the ropes stretched under his massive weight. Once on the other side, the elephant turned around to look at the bridge. It was still swaying in the wake of his weight. The flea exclaimed in the elephant's ear, "Wow! Did *we* ever shake that bridge!"

The truth is the flea did nothing. The elephant was the one responsible for the results. Likewise, Shadrach, Meshach, and Abednego didn't cause the miracle in the furnace. The fourth person in the fire, whether an angel or God himself, was responsible for the miracle. The three friends were recipients of God's miraculous protection as they were carried through the fire unharmed.

3. The courage necessary to face uncertainty. Shadrach, Meshach, and Abednego were given no guarantee of being rescued from the fire. They told the king, "If the God we serve exists, then he can rescue us from the furnace of blazing fire, and he can rescue us from the power of you, the king. *But even if he does not rescue us*, we want you as king to know that we will not serve your gods" (vv. 17–18). The three friends never assumed that God was on their side, but they made every effort to ensure that they were on God's side.

The outcome of this story is seen far beyond the pages of Daniel's book. God ultimately restored the nation of Judah, in part because of faithful individuals like Shadrach, Meshach, and Abednego. Just as the Babylonians had replaced the Assyrians as the world's superpower, so the new Persian superpower was destined to absorb the Babylonians. The Persian rise to power would open the door for Jewish refugees to return to their homeland. This restoration wouldn't have happened if the Jews had smugly assumed that God was on their side. Restoration came because

God's people determined to be on God's side, come what may. Such attitudes make and change the course of history.

FOR REFLECTION

Can you recall a specific circumstance when you sensed the unmistakable presence of God during a test or trial? Even if you can't recall an exact situation, the truth is this: you are never truly alone. The promise of God for the Christ follower is summed up in Hebrews 13:5: "I will never leave you or abandon you." Indeed, you never face the fires of life by yourself.

Daniel 6

¹ Darius decided to appoint 120 satraps over the kingdom, stationed throughout the realm, ² and over them three administrators, including Daniel. These satraps would be accountable to them so that the king would not be defrauded. ³ Daniel distinguished himself above the administrators and satraps because he had an extraordinary spirit, so the king planned to set him over the whole realm. ⁴ The administrators and satraps, therefore, kept trying to find a charge against Daniel regarding the kingdom. But they could find no charge or corruption, for he was trustworthy, and no negligence or corruption was found in him. ⁵ Then these men said, "We will never find any charge against this Daniel unless we find something against him concerning the law of his God."

⁶ So the administrators and satraps went together to the king and said to him, "May King Darius live forever. ⁷ All the administrators of the kingdom, the prefects, satraps, advisers, and governors have agreed that the king should establish an ordinance and enforce an edict that for thirty days, anyone who petitions any god or man except you, the king, will be thrown into the lions' den. ⁸ Therefore, Your Majesty, establish the edict and sign the document so that, as a law of the Medes and Persians, it is irrevocable and cannot be changed." ⁹ So King Darius signed the written edict.

¹⁰ When Daniel learned that the document had been signed, he went into his house. The windows in its upstairs room opened toward Jerusalem, and three times a day he got down on his knees, prayed, and gave thanks to his God, just as he had done before. ¹¹ Then these men went as a group and found Daniel petitioning and imploring his God. ¹² So they approached the king and asked about his edict: "Didn't you sign an edict that for thirty days any person who petitions any god or man except you, the king, will be thrown into the lions' den?"

The king answered, "As a law of the Medes and Persians, the order stands and is irrevocable."

¹³ Then they replied to the king, "Daniel, one of the Judean exiles, has ignored you, the king, and the edict you signed, for he prays three times a day." ¹⁴ As soon as the king heard this, he was very displeased; he set his mind on rescuing Daniel and made every effort until sundown to deliver him.

¹⁵ Then these men went together to the king and said to him, "You know, Your Majesty, that it is a law of the Medes and Persians that no edict or ordinance the king establishes can be changed."

¹⁶ So the king gave the order, and they brought Daniel and threw him into the lions' den. The king said to Daniel, "May your God, whom you continually serve, rescue you!" ¹⁷ A stone was brought and placed over the mouth of the den. The king sealed it with his own signet ring and with the signet rings of his nobles, so that nothing in regard to Daniel could be changed. ¹⁸ Then the king went to his palace and spent the night fasting. No diversions were brought to him, and he could not sleep.

¹⁹ At the first light of dawn the king got up and hurried to the lions' den. ²⁰ When he reached the den, he cried out in anguish to Daniel. "Daniel, servant of the living God," the king said, "has your God, whom you continually serve, been able to rescue you from the lions?"

²¹ Then Daniel spoke with the king: "May the king live forever. ²² My God sent his angel and shut the lions' mouths; and they haven't harmed me, for I was found innocent before him. And also before you, Your Majesty, I have not done harm."

²³ The king was overjoyed and gave orders to take Daniel out of the den. When Daniel was brought up from the den, he was found to be unharmed, for he trusted in his God. ²⁴ The king then gave the command, and those men who had maliciously accused Daniel were brought and thrown into the lions' den — they, their children, and their wives. They had not reached the bottom of the den before the lions overpowered them and crushed all their bones.

²⁵ Then King Darius wrote to those of every people, nation, and language who live on the whole earth: "May your prosperity abound. ²⁶ I issue a decree that in all my royal dominion, people must tremble in fear before the God of Daniel:

For he is the living God,
and he endures forever;
his kingdom will never be destroyed,
and his dominion has no end.
²⁷ He rescues and delivers;
he performs signs and wonders

in the heavens and on the earth,
for he has rescued Daniel
from the power of the lions."

²⁸ So Daniel prospered during the reign of Darius and the reign of Cyrus the Persian.

19

Integrity under Fire
Daniel 6

Daniel was an individual of unquestionable integrity. If one truth is remembered from his story and experiences, it's certainly this one. In a world overrun with sketchy personalities and shady organizations, it's refreshing to encounter at least one person who lived indifferent to the pressure to conform. Daniel reminds us that life is lived best when we compromise least.

The word *integrity* shares an obvious kinship with a mathematical term—*integer*. An integer is a whole number. An integer is complete, total, and full. Likewise, integrity describes a person who chooses to be whole and undivided in personality. Blessed are those who have "nothing to hide."[1] A person of integrity refuses to wear two faces or cultivate two sides to his or her character.

Frédéric Bartholdi designed the Statue of Liberty. Fabricated in France and shipped a piece at a time across the Atlantic Ocean, the statue was assembled in New York Harbor, where it has stood since October 1886.

It wasn't until the dawn of the twentieth century—1903 to be exact—that humanity first achieved mechanized flight. As airplanes flew over the Statue of Liberty for the first time, passengers made an astonishing discovery. Bartholdi had employed the same exacting detail in sculpting the sections at the very top of the statue as he had for the most visible parts. He crafted the top of Lady Liberty's head, believing only the seagulls would ever see it.

Integrity is a head-to-toe commitment. A person of integrity chooses to be the same person from top to bottom, no matter who sees, or whether anyone sees at all. Here's a glimpse of Daniel's integrity:

> Daniel distinguished himself above the administrators and satraps because he had an extraordinary spirit, so the king planned to set him over the whole realm. The administrators and satraps, therefore, kept trying to find a charge against Daniel regarding the kingdom. But they could find no charge or corruption, for he was trustworthy, and no negligence or corruption was found in him. Then these men said, "We will never find any charge against this Daniel unless we find something against him concerning the law of his God." (Dan. 6:3–5)

Daniel served during a tense time in history. Among the best and brightest of the Jews deported from Judah into Babylonian captivity, Daniel distinguished himself in the science of politics and the art of administration. Even when the Persian Empire absorbed Babylon, Daniel's expertise made him indispensable to the new regime.

Strange as it sounds, the best in us can bring out the worst in others. Daniel's closest associates, who proved to be his most jealous rivals, searched for any evidence of intentional corruption or unintentional negligence. Finding nothing, they determined that his weakest point was the strength of his commitment to the Lord. Doesn't this say something about Daniel's integrity? (Could the same be said of you or me?)

Verses 6–9 record a plot that Daniel's political rivals hatched to force him into choosing obedience to God or loyalty to the government.

Daniel's reaction reveals strong wisdom: it's easier to be a thermometer than a thermostat. Here's what I mean: a thermometer reacts to temperature, while a thermostat regulates temperature. We see people acting like thermometers all the time. Indeed, most of us are prone to reaction and overreaction. Reacting as a thermometer is common; responding like a thermostat is rare. When circumstances heat up, the challenge is to keep cool and choose intentional action. Integrity asks the question, "How can I act, not react, in a way that will honor God in my current crisis?"

Daniel didn't blatantly challenge King Darius's ruling. Nor did Daniel change his daily discipline of prayer. He made no grandiose demonstration; he simply upheld his standards. Daniel went about his business as he always had. He knelt toward Jerusalem and prayed for God's graciousness and mercy. No flash. No pomp. Just faithfulness. Whether others noticed or not, Daniel's actions remained unaltered; his integrity remained intact. It's worth mentioning that Daniel's name in Hebrew means "God is the judge." Daniel was so concerned with the judgment of God that the judgment of others became inconsequential.

While the variety of life in the ocean is vast, it is easy to imagine two categories of aquatic life: drifters and swimmers. Drifters do as their name suggests. They move with the current. Their destination is determined by chance as the tides direct them. Swimmers, on the other hand, have a say in their direction. They exert will and effort, even if it means moving against the current. Drifting falls short of true living. Obedience to God requires great effort, especially when we find ourselves moving against the flow of comfort and convenience.

For his integrity, Daniel was thrown into a lions' den. It was a common custom among ancient kings to keep an enclosure filled with living lions. On occasion a lion would be released into the king's gardens for the monarch to hunt. Killing a lion was a way of illustrating the absolute power of the king's office. A den of lions also happened to come in handy when an occasional execution was required.

What happened—or rather what didn't happen—to Daniel is nothing short of miraculous. The lions refused to devour him. Under the supernatural protection of God, Daniel's body, like his integrity, remained untouchable. The story was different for Daniel's political rivals when they were tossed into the lions' enclosure. From the fate of these men we learn that Daniel's life was spared not because the lions lacked an appetite but because of God's abundant protection.

Neal Bascomb's book *The Perfect Mile* recounts the journey of three men who set out to break the four-minute mile. John Landy, Roger Bannister, and Wes Santee endured enormous hardship and immense sacrifice in their attempts to accomplish the feat.

As a training exercise, Wes Santee ran a half marathon against twenty-seven other men. While Santee ran the full distance of the race, the other men ran the race relay style. Each man ran half a mile, whereupon the next runner would take over. Santee beat the team by four hundred yards. An entire team's effort was no match for one man's training.[2]

Likewise, the intrigue of an entire group of politicians was no match for the integrity of one individual. Some scholars believe that Daniel celebrated his one-hundredth birthday during the reign of King Darius. Perhaps his age gave him an edge in understanding. He understood that intimidation isn't as frightening as it appears. Daniel believed there were fates worse than death. He grasped the truth that people may attempt to destroy our lives, but our reputations are untouchable apart from our permission.

Daniel's integrity should inform and inspire our own. As we face our own critics and lions, enemies and intrigue, we need to recognize that God is our only true and ultimate judge.

Jonathan Edwards, an American theologian from the eighteenth century, once said, "Resolved: That every man should live to the glory of God. Resolved second: That whether others do this or not, I will."[3] May integrity be the resolution of our entire lives, no matter what others choose to do with theirs.

FOR REFLECTION

John Stott once said, "Apathy is the acceptance of the unacceptable."[4] Have you accepted apathy in some area of your life that demands integrity? Is it a relationship? Your marriage? A private matter? Your job? Integrity involves fighting against apathy to live a life honoring to God. Listen to God speak to you today. Reject apathy. Embrace integrity.

Jonah 1

¹ The word of the LORD came to Jonah son of Amittai: ² "Get up! Go to the great city of Nineveh and preach against it because their evil has come up before me." ³ Jonah got up to flee to Tarshish from the LORD's presence. He went down to Joppa and found a ship going to Tarshish. He paid the fare and went down into it to go with them to Tarshish from the LORD's presence.

⁴ But the LORD threw a great wind onto the sea, and such a great storm arose on the sea that the ship threatened to break apart. ⁵ The sailors were afraid, and each cried out to his god. They threw the ship's cargo into the sea to lighten the load. Meanwhile, Jonah had gone down to the lowest part of the vessel and had stretched out and fallen into a deep sleep.

⁶ The captain approached him and said, "What are you doing sound asleep? Get up! Call to your god. Maybe this god will consider us, and we won't perish."

⁷ "Come on!" the sailors said to each other. "Let's cast lots. Then we'll know who is to blame for this trouble we're in." So they cast lots, and the lot singled out Jonah. ⁸ Then they said to him, "Tell us who is to blame for this trouble we're in. What is your business, and where are you from? What is your country, and what people are you from?"

⁹ He answered them, "I'm a Hebrew. I worship the LORD, the God of the heavens, who made the sea and the dry land."

¹⁰ Then the men were seized by a great fear and said to him, "What is this you've done?" The men knew he was fleeing from the LORD's presence because he had told them. ¹¹ So they said to him, "What should we do to you so that the sea will calm down for us?" For the sea was getting worse and worse.

¹² He answered them, "Pick me up and throw me into the sea so that it will calm down for you, for I know that I'm to blame for this great storm that is against you." ¹³ Nevertheless, the men rowed hard to get back to dry land, but they couldn't because the sea was raging against them more and more.

¹⁴ So they called out to the LORD: "Please, LORD, don't let us perish because of this man's life, and don't charge us with innocent blood! For you, LORD, have done just as you pleased." ¹⁵ Then they picked up Jonah and threw him into the sea, and the sea stopped its raging. ¹⁶ The men

were seized by great fear of the LORD, and they offered a sacrifice to the LORD and made vows.

¹⁷ The LORD appointed a great fish to swallow Jonah, and Jonah was in the belly of the fish three days and three nights.

20

Man on the Run
Jonah 1

Jonah was a minor prophet with major name recognition. The book bearing his name takes all of five minutes to read, yet its impact is exponentially out of proportion to its size. Although Jonah is a sliver of a book, Jonah the prophet has become significant to understanding the Bible. What is it about Jonah that we find so memorable?

I personally treasure the fact that Jonah was simultaneously an extraordinary prophet and an ordinary person. Here's a man we assume would be faithful to God but chose instead to be self-serving at a critical moment. What draws me into this story isn't a great fish but a great failure. Jonah was a man on the run from God.

My friend Brian is an Alabama police officer. During his off-duty hours, he works security at a shopping mall. One hot afternoon, a shoplifter sprinted from a store with stolen goods in hand. Brian gave chase. Apparently the thief hadn't given thought to his escape. As he ran, the flip-flops on his feet slowed his getaway.

Finally the bandit kicked off his flip-flops, but the additional speed was short lived. On such a hot day, the parking lot was molten asphalt. By the time Brian tackled the bandit at the far end of the parking lot, several layers of skin had been stripped from the bottom of the thief's feet. This gruesome account parallels a spiritual reality: to run from God is not only disobedient; it's ultimately self-destructive.

Here's how the prophet Jonah's adventure began: "The word of the LORD came to Jonah son of Amittai: 'Get up! Go to the great city of Nineveh and preach against it because their evil has come up before me'" (Jon. 1:1–2).

Every era of history has had at least one nation intent on threatening the well-being of its neighbors. In Jonah's day—approximately 750 years before Jesus—the bully of the Middle East was the Assyrian Empire. With its "great city" of Nineveh, Assyria threatened conquest and destruction on every neighbor within its reach, including Jonah's nation of the northern kingdom of Israel. Jonah's culture assumed that God wanted nothing more than to punish the Assyrians. But it turns out that public opinion was the opposite of God's viewpoint.

Martin Niemöller was a German pastor during World War II who didn't support Hitler or the Nazi regime. As Hitler threatened to destroy the German churches, Niemöller employed every political maneuver available to protect Christians. Niemöller ultimately survived the war and died in 1984. Just prior to his death, he complained to friends of a recurring nightmare. In his dream he witnessed Adolf Hitler standing before Jesus.

Jesus said, "Adolf, Adolf, why did you do so many vile and evil things?"

Hitler hung his head and gave the reply, "I did those things because no one ever told me how much you loved me."

Niemöller awoke to the realization that in his many meetings with the führer, never once had he seen Hitler as a man in need of God's forgiveness and love.

We, along with Niemöller and Jonah, often forget that God's love for all people is greater than our hatred for even our worst enemies. God will stop at nothing to share his love, even with the very people we refuse to stop hating.

God commanded Jonah to enter enemy territory, but the prophet had other ideas: "Jonah got up to flee to Tarshish from the LORD's presence" (v. 3). Without going into the geographical details, suffice it to say that Tarshish lay in the opposite direction of Nineveh. Simply put, Jonah's response was the exact opposite of God's clear command.

While Jonah was at the center of this account, God was the one directing the drama. At every critical point in the unfolding drama of Jonah's life, God was the one silently and skillfully moving the plot along. The Lord sent a "great fish" (1:17), provided a plant for shade (4:6), sent a worm to eat the plant (v. 7), and summoned a scorching breeze (v. 8).

At the top of the list of all the Lord sent Jonah's way was a great wind: "The LORD threw a great wind onto the sea, and such a great storm arose on the sea that the ship threatened to break apart" (1:4). God sent a great wind to blow Jonah back on course.

In response to the storm, the sailors on board the ship resorted to their superstitions. Each one began to cry out to his native god for help. The sailors also began searching for the cause of the calamity that had befallen them. Discovering that the cause of their problem was Jonah, amazingly, they decided to make every effort to save Jonah's life.

Two great lessons can be learned from Jonah 1. First, at times non-Christians act with greater integrity than Christians. It's an unfortunate and uncomfortable truth that many non-Christians act more like Christ than do some who claim to be Jesus's followers.

The pagan sailors stood in stark contrast to the God-fearing, God-fleeing Jonah. Jonah knew that running would bring him under God's judgment. Jonah was no doubt aware that boarding a ship filled with sailors put everyone at risk. The sailors, by contrast, did their noble best to save Jonah. Even after discovering that Jonah was the root of their dilemma, they continued fighting the waves to save his life. The sailors' willingness to risk their lives reflected the character of God more than Jonah's running.

Yet a glimmer of hope in Jonah 1 highlights the second profound point: building trust with others leads to changed lives. Once every option had been exhausted, Jonah instructed the sailors to throw him into the sea to spare their lives. Jonah's self-sacrifice resulted in a moment of transformation for the pagan crew. Each sailor had cried out to his own god, but now "the men were seized by great fear of the LORD, and they offered a sacrifice to the LORD and made vows" (v. 16). Jonah's simple self-sacrifice built enough trust with the sailors that they turned away from their pagan superstitions and toward the Lord. The challenge is to be Jesus followers who fully reflect the character of Jesus. Our character becomes credible as we move from selfish to selfless.

Don Everts and Doug Schaupp have written about the importance of building trust with those in our culture. They say, "In another day and age, God, religion and church enjoyed the general respect of the culture. Not today. Religion is suspect, church is weird, and Christians are hypocrites. Distrust has become the norm."[1] Before we can expect to see change occur in the lives of others, we must be credible people ourselves.

How does the story of Jonah end? Eventually God set Jonah back on course for Nineveh. This time, although reluctant, Jonah was obedient. However, the story ends with Jonah still stewing in his own selfishness.

Beyond the pages of this short book, Jonah serves a larger purpose in the Bible. He is an important figure in understanding Jesus. Even in his own teachings, Jesus cited Jonah as a foreshadowing of his own work among God's people. Jesus also traveled from the safety of home (heaven) to unfriendly territory (earth). In Matthew 12:40, he said, "For as Jonah was in the belly of the huge fish three days and three nights, so the Son of Man will be in the heart of the earth three days and three nights." Just as Jonah emerged from the fish, Jesus emerged from the grave, fulfilling God's quest for our restoration.

FOR REFLECTION

When asked to test a pen, the vast majority of people will write their own name. Like Jonah, our natural tendency is toward selfish behavior. It's a constant challenge to set aside the focus on ourselves to follow our Savior, who asks for immediate obedience.

Practice self-sacrifice today, asking God to bring someone to mind whom you can serve. Don't be surprised if he calls you to serve someone you consider an enemy. Whomever God brings to mind, consider this question: How can I serve this person in a manner that reveals the reality of Jesus in my character?

Why Two Testaments?

For me, the best summary of why the Bible contains two testaments is captured in Hebrews 1:1. Loosely paraphrased, the beginning of this verse says, "For as long as humanity has existed, God has been speaking. In fact, God has spoken to many, many people and in multiple ways."

Come to think of it, this is an accurate description of the twenty Bible chapters you've read so far. You've inched your way through the Bible's Older Testament, and yet look at the ground you've covered! You've watched the creation of the world culminate with Adam and Eve. You've witnessed the creation of a nation—God's special people promised to Abraham. You've seen these same people endure slavery in Egypt, and you've vicariously experienced their exodus thanks to God's delivering power.

The Israelites finally claimed the land God had promised. Through fair and foul times, God sent a long succession of kings and judges and prophets and priests who lent their influence and spent their words in attempts to convince God's people to remain faithful to him.

In the Older Testament, God spoke through the likes of Noah and Moses and Samson and Solomon and Jonah and Jeremiah. And the list goes on.

Again, God has spoken to many, many people in multiple ways.

So does the story end here?

Absolutely not.

The balance of Hebrews 1 (again, my loose paraphrase) offers this observation: "Now God has decided to show us who he is by sending his Son, Jesus."

Please don't make the mistake of thinking God sent Jesus as a last-ditch effort to get our attention or win our affection. It's not as though God one day said to himself, "Well, all these other ways of communicating with my people haven't panned out, so let me try *this*."

Far from it. Jesus was God's plan all along. God knew from the beginning that we could never fully grasp a restored relationship with him apart from his flesh-and-blood intervention.

Intuitively we know the most powerful way to teach is to show rather than tell. All the explanation in the world is little help compared with the power of example. No matter how detailed the instructions, demonstration carries greater impact.

For years Bob Ross was a staple in many American homes. His program, *The Joy of Painting*, operated on a simple principle: show people how to paint. Each episode found Bob sitting in front of a television camera with a fresh canvas. With brush and palette in hand, he showed people step by step how to create a masterpiece.

The truth is that fewer than 10 percent of Ross's viewers ever dabbed a paintbrush.[1] It seems that the power of his program went beyond artistic adventure. A generation of latchkey kids grew up listening to Ross's calm voice. For them, Bob Ross was an adult who talked *with* them rather than *at* them. Homebound elderly, at least for a short time each day, enjoyed a respite from their loneliness. Viewers everywhere were drawn to the show because *The Joy of Painting* existed in stark contrast to the negativity of daily life.

Even though God had been speaking to the human race for a long, long time, few bothered to listen. So at the perfect time, he decided to show us the full extent of his love for us.

Enter Jesus.

In Jesus, God isn't talking down to us; God is speaking with us face to face. In Jesus, those living in isolation and loneliness discover they'll never be alone again. And most important, Jesus is living proof that God is willing to take the canvases of our lives and transform them into masterpieces through our relationship with him. This fully restored relationship with God in Jesus is so big that only one word can truly describe it: *salvation.*

If I were to choose another name for the New Testament, I would call it *The Joy of Living.* The star is Jesus. With little pomp and circumstance, his presence in the world allows us to experience the love of God in all its intense color and infinite detail.

So let's look intently into the New Testament. It is here we'll see the full magnitude of God's love in the face of Jesus.

JESUS HAS JUST ENTERED THE BUILDING

John 1

¹ In the beginning was the Word, and the Word was with God, and the Word was God. ² He was with God in the beginning. ³ All things were created through him, and apart from him not one thing was created that has been created. ⁴ In him was life, and that life was the light of men. ⁵ That light shines in the darkness, and yet the darkness did not overcome it.

⁶ There was a man sent from God whose name was John. ⁷ He came as a witness to testify about the light, so that all might believe through him. ⁸ He was not the light, but he came to testify about the light. ⁹ The true light that gives light to everyone, was coming into the world.

¹⁰ He was in the world, and the world was created through him, and yet the world did not recognize him. ¹¹ He came to his own, and his own people did not receive him. ¹² But to all who did receive him, he gave them the right to be children of God, to those who believe in his name, ¹³ who were born, not of natural descent, or of the will of the flesh, or of the will of man, but of God.

¹⁴ The Word became flesh and dwelt among us. We observed his glory, the glory as the one and only Son from the Father, full of grace and truth. ¹⁵ (John testified concerning him and exclaimed, "This was the one of whom I said, 'The one coming after me ranks ahead of me, because he existed before me.'") ¹⁶ Indeed, we have all received grace upon grace from his fullness, ¹⁷ for the law was given through Moses; grace and truth came through Jesus Christ. ¹⁸ No one has ever seen God. The one and only Son, who is himself God and is at the Father's side — he has revealed him.

¹⁹ This was John's testimony when the Jews from Jerusalem sent priests and Levites to ask him, "Who are you?"

²⁰ He didn't deny it but confessed: "I am not the Messiah."

²¹ "What then?" they asked him. "Are you Elijah?"

"I am not," he said.

"Are you the Prophet?"

"No," he answered.

²² "Who are you, then?" they asked. "We need to give an answer to those who sent us. What can you tell us about yourself?"

²³ He said, "I am a voice of one crying out in the wilderness: Make straight the way of the Lord — just as Isaiah the prophet said."

²⁴ Now they had been sent from the Pharisees. ²⁵ So they asked him, "Why then do you baptize if you aren't the Messiah, or Elijah, or the Prophet?"

²⁶ "I baptize with water," John answered them. "Someone stands among you, but you don't know him. ²⁷ He is the one coming after me, whose sandal strap I'm not worthy to untie." ²⁸ All this happened in Bethany across the Jordan, where John was baptizing.

²⁹ The next day John saw Jesus coming toward him and said, "Here is the Lamb of God, who takes away the sin of the world! ³⁰ This is the one I told you about: 'After me comes a man who ranks ahead of me, because he existed before me.' ³¹ I didn't know him, but I came baptizing with water so he might be revealed to Israel." ³² And John testified, "I saw the Spirit descending from heaven like a dove, and he rested on him. ³³ I didn't know him, but he who sent me to baptize with water told me, 'The one you see the Spirit descending and resting on — he is the one who baptizes with the Holy Spirit.' ³⁴ I have seen and testified that this is the Son of God."

³⁵ The next day, John was standing with two of his disciples. ³⁶ When he saw Jesus passing by, he said, "Look, the Lamb of God!"

³⁷ The two disciples heard him say this and followed Jesus. ³⁸ When Jesus turned and noticed them following him, he asked them, "What are you looking for?"

They said to him, "Rabbi" (which means "Teacher"), "where are you staying?"

³⁹ "Come and you'll see," he replied. So they went and saw where he was staying, and they stayed with him that day. It was about four in the afternoon.

⁴⁰ Andrew, Simon Peter's brother, was one of the two who heard John and followed him. ⁴¹ He first found his own brother Simon and told him, "We have found the Messiah" (which is translated "the Christ"), ⁴² and he brought Simon to Jesus.

When Jesus saw him, he said, "You are Simon, son of John. You will be called Cephas" (which is translated "Peter").

⁴³ The next day Jesus decided to leave for Galilee. He found Philip and told him, "Follow me."

⁴⁴ Now Philip was from Bethsaida, the hometown of Andrew and Peter. ⁴⁵ Philip found Nathanael and told him, "We have found the one

Moses wrote about in the law (and so did the prophets): Jesus the son of Joseph, from Nazareth."

⁴⁶ "Can anything good come out of Nazareth?" Nathanael asked him.

"Come and see," Philip answered.

⁴⁷ Then Jesus saw Nathanael coming toward him and said about him, "Here truly is an Israelite in whom there is no deceit."

⁴⁸ "How do you know me?" Nathanael asked.

"Before Philip called you, when you were under the fig tree, I saw you," Jesus answered.

⁴⁹ "Rabbi," Nathanael replied, "You are the Son of God; you are the King of Israel!"

⁵⁰ Jesus responded to him, "Do you believe because I told you I saw you under the fig tree? You will see greater things than this." ⁵¹ Then he said, "Truly I tell you, you will see heaven opened and the angels of God ascending and descending on the Son of Man."

21

Jesus—God with Skin On
John 1

Shortly after my family moved to Tulsa, a man named Walt befriended me. With his business and life experience, Walt was an endless source of stories and practical wisdom. Having made more money than he could possibly enjoy, he was intentional about giving to the community in the form of hospital wings, parks, and museums.

Walt commissioned a painting that hangs in the rotunda of the Oklahoma City capitol building. The painting depicts the morning in 1907 when Teddy Roosevelt signed Oklahoma into statehood. Following a centuries-old tradition, the painter placed the patron within the painting. Among the group surrounding Teddy Roosevelt with his signature smile is my friend Walt, staring out from the canvas with a gentle look of approval.

This painting reminds me of what I experience in the Gospels. As I read the four accounts of the life of Christ, I sense Jesus softly smiling from the canvas of Scripture. It's as though he's looking out at me, wanting me to know him better so that I can grasp and grapple with his powerful love.

The gospels of Matthew, Mark, Luke, and John offer four spiritual biographies of Jesus. For reasons known only to each writer, the four accounts begin in different places. Mark began his telling of the story with the public appearances of Jesus when he was about thirty years old. Luke began earlier, launching his story in the year Jesus was born—around 5 BC. Matthew stretched even further into the past, tracing the lineage of Jesus all the way back to Abraham, the father of the Hebrew people and the Jewish faith.

John topped them all. His gospel reaches back in time—way back before time existed. In many ways, John 1 is a retelling of Genesis 1. The opening chapter takes us to the moment of creation. With such phrasing as "in the beginning" (John 1:1) and "light shines in the darkness" (v. 5), John transports us back to the beginning of reality as we know it. Before anything or anyone else existed, there was someone—and this someone was Jesus.

John opened his account with an important statement about Jesus's divine identity: "In the beginning was the Word, and the Word was with God, and the Word was God" (v. 1).

Why did John speak of Jesus as "the Word"? History provides a bit of clarity.

Five hundred years before Jesus, there lived a Greek philosopher by the name of Heraclitus, to whom we attribute the adage "You never step in the same river twice." As his famous quote suggests, Heraclitus believed the world was ever changing. The universe was constantly in flux and never the same from one moment to the next. So what prevents our ever-changing world from spiraling out of control into utter chaos?

To address this dilemma, Heraclitus used a term to describe the aspect of the universe that holds everything together in harmony and unity. You might guess that he chose the term *word* (or in the Greek language, *logos*). The *logos* represents the order behind all that is unpredictable.

John picked up on this centuries-old word, which readers of his day still understood. Though John's gospel situates Jesus within human history, it also tells us that his true identity stretches back into eternity. Jesus is the cosmic glue that holds the universe and all reality together.

While Jesus is divine, he refuses to remain distant. John tells us that "the Word became flesh and dwelt among us. We observed his glory, the glory as the one and only Son from the Father, full of grace and truth" (v. 14).

Sometimes it's challenging to understand Jesus because we're asked to accept two truths that seem contradictory. Jesus is God, and yet he is also distinct from God. Jesus is one and the same as God, yet he maintains his own unique personality.

These challenges are wrapped up in the mystery of the incarnation. Though *incarnation* is a weighty spiritual term, I find it easy to understand when I break it down. The word *carnation* (a common name for a flower) means "flesh-colored." *In*carnation is another way of saying "*in* the color of flesh." God has come to us in the color of flesh, in the person of Jesus.

Elton Trueblood, a famous Quaker theologian, pointed out that "the historic Christian doctrine of the divinity of Christ does not simply mean that Jesus is like God. It is far more radical than that. It means that God is like Jesus."[1]

John wrote his gospel in a manner that was intensely personal. Three words show up repeatedly in John's account of Jesus. Collectively they remind us that knowing God is no longer a matter of guesswork. While Jesus fully identifies with humans, he also fully reveals the identity of God.

Light. "In him was life, and that life was the light of men" (v. 4). Remember that Genesis 1 indicates that the first thing God created was light. Just as physical light is essential for existence, spiritual light is necessary for our being. Jesus and the life he offers are indispensable to a relationship with God.

Grace. Even though our relationship with God seems strained beyond repair, he has initiated a project of restoration through Jesus. Grace is God's decision to outlast our every attempt to avoid him, to outdistance our attempts to run from him, and to outwait our stubbornness in resisting him. God's grace doesn't merely offer to make us better; it promises to make us new. Grace reconciles our past with forgiveness and empowers our future with hope.

Truth. Another word for "truth" is *reality*. Jesus is God as God really is. For Christians, truth or reality is more than a collection of statements or propositions; truth is personal. For this reason, as John concludes this first section of his book, he says, "For the law was given through Moses; grace and truth came through Jesus Christ" (v. 17).

God wants all humanity to know, love, and understand him. Jesus is the epitome of light, grace, and truth. He is the embodiment of God's full identity. While Jesus has impact in history, the beginnings of his earthly story stretch back into eternity.

In the 1960s, a meteorologist named Edward Lorenz posed a simple question: Could the flap of a butterfly's wings in one hemisphere affect a hurricane in the other hemisphere? Lorenz's theory of small actions having exponential impact has become known as the butterfly effect. God uttered one small word: Jesus. And the effects have been everlasting.

FOR REFLECTION

Do you find it difficult to accept that God loves you deeply and desires an intimate relationship with you? Why or why not?

John 3:16, easily the most quoted verse in the New Testament, says, "For God loved the world in this way: He gave his one and only Son, so that everyone who believes in him will not perish but have eternal life." Say this verse aloud, and put your name in place of the words *the world*. Even if it's hard to understand, take time today to accept that God loves you for being you.

Luke 2

¹ In those days a decree went out from Caesar Augustus that the whole empire should be registered. ² This first registration took place while Quirinius was governing Syria. ³ So everyone went to be registered, each to his own town.

⁴ Joseph also went up from the town of Nazareth in Galilee, to Judea, to the city of David, which is called Bethlehem, because he was of the house and family line of David, ⁵ to be registered along with Mary, who was engaged to him and was pregnant. ⁶ While they were there, the time came for her to give birth. ⁷ Then she gave birth to her firstborn Son, and she wrapped him tightly in cloth and laid him in a manger, because there was no guest room available for them.

⁸ In the same region, shepherds were staying out in the fields and keeping watch at night over their flock. ⁹ Then an angel of the Lord stood before them, and the glory of the Lord shone around them, and they were terrified. ¹⁰ But the angel said to them, "Don't be afraid, for look, I proclaim to you good news of great joy that will be for all the people: ¹¹ Today in the city of David a Savior was born for you, who is the Messiah, the Lord. ¹² This will be the sign for you: You will find a baby wrapped tightly in cloth and lying in a manger."

¹³ Suddenly there was a multitude of the heavenly host with the angel, praising God and saying:

¹⁴ Glory to God in the highest heaven,
and peace on earth to people he favors!

¹⁵ When the angels had left them and returned to heaven, the shepherds said to one another, "Let's go straight to Bethlehem and see what has happened, which the Lord has made known to us."

¹⁶ They hurried off and found both Mary and Joseph, and the baby who was lying in the manger. ¹⁷ After seeing them, they reported the message they were told about this child, ¹⁸ and all who heard it were amazed at what the shepherds said to them. ¹⁹ But Mary was treasuring up all these things in her heart and meditating on them. ²⁰ The shepherds returned, glorifying and praising God for all the things they had seen and heard, which were just as they had been told.

²¹ When the eight days were completed for his circumcision, he was named Jesus — the name given by the angel before he was conceived. ²² And when the days of their purification according to the law of Moses were finished, they brought him up to Jerusalem to present him to the Lord ²³ (just as it is written in the law of the Lord, Every firstborn male will be dedicated to the Lord) ²⁴ and to offer a sacrifice (according to what is stated in the law of the Lord, a pair of turtledoves or two young pigeons).

²⁵ There was a man in Jerusalem whose name was Simeon. This man was righteous and devout, looking forward to Israel's consolation, and the Holy Spirit was on him. ²⁶ It had been revealed to him by the Holy Spirit that he would not see death before he saw the Lord's Messiah. ²⁷ Guided by the Spirit, he entered the temple. When the parents brought in the child Jesus to perform for him what was customary under the law, ²⁸ Simeon took him up in his arms, praised God, and said,

> ²⁹ Now, Master,
> you can dismiss your servant in peace,
> as you promised.
> ³⁰ For my eyes have seen your salvation.
> ³¹ You have prepared it
> in the presence of all peoples —
> ³² a light for revelation to the Gentiles
> and glory to your people Israel.

³³ His father and mother were amazed at what was being said about him. ³⁴ Then Simeon blessed them and told his mother Mary: "Indeed, this child is destined to cause the fall and rise of many in Israel and to be a sign that will be opposed — ³⁵ and a sword will pierce your own soul — that the thoughts of many hearts may be revealed."

³⁶ There was also a prophetess, Anna, a daughter of Phanuel, of the tribe of Asher. She was well along in years, having lived with her husband seven years after her marriage, ³⁷ and was a widow for eighty-four years. She did not leave the temple, serving God night and day with fasting and prayers. ³⁸ At that very moment, she came up and began to thank God and to speak about him to all who were looking forward to the redemption of Jerusalem.

³⁹ When they had completed everything according to the law of the Lord, they returned to Galilee, to their own town of Nazareth. ⁴⁰ The boy grew up and became strong, filled with wisdom, and God's grace was on him.

⁴¹ Every year his parents traveled to Jerusalem for the Passover Festival. ⁴² When he was twelve years old, they went up according to the custom of the festival. ⁴³ After those days were over, as they were returning, the boy Jesus stayed behind in Jerusalem, but his parents did not know it. ⁴⁴ Assuming he was in the traveling party, they went a day's journey. Then they began looking for him among their relatives and friends. ⁴⁵ When they did not find him, they returned to Jerusalem to search for him. ⁴⁶ After three days, they found him in the temple sitting among the teachers, listening to them and asking them questions. ⁴⁷ And all those who heard him were astounded at his understanding and his answers. ⁴⁸ When his parents saw him, they were astonished, and his mother said to him, "Son, why have you treated us like this? Your father and I have been anxiously searching for you."

⁴⁹ "Why were you searching for me?" he asked them. "Didn't you know that it was necessary for me to be in my Father's house?" ⁵⁰ But they did not understand what he said to them.

⁵¹ Then he went down with them and came to Nazareth and was obedient to them. His mother kept all these things in her heart. ⁵² And Jesus increased in wisdom and stature, and in favor with God and with people.

22

Welcome to Our World
Luke 2

In appreciation for my ten years of service as pastor, my church sent my entire family on a tour of Israel. Our love for faraway places and our affection for history made for the perfect adventure. A personal highlight was the day we crossed the Palestinian border into Bethlehem. Once in the city, we visited the Church of the Nativity, the oldest continuously operating church in the world. This church was built over the very cave where it is believed Jesus was born.

The main door of the church is unspectacular—so small, in fact, that a full-grown person must bend to enter. It's a fitting gesture, if you stop to consider it. Jesus himself stooped low to enter our world in Bethlehem. Jesus laid aside his rights as divinity to enter into the full experience of humanity.

The previous chapter's reading in John 1 unveiled the incarnation from an eternal vantage point. Luke 2, by contrast, captures the incarnation from earth's angle.

Caesar Augustus, mentioned in verse 1, reigned as emperor of Rome from 27 BC to AD 14. Using these dates and other clues from within and outside the Bible, historians place the birth of Jesus near the year 5 BC. The original intent of the calendar we use today was to divide time at Jesus's birth, starting the new era with AD 1. Over the centuries, better scholarship has adjusted the date of Jesus's birth. But we honor the intent of our calendar's creators by leaving the years as they are.

Luke's intent was to place the birth of Jesus firmly within a chronological context, thereby reminding all readers that his birth was an actual event. It was a historical occurrence. Almighty God became an ordinary human. The infinite squeezed himself down to the size of an infant.

When I read Luke 2, it has the feel of a parade. No sooner was Jesus born than a long procession of people filed by to welcome the newborn Christ child.

First, we meet Mary and Joseph. Tradition tells us that Mary was no more than a teenager at the time of Jesus's birth, while Joseph was considerably older. We have no way of knowing their ages because we aren't told. But two things we know for certain. First, Mary was pregnant without the involvement of a man. The virgin birth was the first—and only—of its kind, and it stands as a miraculous reminder of the truth that salvation is ultimately God's doing, not ours. He initiates; we receive. Second, we know that Mary and Joseph were poor. Poverty stricken, in fact. They had no clout to warrant them a place in an overcrowded town. Their only refuge was a cave turned cattle pen. Jesus's first crib was a feeding trough called a manger. Jesus moved from the halls of heaven to birth in a barn. To say Jesus stooped down is an understatement.

The shepherds were next in the procession. The angel's appearance was certainly a surprise to the herders. But the original readers of Luke's gospel would have been equally surprised that such men were the first to learn of Jesus's birth. In short, shepherds were viewed as outcasts among the religious establishment of the day.

Temple worship in Jerusalem required rigorous rituals to ensure ceremonial cleanliness. Without these rituals, a person was deemed unclean. Uncleanness translated into being cut off from the temple. No admittance to the temple meant no access to worshipping God. Because of the constant occupational demands, shepherds were unable to perform the rituals that would have qualified them to worship in the temple.

So why would God choose people so outside the religious norm to be the first hearers of the good news? The angel's pronouncement of Jesus's birth was the main message. But those chosen to receive the message provided yet another message. If the shepherds aren't excluded from the auspicious announcement of Jesus's arrival, then perhaps no soul is outside the reach of God's love. The good news of Jesus isn't only for the in-crowd. The good news is for everybody.

The 1989 *Oxford English Dictionary* contains more than 250,000 words, which make up the English language. Of all the words in all the lexicons of human language, God chose the word *peace* to accompany the announcement of Jesus's arrival: "Glory to God in the highest heaven, and *peace* on earth to people he favors!" (v. 14). By announcing the good news to shepherds, God made clear that his favor rests on all people. No exceptions. No exclusions.

Several days after Jesus's birth, Mary and Joseph made their way to the temple in Jerusalem, baby in tow. The Jewish custom of the day called for new babies to be dedicated to God. Once inside the temple courts, Mary and Joseph crossed paths with two strangers who had surprising insights to share about this small child.

At some earlier point in life, Simeon had received a promise that he would see God's deliverer before his death. The promise fulfilled in Luke 2 was the culmination of a blessed life.

Then there was Anna. Nowhere are we told that God made any promise to her. In fact, her life had been pockmarked by pain. The loss of a husband and decades of loneliness could have made her a bitter person. Unmet expectations often do.

The contrast of these two strangers couldn't be more obvious. Their brief appearances in the parade-like story of Luke remind us that blessed lives and burdened lives alike have need of an encounter with God. The most blessed lives are incomplete without Christ. And the difficulties of life dissolve when we encounter him.

The meetings with Simeon and Anna may seem to be nothing more than chance. But far from accidental, these meetings were instrumental in making others aware—especially Mary and Joseph—that a unique destiny awaited Jesus.

When my daughter was much younger, we traveled through Europe for several weeks. With each leg of our journey, she became increasingly anxious about flying. The obsessive fear of a plane crash stuck in her mind. The thought of flying over the Atlantic Ocean for our journey home loomed ever larger as our return date drew closer.

Shortly before our return, we were riding on the London Underground. I struck up a conversation with a well-groomed man next to me on the Tube who was a professor at a college in London. He was highly educated and very personable.

He turned to my daughter and said, "I'm one of the most interesting people you'll ever meet because I'm one of only a few to survive an airplane crash."

I was stunned. My blood pressure began to rise from concern that his words would result in even greater fears for my daughter. The professor told a riveting tale of traveling with his family as a child. The collision of the plane with the side of a South American mountain meant the death of one parent and a sibling. He concluded his story with a question.

"Young lady," he said, "do you know what I learned from that event? God taught me that he will always take care of me. And I believe God will always take care of you as well."

With these words the professor stepped off the Tube and out of our lives. Still in disbelief at the content of the conversation, I turned to my daughter and said, "Kira, if ever there was a time that God has spoken to you, this is it."

This was a Simeon and Anna moment. These two very different people spoke words that were beyond their ability to fully comprehend. Perhaps Mary and Joseph recalled these words for years to come and were reminded that God would always take care of their boy, come what may.

Luke 2 ends with the only record we have of Jesus's adolescence. Before Jesus went public, he went through puberty. But even at a young age, he had a singular attraction to God. His early years are summed up in verse 52: "Jesus increased in wisdom and stature, and in favor with God and with people." All the necessary components of maturity were there—mental, physical, spiritual, and relational growth. Jesus grew mentally, with an ever-increasing awareness of his identity. He grew physically, becoming stronger and more agile through his work as a carpenter's apprentice. Spiritually, Jesus developed a deep connection with God that would serve him well. Relationally, he earned the trust and respect of others.

Although he was the embodiment of the eternal God, Jesus still went through every stage of maturing as a man. God stooped down by allowing himself to grow up into a man called Jesus.

FOR REFLECTION

Read Luke 2:52 carefully. In your own growth as a person, where do you need to give more attention and focus? Mental growth? Physical health? Spiritual maturity? Relational development? If Jesus required growth, then don't we all?

Matthew 5

¹ When he saw the crowds, he went up on the mountain, and after he sat down, his disciples came to him. ² Then he began to teach them, saying:

³ "Blessed are the poor in spirit,
for the kingdom of heaven is theirs.
⁴ Blessed are those who mourn,
for they will be comforted.
⁵ Blessed are the humble,
for they will inherit the earth.
⁶ Blessed are those who hunger and thirst for righteousness,
for they will be filled.
⁷ Blessed are the merciful,
for they will be shown mercy.
⁸ Blessed are the pure in heart,
for they will see God.
⁹ Blessed are the peacemakers,
for they will be called sons of God.
¹⁰ Blessed are those who are persecuted because of righteousness,
for the kingdom of heaven is theirs.

¹¹ "You are blessed when they insult you and persecute you and falsely say every kind of evil against you because of me. ¹² Be glad and rejoice, because your reward is great in heaven. For that is how they persecuted the prophets who were before you.

¹³ "You are the salt of the earth. But if the salt should lose its taste, how can it be made salty? It's no longer good for anything but to be thrown out and trampled under people's feet.

¹⁴ "You are the light of the world. A city situated on a hill cannot be hidden. ¹⁵ No one lights a lamp and puts it under a basket, but rather on a lampstand, and it gives light for all who are in the house. ¹⁶ In the same way, let your light shine before others, so that they may see your good works and give glory to your Father in heaven.

¹⁷ "Don't think that I came to abolish the Law or the Prophets. I did not come to abolish but to fulfill. ¹⁸ For truly I tell you, until heaven and earth pass away, not the smallest letter or one stroke of a letter will pass away

from the law until all things are accomplished. [19] Therefore, whoever breaks one of the least of these commands and teaches others to do the same will be called least in the kingdom of heaven. But whoever does and teaches these commands will be called great in the kingdom of heaven. [20] For I tell you, unless your righteousness surpasses that of the scribes and Pharisees, you will never get into the kingdom of heaven.

[21] "You have heard that it was said to our ancestors, Do not murder, and whoever murders will be subject to judgment. [22] But I tell you, everyone who is angry with his brother or sister will be subject to judgment. Whoever insults his brother or sister, will be subject to the court. Whoever says, 'You fool!' will be subject to hellfire. [23] So if you are offering your gift on the altar, and there you remember that your brother or sister has something against you, [24] leave your gift there in front of the altar. First go and be reconciled with your brother or sister, and then come and offer your gift. [25] Reach a settlement quickly with your adversary while you're on the way with him to the court, or your adversary will hand you over to the judge, and the judge to the officer, and you will be thrown into prison. [26] Truly I tell you, you will never get out of there until you have paid the last penny.

[27] "You have heard that it was said, Do not commit adultery. [28] But I tell you, everyone who looks at a woman lustfully has already committed adultery with her in his heart. [29] If your right eye causes you to sin, gouge it out and throw it away. For it is better that you lose one of the parts of your body than for your whole body to be thrown into hell. [30] And if your right hand causes you to sin, cut it off and throw it away. For it is better that you lose one of the parts of your body than for your whole body to go into hell.

[31] "It was also said, Whoever divorces his wife must give her a written notice of divorce. [32] But I tell you, everyone who divorces his wife, except in a case of sexual immorality, causes her to commit adultery. And whoever marries a divorced woman commits adultery.

[33] "Again, you have heard that it was said to our ancestors, You must not break your oath, but you must keep your oaths to the Lord. [34] But I tell you, don't take an oath at all: either by heaven, because it is God's throne; [35] or by the earth, because it is his footstool; or by Jerusalem, because it

is the city of the great King. ³⁶ Do not swear by your head, because you cannot make a single hair white or black. ³⁷ But let your 'yes' mean 'yes,' and your 'no' mean 'no.' Anything more than this is from the evil one.

³⁸ "You have heard that it was said, An eye for an eye and a tooth for a tooth. ³⁹ But I tell you, don't resist an evildoer. On the contrary, if anyone slaps you on your right cheek, turn the other to him also. ⁴⁰ As for the one who wants to sue you and take away your shirt, let him have your coat as well. ⁴¹ And if anyone forces you to go one mile, go with him two. ⁴² Give to the one who asks you, and don't turn away from the one who wants to borrow from you.

⁴³ "You have heard that it was said, Love your neighbor and hate your enemy. ⁴⁴ But I tell you, love your enemies and pray for those who persecute you, ⁴⁵ so that you may be children of your Father in heaven. For he causes his sun to rise on the evil and the good, and sends rain on the righteous and the unrighteous. ⁴⁶ For if you love those who love you, what reward will you have? Don't even the tax collectors do the same? ⁴⁷ And if you greet only your brothers and sisters, what are you doing out of the ordinary? Don't even the Gentiles do the same? ⁴⁸ Be perfect, therefore, as your heavenly Father is perfect."

23

What Does Jesus Want?
Matthew 5

"If you were stranded on a deserted island and were permitted to have only one book, what would it be?"

This was the question English writer G. K. Chesterton was asked. The most pious of his friends chose the Bible. When Chesterton's turn came, he simply said that if he were stranded on an island with only one book, he would choose *Thomas's Guide to Practical Shipbuilding.*[1]

I appreciate the humor. I value the insight. There are times when the least religious answer is the best.

If someone told me I could choose only one tiny piece of the Bible to read for the rest of my life, I would unhesitatingly choose Matthew 5, 6, and 7. Commonly called the Sermon on the Mount, these three chapters offer nitty-gritty guidance on the daily experiment of following Jesus. Stranded here on the island of earth, our call is to pursue a life pleasing to God. Jesus said many things in these chapters that challenged the conventional religion of his day. After two thousand years, his wisdom still surprises.

Matthew 5 sets the opening scene: "When [Jesus] saw the crowds, he went up on the mountain, and after he sat down, his disciples came to him. Then he began to teach them" (vv. 1–2).

At the core of Jesus's message was a simple but significant challenge: *continue to become until you completely become like him.*

But what does this mean? I'm reminded of Michelangelo's approach to creating a sculptural masterpiece. Whenever a new stone was brought into his studio, the artist would spend the next few days eating, sleeping, and existing with that piece of marble. Over and over he would circle the stone, taking note of its contour and composition. In the early morning, when the angle of the sun was just right, Michelangelo could see through the translucent marble for a few precious moments, observing its veins and flaws. Only after understanding the stone's strengths and weaknesses would he pick up hammer and chisel to begin his work.

Much as Michelangelo worked with the strengths and weaknesses of the marble, so Jesus works with the gifts and flaws of our personalities. We're transparent to his ever-seeing, always-loving eyes, and like a great artist, he patiently shapes our lives so we can continue to become until we completely become like him.

Matthew 5:3–12 contains a series of short sayings called the Beatitudes. To Jesus, attitude is important. Psychologists speak of a person's explanatory style. Good and bad happen to us all. A positive or negative attitude originates from how we explain these circumstances to ourselves. Jesus holds in front of us the perpetual truth that even when life is unfair, God is still good. That should become our explanatory style as well.

In these beatitudes are qualities we consider to be strengths—being merciful, having a pure heart, and becoming a peacemaker. There are also aspects that sound more like weaknesses—poverty, mourning, and persecution. Jesus often uses the weakest, most difficult areas of our lives to mold us into his likeness. He is both creative and powerful, letting nothing go to waste.

When my family and I toured Israel many years ago, we faced several unseasonably hot days in Jerusalem. Late on one particular morning, as we walked across rough terrain, my thirteen-year-old daughter voiced her discontent. "Dad, can't we just go back to the hotel?"

My reply was part parental and part pastoral. "Honey, do you realize what you're getting to do? You have the opportunity to walk where Jesus walked."

"Daddy," she said with every ounce of teenage attitude, "I don't want to walk where Jesus walked. I would rather *drive* where Jesus walked."

In my daughter's complaint was a great truth: following Jesus is hard work. I sometimes wish it were easier. But the journey is more rewarding when we're able to accept the delights and endure the difficulties, trusting that God will use both our strengths and our weaknesses to shape us into the image of Christ.

In addition to attitude, Jesus spoke about identity in Matthew 5:13–16. Two pictures in particular capture the character of a Jesus follower.

1. "You are the salt of the earth" (v. 13). In Jesus's culture, salt was a symbol of wisdom. In fact, the phrase "lose its taste" is a single Greek word: *moranthe*. This is a word that ultimately found its way into English as the word *moron*. Jesus commands his followers to reflect wisdom to the whole world. More dangerous than thinking the wrong thoughts is the refusal to think at all. "Engage your mind!" commands Christ. We're exhorted to live wisely and reject the moronic norm.

2. "You are the light of the world" (v. 14). In this second picture, Jesus mentioned two lights of varying intensities: the light of a thriving city that pierces the darkness for miles, and the light of a simple candle that illuminates a single room. Why mention these two degrees of light? Jesus was pointing out that while all Jesus followers are to shine with the same *integrity*, each follower shines with a different *intensity*. Stay-at-home parents may shed light only on the few lives under their care, while those with a public platform may influence thousands. Whether public or private, each of us is called to live a life that reflects the brightness of God, making integrity our primary concern and leaving it to God to determine the level of intensity.

Salt—wisdom. Light—integrity. Wise judgment and luminous lives take great effort to develop. This is why we strive to *continually become* until we *completely become* like Jesus.

In the final paragraphs of Matthew 5, Jesus repeated a phrase several times: "You have heard that it was said ... But I tell you" (vv. 21–22, 27–28, 31–34, 38–39, 43–44). With each repetition, Jesus cited a familiar commandment from the Older Testament and then exposed the heart attitude from which these evil doings originate. Perhaps Jesus is teaching us that character doesn't originate from outer appearances or actions but from inner decisions and devotion.

For most people, murder is easy to avoid. But it can be difficult to free ourselves from the anger in which murder incubates. We may not commit adultery because we fear getting caught. But it's tempting to indulge in lust because it's often an invisible sin. Jesus calls us further—to a level of honesty where looking good on the outside flows from being good on the inside. That's the meaning of integrity, when outside and inside match, forming a flawless whole.

Perhaps the advice that takes us most aback is Christ's counsel on avoiding sin. Matthew 5:29 says, "If your right eye causes you to sin, gouge it out and throw it away." What could these words possibly mean? Jesus isn't commanding us to perform literal amputation. Instead, he is asking us to purposefully address the sin that exists in our lives.

In 2003 a climber named Aron Ralston was biking and hiking alone in the Bluejohn Canyon of Utah. An eight-hundred-pound boulder shifted as he moved across its surface, trapping his hand beneath its immovable weight. For several days Ralston awaited rescue. After his water supply was depleted, he made the ghastly decision to sever his forearm to save his life.

Serious sins call for drastic decisions. There will be pain. We must deal with it and then move on—continuing to become until we completely become like Christ.

FOR REFLECTION

What is your greatest weakness as a follower of Jesus? As you consider this question, you may want to look through the list of sins Jesus mentioned in Matthew 5, asking God to show you how you've failed. But don't limit yourself to confessing your sins and asking for forgiveness. Consider your greatest strengths as well. Take a few moments to thank God for how he has gifted you.

Matthew 6

[1] "Be careful not to practice your righteousness in front of others to be seen by them. Otherwise, you have no reward with your Father in heaven. [2] So whenever you give to the poor, don't sound a trumpet before you, as the hypocrites do in the synagogues and on the streets, to be applauded by people. Truly I tell you, they have their reward. [3] But when you give to the poor, don't let your left hand know what your right hand is doing, [4] so that your giving may be in secret. And your Father who sees in secret will reward you.

[5] "Whenever you pray, you must not be like the hypocrites, because they love to pray standing in the synagogues and on the street corners to be seen by people. Truly I tell you, they have their reward. [6] But when you pray, go into your private room, shut your door, and pray to your Father who is in secret. And your Father who sees in secret will reward you. [7] When you pray, don't babble like the Gentiles, since they imagine they'll be heard for their many words. [8] Don't be like them, because your Father knows the things you need before you ask him.

[9] "Therefore, you should pray like this:

Our Father in heaven,
your name be honored as holy.
[10] Your kingdom come.
Your will be done
[11] on earth as it is in heaven.
Give us today our daily bread.
[12] And forgive us our debts,
as we also have forgiven our debtors.
[13] And do not bring us into temptation,
but deliver us from the evil one.

[14] "For if you forgive others their offenses, your heavenly Father will forgive you as well. [15] But if you don't forgive others, your Father will not forgive your offenses.

[16] "Whenever you fast, don't be gloomy like the hypocrites. For they make their faces unattractive so that their fasting is obvious to people.

Truly I tell you, they have their reward. [17] But when you fast, put oil on your head and wash your face, [18] so that your fasting isn't obvious to others but to your Father who is in secret. And your Father who sees in secret will reward you.

[19] "Don't store up for yourselves treasures on earth, where moth and rust destroy and where thieves break in and steal. [20] But store up for yourselves treasures in heaven, where neither moth nor rust destroys, and where thieves don't break in and steal. [21] For where your treasure is, there your heart will be also.

[22] "The eye is the lamp of the body. If your eye is healthy, your whole body will be full of light. [23] But if your eye is bad, your whole body will be full of darkness. So if the light within you is darkness, how deep is that darkness!

[24] "No one can serve two masters, since either he will hate one and love the other, or he will be devoted to one and despise the other. You cannot serve both God and money.

[25] "Therefore I tell you: Don't worry about your life, what you will eat or what you will drink; or about your body, what you will wear. Isn't life more than food and the body more than clothing? [26] Consider the birds of the sky: They don't sow or reap or gather into barns, yet your heavenly Father feeds them. Aren't you worth more than they? [27] Can any of you add one moment to his life-span by worrying? [28] And why do you worry about clothes? Observe how the wildflowers of the field grow: They don't labor or spin thread. [29] Yet I tell you that not even Solomon in all his splendor was adorned like one of these. [30] If that's how God clothes the grass of the field, which is here today and thrown into the furnace tomorrow, won't he do much more for you — you of little faith? [31] So don't worry, saying, 'What will we eat?' or 'What will we drink?' or 'What will we wear?' [32] For the Gentiles eagerly seek all these things, and your heavenly Father knows that you need them. [33] But seek first the kingdom of God and his righteousness, and all these things will be provided for you. [34] Therefore don't worry about tomorrow, because tomorrow will worry about itself. Each day has enough trouble of its own."

24

Why Worry Never Works
Matthew 6

Jesus's Sermon on the Mount is contained in the 107 verses of Matthew 5, 6, and 7. The sermon is a guide for the day-to-day practice of following Jesus. The key word in this statement is *practice*.

Pablo Casals is among the greatest musicians of human history. Proficient in piano, organ, and violin, he especially excelled on the cello. His late-1930s recording of the Bach cello suites was considered flawless. Casals was certainly talented. But he also knew the value of training. Until he was ninety-six, Casals practiced his scales four to six hours each day. He correctly understood that to command scales was to master music. Attention to the basics served to unleash beauty.

For Casals, and for us, practice is key. To unleash the full beauty of following Jesus, we must rehearse simple disciplines each day that result in the transformation of our character. To play a symphony, we must practice the scales.

Among the many spiritual exercises of Jesus's day, he pointed to three as indispensable: generosity, prayer, and fasting (Matt. 6:1–18). For these spiritual disciplines to produce their full intended result, we must heed Jesus's reminder to practice them in privacy. Dallas Willard, a wise voice among Jesus followers, once said, "What Jesus is teaching us to do in this important passage from his Discourse is to be free of control by the opinions of others."[1] Genuine spirituality longs for the approval of God, not the applause of people. The secrecy of these practices ensures their authenticity.

Generosity is the practice of sharing our resources with others in the spirit of Christ (vv. 1–4). Stinginess isn't spiritual. Resources can be used for selfish or selfless purposes. The choice for the follower of Christ is obvious.

Prayer is developing an unpretentious and conversational relationship with God (vv. 5–15). Philip Yancey captures the heart of Jesus's teaching on prayer when he encourages us to "keep it honest, keep it simple, and keep it up."[2]

Fasting is the practice of refusing physical food for the purpose of discovering spiritual sustenance (vv. 16–18). Fasting is a self-reminder that life isn't to be dictated by our wants but by the will of God. Our desire to please God takes priority even over our natural appetites.

When my son was younger, he would get out of bed early in the morning and find his way to my study, where I was reading in my recliner. He would stretch out beside me, and the two of us, without saying a word, would hug for a while. My son's habit was to adjust his rate of breathing to match mine. For a few moments, father and son were in sync. The spiritual practices Jesus mentioned—generosity, prayer, and fasting—are simple ways of ensuring our harmony with the heart and mind of God.

As important as it is to integrate good habits into our character, it's equally important to avoid habits that may prove destructive. The final section of Matthew 6 is Jesus's full-frontal assault on the damaging habit of worry. The word *worry* is used seven times throughout Matthew, six of which appear in the latter part of this chapter.

The New Testament word for *worry* reveals why the condition is so damaging. The Greek term *merimnate* could also be translated "don't go to pieces." Worry can fracture our hearts and minds, and it may even ultimately break our trust in God. Worry distracts us from our greatest focus: becoming like Jesus himself. Following Jesus is difficult with a fragmented soul.

Jesus's teaching on worry was nothing short of sheer genius. He spoke of birds and flowers so that whether we look up to the sky or down to the ground, a living illustration of the uselessness of worry is constantly before us. Jesus commands us not to be concerned with what is around us (clothes) or what is in us (food). Both external matters and internal concerns are under God's watchful care.

Jesus speaks of the birds sowing and reaping—farming being a man's job in Jesus's day. Then he refers to the flowers not needing to spin—weaving being part of a woman's typical household tasks. No matter whether we're male or female, with our different reasons and responses to anxiety, Jesus reminds us that worry is impractical and not beneficial.

Like every person living in the midwestern United States, I'm accustomed to hailstorms, the kind that damage roofs and dent cars. An official scale has even been developed to measure hailstones. The TORRO Hailstorm Intensity Scale describes the size of hail that approaching storms might produce by referring to objects of various sizes. The scale begins with pea-sized hail and moves progressively to mothball-sized hail, walnut-sized hail, golf ball–sized hail, softball-sized hail, to the largest measure of melon-sized hail. Beyond these descriptions, hailstones are typically measured by diameter.[3] The largest recorded piece of hail fell near Vivian, South Dakota, in 2010. The hailstone, more than eight inches in diameter, weighed just less than two pounds.[4]

Like hailstones, worries of all sizes fall on our lives at unwelcome and unexpected times. We worry about the weather and the possibility of cancer. We obsess over our weight and our finances. We're concerned about our marriages and whether or not we closed the garage door when we left the house. But God's goodness addresses our small concerns and overtakes even our most massive problems. Jesus invites us to engage in the practice of worry-free living, which is a rehearsal of daily trust in God.

Jesus concluded his teachings on worry with one of his best-remembered quotes from the Sermon on the Mount: "Seek first the kingdom of God and his righteousness, and all these things will be provided for you. Therefore don't worry about tomorrow, because tomorrow will worry about itself. Each day has enough trouble of its own" (vv. 33–34).

Two words in Jesus's declaration deserve clarification: *kingdom* and *righteousness*.

Kingdom. Simply stated, God's kingdom is God's rule in the hearts of people. To cut off the suffix -*dom* from this word exposes the word *king*. God wants nothing more than to be king of your life and my life, your heart and my heart. Jesus doesn't want to make us more religious; he wants to make us more alive. When the rule of God becomes the defining reality of our lives, worry is no longer welcome.

Righteousness. As mentioned earlier, righteousness is to be in right relationship with another person. For the Jesus follower, if our relationship with God is in good standing, no circumstance can alarm us because nothing can truly harm us.

Quaker Christians have a prayer practice called "palms down, palms up." Those praying begin by placing palms facedown in their laps as an act of surrendering every anxiety, concern, worry, or doubt to God. Then they flip their hands with palms facing up as a means of symbolically receiving the goodness and blessings of God.

In the journey of following Jesus, we're invited to receive vital disciplines to ensure a growing relationship with him— generosity, prayer, and fasting. We're also asked to surrender all that is unnecessary in our lives—worry, anxiety, and fear. Jesus's kingdom and God's righteousness demand nothing less.

FOR REFLECTION

Practice the palms-down, palms-up prayer for a few minutes. Which part of this prayer comes more naturally to you? Are you more comfortable asking for God's help or giving yourself over to his care? Are you more inclined to receive or surrender as you pray? God's kingship over our lives means that we're free to ask him to provide and protect.

Matthew 7

"Do not judge, so that you won't be judged. ² For you will be judged by the same standard with which you judge others, and you will be measured by the same measure you use. ³ Why do you look at the splinter in your brother's eye but don't notice the beam of wood in your own eye? ⁴ Or how can you say to your brother, 'Let me take the splinter out of your eye,' and look, there's a beam of wood in your own eye? ⁵ Hypocrite! First take the beam of wood out of your eye, and then you will see clearly to take the splinter out of your brother's eye. ⁶ Don't give what is holy to dogs or toss your pearls before pigs, or they will trample them under their feet, turn, and tear you to pieces.

⁷ "Ask, and it will be given to you. Seek, and you will find. Knock, and the door will be opened to you. ⁸ For everyone who asks receives, and the one who seeks finds, and to the one who knocks, the door will be opened. ⁹ Who among you, if his son asks him for bread, will give him a stone? ¹⁰ Or if he asks for a fish, will give him a snake? ¹¹ If you then, who are evil, know how to give good gifts to your children, how much more will your Father in heaven give good things to those who ask him. ¹² Therefore, whatever you want others to do for you, do also the same for them, for this is the Law and the Prophets.

¹³ "Enter through the narrow gate. For the gate is wide and the road broad that leads to destruction, and there are many who go through it. ¹⁴ How narrow is the gate and difficult the road that leads to life, and few find it.

¹⁵ "Be on your guard against false prophets who come to you in sheep's clothing but inwardly are ravaging wolves. ¹⁶ You'll recognize them by their fruit. Are grapes gathered from thornbushes or figs from thistles? ¹⁷ In the same way, every good tree produces good fruit, but a bad tree produces bad fruit. ¹⁸ A good tree can't produce bad fruit; neither can a bad tree produce good fruit. ¹⁹ Every tree that doesn't produce good fruit is cut down and thrown into the fire. ²⁰ So you'll recognize them by their fruit.

²¹ "Not everyone who says to me, 'Lord, Lord,' will enter the kingdom of heaven, but only the one who does the will of my Father in heaven. ²² On that day many will say to me, 'Lord, Lord, didn't we prophesy in your name, drive out demons in your name, and do many miracles in

your name?' ²³ Then I will announce to them, 'I never knew you. Depart from me, you lawbreakers!'

²⁴ "Therefore, everyone who hears these words of mine and acts on them will be like a wise man who built his house on the rock. ²⁵ The rain fell, the rivers rose, and the winds blew and pounded that house. Yet it didn't collapse, because its foundation was on the rock. ²⁶ But everyone who hears these words of mine and doesn't act on them will be like a foolish man who built his house on the sand. ²⁷ The rain fell, the rivers rose, the winds blew and pounded that house, and it collapsed. It collapsed with a great crash."

²⁸ When Jesus had finished saying these things, the crowds were astonished at his teaching, ²⁹ because he was teaching them like one who had authority, and not like their scribes.

25

Life over the Long Haul
Matthew 7

Stephen Ambrose's book *Nothing Like It in the World* recounts the construction of the transcontinental railroad, the first modern means of transportation between the East and West Coasts of the United States. Early on, a handful of the project's investors suggested a celebration to launch construction. One major financer, Collis Huntington, objected to the festivities, saying, "If you want to jubilate over driving the first spike, go ahead and do it. I don't.... Anybody can drive the first spike, but there are many months of labor and unrest between the first and last spike."[1]

Entering a relationship with Jesus is quite simple. Taking on the title of *Christian* isn't unlike driving the first spike. The immense challenge, however, is the process of following Jesus daily and allowing his presence to transform our character into something more like his own. This process necessitates a lifetime of labor and unrest. Following Jesus is out-and-out effort until we drive home the final spike when we draw our last earthly breath. Jesus's Sermon on the Mount addresses the complexity and the tenacity essential for a lifelong Jesus follower.

Matthew 7 can be condensed into one word: *choices*. The choices we make, both big and small, matter to Jesus and bear consequences in the development of our character. Therefore, Jesus invites us to live by intention instead of impulse in our relationships with others, our relationship with God, and even our relationship with ourselves. A number of choices determine the kind of character we develop over a lifetime.

We choose an attitude of judgment or generosity (vv. 1–6). How easy it is to look on others with suspicion and skepticism. Certainly, Christ doesn't call us to live in naïveté regarding the fact that evil people exist in our imperfect world. But neither are we to allow unchecked negativity toward others to become a standard character trait.

Recently I met a visitor to our church whom I sized up as a homeless person. I made this assumption based on his ragged beard and wrinkled clothes. It turned out this man had just arrived with a traveling theater company for a production of *Fiddler on the Roof*. His recent arrival made for rumpled apparel, and his beard helped portray Tevye, the lead character in the play. Jesus followers can choose to be generous in our opinions of others. I think Jesus would agree with the maxim, "Great minds discuss ideas; average minds discuss events; small minds discuss people."

We choose between a life of prayerfulness and a life of prayerless-ness (vv. 7–11). Jesus gives his followers permission to ask, seek, and knock. For fear of praying the wrong way, some choose not to pray at all. But Richard Foster offers this insight: "In the same way that a small child cannot draw a bad picture so a child of God cannot offer a bad prayer."[2]

Pray as best you know how. Like any patient parent, God will encourage where you succeed and correct when mistakes are made. In short, Jesus invites the exploration of a relationship with God marked by authenticity and candor. Posturing and politeness may be necessary for pleasing others, but such politics have no room in a relationship with God.

We choose how we treat other people (v. 12). "Therefore, whatever you want others to do for you, do also the same for them, for this is the Law and the Prophets." This verse is one of Jesus's most iconic statements. Confucius, Plato, and the noted Jewish rabbi Hillel all said something along the same lines, and they said it well before the time of Jesus. But their statements suggested that *what you don't want done to yourself, don't do to others.* Their version of the Golden Rule was a prohibition against bad, whereas Jesus encourages initiative in doing good. Jesus's command doesn't restrict us but frees us to act in the best interests of others at all times.

We choose our path in life (vv. 13–14). In most major decisions, I've found a simple principle at work: the most difficult course of action is typically the correct course of action. The easy way out is typically the wrong way. This principle is embedded in Jesus's instruction about the path of life we choose. Electing to follow Jesus is the quintessential small gate and narrow road.

Following him requires an agility and obedience few things in life demand. While it's far easier not to follow Jesus, that broad road is also far from being the best.

We choose whom we allow to influence our lives (vv. 15–23). Jesus warns us against false leaders. As much as we'd like to believe that everyone is honest and shares our good intentions, actual experience tells a very different story.

Years ago as a young pastor, I befriended a fellow minister who quickly gained my trust and affection. Not only did I respect him professionally, but I also trusted him enough to introduce him to my family. He became a regular fixture at birthday parties and family gatherings. After years of friendship, it became known that my friend had attempted to embezzle money from his church. Even when the evidence against him became undeniable, he could only blame others for the mistakes he had made.

Jesus asks that we take a realistic view of the world and the people in it. He doesn't advocate suspicion toward others, but he does caution us to select carefully those we place in positions of influence over us.

We choose who we become (vv. 24–27). Jesus used the picture of a house to describe the life of a follower. In Jesus's day, many people living in Israel built their homes into the sides of hills. Chiseling a house into the side of a rock was a laborious task. The steeper the grade of the hillside, the more tempting it must have been to build a house on the sandy, flat surface of the valley floor.

And why not do this in the first place? The reason was quite simple. While the better part of the year in Israel is dry, with only a trickle of precipitation, the rainy season brings torrential rains. Valley floors, dry for most of the year, can quickly become raging rapids. Any home built in the path of these flash floods would face sure destruction. Any homebuilder foolish enough to ignore this certain reality was just that—foolish.

Kansai International Airport, Japan's first twenty-four-hour airport, opened in September 1994. It sits on a man-made island in Osaka Bay. The artificial island presents structural issues for the airport, given that it will continue to settle for years to come. To compensate, engineers dropped some nine hundred concrete columns with an intricate system of hydraulic jacks beneath. A central computer can raise or lower each column as needed to keep the airport level.[3] Without this firm and flexible foundation, the airport would become uneven, unstable, and eventually useless.

Jesus challenges us to build our lives firmly on his words. His teachings are also flexible enough to expand with our understanding and the ever-changing circumstances of life.

FOR REFLECTION

The Sermon on the Mount ends with the reaction of Jesus's listeners: "When Jesus had finished saying these things, the crowds were astonished at his teaching, because he was teaching them like one who had authority, and not like their scribes" (vv. 28–29).

Jesus's teachings command an authority all their own. Have you permitted Jesus and his teachings to have the final say in your life? Why or why not? Is it time to acknowledge his authority over you today? Jesus's teachings are a narrow road, to be sure. But this also happens to be the best possible way to live.

JESUS WON'T LEAVE US AS WE ARE

Luke 8

¹ Afterward he was traveling from one town and village to another, preaching and telling the good news of the kingdom of God. The Twelve were with him, ² and also some women who had been healed of evil spirits and sicknesses: Mary, called Magdalene (seven demons had come out of her); ³ Joanna the wife of Chuza, Herod's steward; Susanna; and many others who were supporting them from their possessions.

⁴ As a large crowd was gathering, and people were coming to Jesus from every town, he said in a parable: ⁵ "A sower went out to sow his seed. As he sowed, some seed fell along the path; it was trampled on, and the birds of the sky devoured it. ⁶ Other seed fell on the rock; when it grew up, it withered away, since it lacked moisture. ⁷ Other seed fell among thorns; the thorns grew up with it and choked it. ⁸ Still other seed fell on good ground; when it grew up, it produced fruit: a hundred times what was sown." As he said this, he called out, "Let anyone who has ears to hear listen."

⁹ Then his disciples asked him, "What does this parable mean?" ¹⁰ So he said, "The secrets of the kingdom of God have been given for you to know, but to the rest it is in parables, so that

> Looking they may not see,
> and hearing they may not understand.

¹¹ "This is the meaning of the parable: The seed is the word of God. ¹² The seed along the path are those who have heard and then the devil comes and takes away the word from their hearts, so that they may not believe and be saved. ¹³ And the seed on the rock are those who, when they hear, receive the word with joy. Having no root, these believe for a while and fall away in a time of testing. ¹⁴ As for the seed that fell among thorns, these are the ones who, when they have heard, go on their way and are choked with worries, riches, and pleasures of life, and produce no mature fruit. ¹⁵ But the seed in the good ground — these are the ones who, having heard the word with an honest and good heart, hold on to it and by enduring, produce fruit.

¹⁶ "No one, after lighting a lamp, covers it with a basket or puts it under a bed, but puts it on a lampstand so that those who come in may see its

light. ¹⁷ For nothing is concealed that won't be revealed, and nothing hidden that won't be made known and brought to light. ¹⁸ Therefore take care how you listen. For whoever has, more will be given to him; and whoever does not have, even what he thinks he has will be taken away from him."

¹⁹ Then his mother and brothers came to him, but they could not meet with him because of the crowd. ²⁰ He was told, "Your mother and your brothers are standing outside, wanting to see you."

²¹ But he replied to them, "My mother and my brothers are those who hear and do the word of God."

²² One day he and his disciples got into a boat, and he told them, "Let's cross over to the other side of the lake." So they set out, ²³ and as they were sailing he fell asleep. Then a fierce windstorm came down on the lake; they were being swamped and were in danger. ²⁴ They came and woke him up, saying, "Master, Master, we're going to die!"

Then he got up and rebuked the wind and the raging waves. So they ceased, and there was a calm. ²⁵ He said to them, "Where is your faith?"

They were fearful and amazed, asking one another, "Who then is this? He commands even the winds and the waves, and they obey him!"

²⁶ Then they sailed to the region of the Gerasenes, which is opposite Galilee. ²⁷ When he got out on land, a demon-possessed man from the town met him. For a long time he had worn no clothes and did not stay in a house but in the tombs. ²⁸ When he saw Jesus, he cried out, fell down before him, and said in a loud voice, "What do you have to do with me, Jesus, Son of the Most High God? I beg you, don't torment me!" ²⁹ For he had commanded the unclean spirit to come out of the man. Many times it had seized him, and though he was guarded, bound by chains and shackles, he would snap the restraints and be driven by the demon into deserted places.

³⁰ "What is your name?" Jesus asked him.

"Legion," he said, because many demons had entered him. ³¹ And they begged him not to banish them to the abyss.

³² A large herd of pigs was there, feeding on the hillside. The demons begged him to permit them to enter the pigs, and he gave them permission. ³³ The demons came out of the man and entered the pigs, and the herd rushed down the steep bank into the lake and drowned.

³⁴ When the men who tended them saw what had happened, they ran off and reported it in the town and in the countryside. ³⁵ Then people went out to see what had happened. They came to Jesus and found the man the demons had departed from, sitting at Jesus's feet, dressed and in his right mind. And they were afraid. ³⁶ Meanwhile, the eyewitnesses reported to them how the demon-possessed man was delivered. ³⁷ Then all the people of the Gerasene region asked him to leave them, because they were gripped by great fear. So getting into the boat, he returned.

³⁸ The man from whom the demons had departed begged him earnestly to be with him. But he sent him away and said, ³⁹ "Go back to your home, and tell all that God has done for you." And off he went, proclaiming throughout the town how much Jesus had done for him.

⁴⁰ When Jesus returned, the crowd welcomed him, for they were all expecting him. ⁴¹ Just then, a man named Jairus came. He was a leader of the synagogue. He fell down at Jesus's feet and pleaded with him to come to his house, ⁴² because he had an only daughter about twelve years old, and she was dying.

While he was going, the crowds were nearly crushing him. ⁴³ A woman suffering from bleeding for twelve years, who had spent all she had on doctors and yet could not be healed by any, ⁴⁴ approached from behind and touched the end of his robe. Instantly her bleeding stopped.

⁴⁵ "Who touched me?" Jesus asked.

When they all denied it, Peter said, "Master, the crowds are hemming you in and pressing against you."

⁴⁶ "Someone did touch me," said Jesus. "I know that power has gone out from me." ⁴⁷ When the woman saw that she was discovered, she came trembling and fell down before him. In the presence of all the people, she declared the reason she had touched him and how she was instantly healed. ⁴⁸ "Daughter," he said to her, "your faith has saved you. Go in peace."

⁴⁹ While he was still speaking, someone came from the synagogue leader's house and said, "Your daughter is dead. Don't bother the teacher anymore."

⁵⁰ When Jesus heard it, he answered him, "Don't be afraid. Only believe, and she will be saved." ⁵¹ After he came to the house, he let no one enter with him except Peter, John, James, and the child's father and mother. ⁵² Everyone was crying and mourning for her. But he said, "Stop crying, because she is not dead but asleep."

[53] They laughed at him, because they knew she was dead. [54] So he took her by the hand and called out, "Child, get up! " [55] Her spirit returned, and she got up at once. Then he gave orders that she be given something to eat. [56] Her parents were astounded, but he instructed them to tell no one what had happened.

26

Is Jesus Strong Enough?
Luke 8

The iconic statue of Atlas stands on the west side of Fifth Avenue in New York City. The mythical figure of strength is perfectly proportioned, yet he can barely support the weight of the sky bearing down on his shoulders. The statue captures the way many people feel under the burden of daily life.

On the opposite side of Fifth Avenue sits Saint Patrick's Cathedral. Behind the high altar, almost hidden, stands a very different statue. This statue depicts the boy Jesus—perhaps six or seven years old—holding the world in one cupped hand. The contrast is clear: the burden of the world is more than we can bear alone, but Jesus's strength is sufficient to carry the weight of our world with ease.

Taking into account all four gospels—Matthew, Mark, Luke, and John—Jesus performed a total of thirty-five miracles. We can separate these miracles into four categories. Nine miracles were actions that overrode nature. Six were exorcisms—the forcible removal of the demonic from a person's life. Seventeen involved physical healing. And three were resuscitations. Luke 8 contains a miracle from each of these categories.

The first miracle took place on the Sea of Galilee (vv. 22–25). Jesus climbed into a boat with his closest followers. Exhausted from the rigors of ministry, he quickly fell asleep. The Sea of Galilee was notorious for its sudden and severe squalls, and the water suddenly began to churn under the small boat. Panicked, the disciples awakened Jesus. Without hesitation Jesus commanded the wind and the waves to be still.

This wonderful story impressed King Canute, an eleventh-century Danish king who had grown weary of the worshipful attention of his flattering courtiers. In an attempt to correct their view of him, Canute led his entourage to a beach. While the tide was rising, he walked to the edge of the waves and commanded them not to soak him. Of course the tide continued to rise, inattentive to the king's command. Canute was making this point: "Am I God that I can command and control nature?"

Jesus is. And Jesus did. His power over nature reveals that he was more than a man. Only divinity can command and countermand the natural order. Jesus is strong enough to handle your world, even when you find yourself in the middle of a terrible storm.

After landing safely on shore, Jesus confronted a demon-possessed man (vv. 26–39). This wasn't his first encounter with the demonic, but it was a different order of magnitude. The demon referred to himself as Legion. A Roman legion consisted of troops numbering no less than six thousand soldiers. Apparently a detachment of demons was marching in chaotic formation through this man's mind. The demonic invasion remained unchecked and unchallenged, until this moment.

Jesus was clearly outnumbered, but he wasn't overpowered. In calm rebuke, he removed the demons from the man's life. The darkest forces of evil couldn't stand against him. Jesus is strong enough to stand against any evil we may encounter.

The miracles of Luke 8 continue with two healings (vv. 40–56). The first began when a man made his way through the crowd to plead with Jesus, asking him to visit his dying twelve-year-old daughter. As Jesus was on his way, a nameless woman in the crowd touched the edge of Jesus's robe, and power went out from him. This woman had been suffering from an incurable blood disorder for as long as the sick girl had been alive, and she yearned to be healed. Despite the urgency of the girl's condition, Jesus stopped and gave the woman his full attention.

Noting Jesus's characteristic calm, J. B. Phillips remarked, "It is refreshing ... to study the poise and quietness of Christ. His task and responsibility might well have driven a man out of his mind. But He was never in a hurry, never impressed by numbers, never a slave of the clock. He was acting, He said, as He observed God to act—never in a hurry."[1] Jesus's power over sickness is obvious. Jesus's supremacy over the pressure of the clock and the expectations of others is inspiring.

Jesus reveals to us a God who notices our deepest needs. Perhaps he realized that the woman with the bleeding disorder needed healing not merely from her ongoing illness but also from her lingering loneliness. The hem of his robe brought physical healing, but his full attention brought emotional wholeness. Jesus is strong enough to cure all that ails us.

After healing the woman, Jesus arrived at the home of the young girl, having been told that she was already dead. It seemed he had come too late. But instead of giving up, Jesus entered her house and combined both word and touch in an ultimate show of strength. Taking her by the hand and speaking tenderly to her, he reclaimed her life from the power of death. Jesus is stronger than nature, evil, sickness, and death. Indeed, Jesus is strong enough.

Thinking about the miracles of Jesus reminds me of *The Jefferson Bible*, a prize piece of history on display at the Smithsonian Institution. Using two copies of the New Testament, Thomas Jefferson cut and pasted his way through the four gospels to eliminate any trace of the miraculous. He kept only the parts that contained Jesus's moral teachings. The result was *The Jefferson Bible: The Life and Morals of Jesus of Nazareth*.

Though I don't question the historical merit of this document, I do question the value of any portrait of Jesus that leaves out his miracles. If Jesus was only a moral and mortal man, he was simply one of many gifted teachers, a remarkable man with lofty ideas and ideals. But he isn't strong enough to help us.

If the miracles of Jesus are true, then they point to a great reality: Jesus is more than a man. He is divine. If Jesus could perform these miracles, then he is strong enough to bear the burden of your world.

FOR REFLECTION

Have you ever asked for a miracle? Unless a request requires God to contradict either his character or his commands, the Bible gives us permission to ask for what we want in any given situation. Jesus is still strong enough to perform miracles in and through our lives.

What miracle would you like to see God do for you? Have you asked him yet? Remember that our challenge is to ask and then trust that Jesus will answer in the best way possible.

John 3

¹ There was a man from the Pharisees named Nicodemus, a ruler of the Jews. ² This man came to him at night and said, "Rabbi, we know that you are a teacher who has come from God, for no one could perform these signs you do unless God were with him."

³ Jesus replied, "Truly I tell you, unless someone is born again, he cannot see the kingdom of God."

⁴ "How can anyone be born when he is old?" Nicodemus asked him. "Can he enter his mother's womb a second time and be born?"

⁵ Jesus answered, "Truly I tell you, unless someone is born of water and the Spirit, he cannot enter the kingdom of God. ⁶ Whatever is born of the flesh is flesh, and whatever is born of the Spirit is spirit. ⁷ Do not be amazed that I told you that you must be born again. ⁸ The wind blows where it pleases, and you hear its sound, but you don't know where it comes from or where it is going. So it is with everyone born of the Spirit."

⁹ "How can these things be?" asked Nicodemus.

¹⁰ "Are you a teacher of Israel and don't know these things?" Jesus replied. ¹¹ "Truly I tell you, we speak what we know and we testify to what we have seen, but you do not accept our testimony. ¹² If I have told you about earthly things and you don't believe, how will you believe if I tell you about heavenly things? ¹³ No one has ascended into heaven except the one who descended from heaven — the Son of Man.

¹⁴ "Just as Moses lifted up the snake in the wilderness, so the Son of Man must be lifted up, ¹⁵ so that everyone who believes in him may have eternal life. ¹⁶ For God loved the world in this way: He gave his one and only Son, so that everyone who believes in him will not perish but have eternal life. ¹⁷ For God did not send his Son into the world to condemn the world, but to save the world through him. ¹⁸ Anyone who believes in him is not condemned, but anyone who does not believe is already condemned, because he has not believed in the name of the one and only Son of God. ¹⁹ This is the judgment: The light has come into the world, and people loved darkness rather than the light because their deeds were evil. ²⁰ For everyone who does evil hates the light and avoids it, so that his deeds may not be exposed. ²¹ But anyone who lives by the truth comes to the light, so that his works may be shown to be accomplished by God."

²² After this, Jesus and his disciples went to the Judean countryside, where he spent time with them and baptized.

²³ John also was baptizing in Aenon near Salim, because there was plenty of water there. People were coming and being baptized, ²⁴ since John had not yet been thrown into prison.

²⁵ Then a dispute arose between John's disciples and a Jew about purification. ²⁶ So they came to John and told him, "Rabbi, the one you testified about, and who was with you across the Jordan, is baptizing — and everyone is going to him."

²⁷ John responded, "No one can receive anything unless it has been given to him from heaven. ²⁸ You yourselves can testify that I said, 'I am not the Messiah, but I've been sent ahead of him.' ²⁹ He who has the bride is the groom. But the groom's friend, who stands by and listens for him, rejoices greatly at the groom's voice. So this joy of mine is complete. ³⁰ He must increase, but I must decrease."

³¹ The one who comes from above is above all. The one who is from the earth is earthly and speaks in earthly terms. The one who comes from heaven is above all. ³² He testifies to what he has seen and heard, and yet no one accepts his testimony. ³³ The one who has accepted his testimony has affirmed that God is true. ³⁴ For the one whom God sent speaks God's words, since he gives the Spirit without measure. ³⁵ The Father loves the Son and has given all things into his hands. ³⁶ The one who believes in the Son has eternal life, but the one who rejects the Son will not see life; instead, the wrath of God remains on him.

27

The Original Come-to-Jesus Meeting
John 3

The gospel of John is composed largely of conversations. Jesus felt free to talk to anyone. He had the unique ability to see opportunity in the most unlikely people. He gave his attention to individuals whom most people found easy to ignore.

Jesus broke through the racial and gender etiquette of his day by talking with a Samaritan woman in John 4. In John 8, a riotous religious band prepared to punish a woman caught in adultery. Jesus not only defended her publicly, but he also gave this nameless woman the dignity of his attention and forgiveness. John 9 records Jesus's conversation with a man Jesus had recently relieved of blindness. John 13–16 captures the dramatic conversation Jesus had with his disciples the night before his death. And at the apex of all conversations in John, John 17 preserves Jesus's longest prayer—his longest conversation with God. All these interactions give us insight into Jesus's character.

Conversation is essential for intimacy. Without it we never know a person well enough to establish trust.

Every Friday morning my wife and I have breakfast together. Nothing is allowed to interfere with our standing date. At a spot that serves the best breakfast in Oklahoma, we share eggs and coffee, biscuits and gravy. More than that, we share conversation about our children, challenges, dreams, difficulties, and future together. Our commitment to conversation keeps our marriage alive and our relationship strong.

The greater part of John 3 is a conversation between Jesus and a man known as Nicodemus. "There was a man from the Pharisees named Nicodemus, a ruler of the Jews. This man came to [Jesus] at night and said, 'Rabbi, we know that you are a teacher who has come from God, for no one could perform these signs you do unless God were with him'" (vv. 1–2).

Nicodemus was a religious leader. Although he was a person of influence, it seems Nicodemus was concerned with what others might think should he be seen talking with Jesus. Many viewed Jesus as a radical. Most religious people were skeptical about this new, young rabbi. To protect his reputation, Nicodemus evidently arranged a covert nighttime meeting.

Nicodemus was also a Pharisee. His brand of Jewish practice tended to reduce one's relationship with God to a list of rules. Dos and don'ts were the depth of Nicodemus's connection with God. These rules were more tradition than Scripture, more fear of God than love for the Lord. Nicodemus was no different from overly religious people today, even within Christianity.

We read this interaction: "Jesus replied, 'Truly I tell you, unless someone is born again, he cannot see the kingdom of God.'

'How can anyone be born when he is old?' Nicodemus asked him. 'Can he enter his mother's womb a second time and be born?'" (vv. 3–4).

In other places we've discussed the kingdom of God. This phrase can be roughly understood as "God's rule in the hearts of people." God wants to be king of you and me. He desires an absolute and unquestioned reign over our lives.

Jesus used another familiar phrase that's a cliché to our twenty-first-century American ears—*born again*. Nicodemus, hearing this for the first time, struggled to understand Jesus's words. The mystery of this phrase can be summed up like this: God offers a new beginning to anyone, anywhere, at any moment. There are no hoops to jump through. No religious rigors to perform. Dirty lives can be made clean. Lives lived distant from God are allowed to come home.

Death Valley is home to the hottest temperatures in the United States. It's also home to the sailing stones. Large boulders, some weighing seven hundred pounds, slide across the desert floor seemingly by themselves. Scientists have only recently solved this mystery. When the temperature in Death Valley plummets at night, "windowpane" sheets of ice form from a thin layer of water beneath the stones. As the temperature climbs the following day, the ice separates into panels that are moved by the breeze. The large rocks, still atop the ice, simply go along for the ride.[1]

As with stones, so with human lives. God's love works in mysterious ways. Through unlikely and often indiscernible events, he offers fresh starts and new beginnings. God is willing to start over with the most unlikely people. Anyone. Anywhere. Anytime. Really, what better way could there be to express it? *Born again.*

We can't experience John 3 without giving attention to the most famous verse in this chapter, indeed in the entire New Testament: "For God loved the world in this way: He gave his one and only Son, so that everyone who believes in him will not perish but have eternal life" (v. 16).

God's dominant attitude toward the world is love. God's dominant attitude toward *you* is love.

Some think God is indifferent to the world. Indeed, some hold that he may not even be involved in the day-to-day details of our existence. Simply stated, he couldn't care less about his creation. John 3:16 disagrees.

Others believe that God bears a grudge against the world and the people who populate it. To hear some of these people talk, usually in an angry tone, it seems that nothing would give God greater delight than to torment us for all eternity. Again, this is a far cry from God's attitude revealed in John 3.

When I was a young man, my pastor visited my home to talk with me about my relationship with God—or rather my lack of relationship with God. I remember his large frame seated on our orange couch. (It was the 1970s, so an orange couch was standard in every home.) He asked me to read John 3:16 and then explained very clearly to my young mind that the phrase "For God loved the world" could just as easily read, "For God loved

Deron." My simple heart embraced a mysterious faith. I made a fresh start. God moved my heart toward him that day.

John 3 doesn't tell us how Jesus's conversation with Nicodemus ended. We're left to wonder how Nicodemus responded, if at all, to the offer of starting fresh with the love of God. Was Nicodemus able to make the spiritual leap from a God of intimidation to a God of intimacy? We're given only one clue. John recorded the burial of Jesus. Jesus's body, once removed from the cross, was placed in a tomb that Joseph of Arimathea owned.

Seemingly out of nowhere, Nicodemus appeared to offer dignity to the dead Christ. It was Nicodemus who donated seventy-five pounds of embalming spice to prepare Jesus's body for burial. This was an enormous amount, a quantity usually reserved for the burial of a king. Could this communicate something of Nicodemus's attitude toward Jesus? Was this Nicodemus's way of expressing his newfound faith and embracing Jesus for who he really was and is—king and Christ? Had Nicodemus entered the kingdom of God and been born again?

FOR REFLECTION

If you could have a face-to-face conversation with Jesus, what is the one thing you would choose to talk about? What would you ask him? What do you suppose Jesus would want to say to you? Realize that you can have this kind of conversation with Jesus at any time. Although his presence isn't visible, it's available to you at any moment.

Luke 15

¹ All the tax collectors and sinners were approaching to listen to him. ² And the Pharisees and scribes were complaining, "This man welcomes sinners and eats with them."

³ So he told them this parable: ⁴ "What man among you, who has a hundred sheep and loses one of them, does not leave the ninety-nine in the open field and go after the lost one until he finds it? ⁵ When he has found it, he joyfully puts it on his shoulders, ⁶ and coming home, he calls his friends and neighbors together, saying to them, 'Rejoice with me, because I have found my lost sheep!' ⁷ I tell you, in the same way, there will be more joy in heaven over one sinner who repents than over ninety-nine righteous people who don't need repentance.

⁸ "Or what woman who has ten silver coins, if she loses one coin, does not light a lamp, sweep the house, and search carefully until she finds it? ⁹ When she finds it, she calls her friends and neighbors together, saying, 'Rejoice with me, because I have found the silver coin I lost!' ¹⁰ I tell you, in the same way, there is joy in the presence of God's angels over one sinner who repents."

¹¹ He also said: "A man had two sons. ¹² The younger of them said to his father, 'Father, give me the share of the estate I have coming to me.' So he distributed the assets to them. ¹³ Not many days later, the younger son gathered together all he had and traveled to a distant country, where he squandered his estate in foolish living. ¹⁴ After he had spent everything, a severe famine struck that country, and he had nothing. ¹⁵ Then he went to work for one of the citizens of that country, who sent him into his fields to feed pigs. ¹⁶ He longed to eat his fill from the pods that the pigs were eating, but no one would give him anything. ¹⁷ When he came to his senses, he said, 'How many of my father's hired workers have more than enough food, and here I am dying of hunger! ¹⁸ I'll get up, go to my father, and say to him, "Father, I have sinned against heaven and in your sight. ¹⁹ I'm no longer worthy to be called your son. Make me like one of your hired workers."' ²⁰ So he got up and went to his father. But while the son was still a long way off, his father saw him and was filled with compassion. He ran, threw his arms around his neck, and kissed him. ²¹ The son said to him, 'Father, I have sinned against heaven and in your sight. I'm no longer worthy to be called your son.'

²² "But the father told his servants, 'Quick! Bring out the best robe and put it on him; put a ring on his finger and sandals on his feet. ²³ Then bring the fattened calf and slaughter it, and let's celebrate with a feast, ²⁴ because this son of mine was dead and is alive again; he was lost and is found!' So they began to celebrate.

²⁵ "Now his older son was in the field; as he came near the house, he heard music and dancing. ²⁶ So he summoned one of the servants, questioning what these things meant. ²⁷ 'Your brother is here,' he told him, 'and your father has slaughtered the fattened calf because he has him back safe and sound.'

²⁸ "Then he became angry and didn't want to go in. So his father came out and pleaded with him. ²⁹ But he replied to his father, 'Look, I have been slaving many years for you, and I have never disobeyed your orders, yet you never gave me a goat so that I could celebrate with my friends. ³⁰ But when this son of yours came, who has devoured your assets with prostitutes, you slaughtered the fattened calf for him.'

³¹ " 'Son,' he said to him, 'you are always with me, and everything I have is yours. ³² But we had to celebrate and rejoice, because this brother of yours was dead and is alive again; he was lost and is found.' "

28

God Is Looking for What He Loves
Luke 15

Luke 15 has been called "the gospel in the gospel." The three stories of Jesus contained within this chapter capture the core message of God's love for all people. Jesus taught repeatedly that God is generous, not grudging, with his forgiveness.

Jesus's stories are commonly called parables. A parable is a simple word picture from everyday life that expresses a truth about the eternal God. All three parables in this chapter point to the one truth of Luke 15:7 (also echoed in verses 10 and 32): "I tell you, in the same way, there will be more joy in heaven over one sinner who repents than over ninety-nine righteous people who don't need repentance." According to Jesus, nothing pleases God more than welcoming people into a right relationship with himself.

In 1970, Bob Russell's car was stolen. He never gave up the search for his beloved 1967 Austin-Healey roadster. His resolve was indefatigable. In 2012, after forty-two years of searching, Russell discovered his long-lost car on eBay.[1] Imagine Russell's pleasure knowing that his car was back under the care of its rightful owner. Like the stories in Luke 15, this story of Russell's search offers a glimpse of God's desire for each of us to be in a fully restored relationship with him.

The first parable (Luke 15:4–7) is an everyday story of a flock of sheep under the watchful eye of a shepherd. For an agrarian society, the image of a shepherd and his sheep would have been as commonplace as parking lots and cars are to our modern mind-set. Everyone in Jesus's audience would have known that the ideal size of a flock of sheep would be around one hundred. At a glance, an adept shepherd would have known that all the sheep were present. In Jesus's story, the shepherd was shocked to discover that one sheep wasn't where it was supposed to be.

Why did the sheep go missing? It was *ignorant*. Sheep mindlessly move from one tuft of grass to the next without giving thought to their direction or their distance from the flock. The sheep never intended to get lost; it just did.

Similarly, some people are estranged from God unintentionally. As a pastor, I talk to many people who were born and raised in a home where God was rarely considered and never mentioned. In this type of environment, it's possible to be genuinely clueless about the God who desires a personal, protective relationship with them. But even in their naïveté, there is good news! They may be unaware of God, but God is fully aware of them.

Jesus's second parable (vv. 8–10) moves the eye of our imagination from a rural field to an urban neighborhood. The typical house of Jesus's day was dark and dirty compared with today's standards. With no electricity and nothing more than a dirt floor, a coin could be easily lost and nearly impossible to find.

The coin in Jesus's story was a drachma, which was equivalent to one day's wage. Jesus's original audience might have imagined a wife entrusted with her husband's hard-earned pay. In an absentminded moment, the coin was dropped. Since the coin represented the only thing standing between the family and hunger, the wife's search would have taken on a tone of desperation. While the lost sheep was a matter of ignorance, the lost coin was *accidental*.

The Alton Towers Corkscrew roller coaster in Staffordshire, England, became operational in April 1980. As the first double-looped roller coaster in Europe, it drew some 43.5 million riders during its years of service. As it was being demolished in 2008, workers discovered an area that collected the items gravity stole from the roller coaster's passengers. Among the items recovered were one diamond wedding ring, fifty-three nonmatching shoes, 604 watches, 237 mobile phones, thousands of hats, ten pieces of underwear, and one prosthetic leg.[2] As much as I wish to comment on the final two items, suffice it to say all these losses were purely accidental.

Life is hard. In response to the grind of daily living, people tend to neglect their commitment to God by accident rather than intent. The urgent tasks of existence can take our eyes off eternal realities. The downward drag can steal years of life and take our attention off the eternal importance of a relationship with God. Many people think they're too busy to seek God, but God is never too busy to continue his search for us.

The final parable of Luke 15 is recognized as one of Jesus's most memorable stories. Timothy Keller, in his book *The Prodigal God*, says, "If the teaching of Jesus is likened to a lake, this famous Parable of the Prodigal Son would be one of the clearest spots where we can see all the way to the bottom."[3]

The word that best describes the estrangement of the son from his father is *intentional*. The son intentionally asked the father for his fair share of the family wealth. This was a not-so-subtle hint that the son wished his father dead. Only when the son hit bottom did he realize the harm he had inflicted on his father. With a guilt-ridden heart and a carefully rehearsed speech on his lips, the son made the long journey home.

Tradition calls this story the parable of the prodigal son. Some assume the word *prodigal* describes a person who lives loosely, when in fact this word defines someone who spends resources too freely. In this case, it appears that both the son and his father were prodigals by nature: the son was prodigal with money, and the father was prodigal with love. The son had been careless with his inherited wealth. The father showed no caution with his affection. Although his son had hurt him, the father was so undignified as to run to meet his wayward boy. Recklessly the father forgave his son as though he had never been gone in the first place.

Several years ago my family and I visited the Grand Canyon. Wanting to take full advantage of the natural beauty, we arranged to fly over the canyon at dawn. We then boarded a boat for a tour through the canyon's chasm. After a day of air and water, we boarded a chartered bus to return to our hotel. Intuitively I assumed the bus ride would require an hour, maybe a bit more. So imagine my surprise when I learned the return trip would require four hours. I didn't realize we were so far from our home base.

It's surprising how far we can remove ourselves from God almost without realizing it. Our intentional decisions can place us at great distance from the eternal God. But one step of return results in the embrace of a loving Father.

Rembrandt's painting *The Return of the Prodigal Son* is a beautiful portrait of Jesus's memorable story. It's worth the time to observe the thought and detail of this masterpiece. You'll notice the feet of the kneeling son. One shoe is reduced to shreds, while the other shoe has completely fallen off. I can almost feel the son's aching arches. What draws my attention are the hands of the father on the shoulders of the son. While one hand is notably masculine, the other hand is nuanced with femininity. With this subtle detail, Rembrandt captured both the stern and nurturing aspects of God's love.

Whether we're displaced from God by our ignorance, by accident, or by impure intentions, God is a God who is always searching for us and forever ready to receive us home with joy.

FOR REFLECTION

As you read Luke 15, notice the decreasing ratios at work in Jesus's series of stories. The lost sheep was one of one hundred. The lost coin was one of ten. The lost son was one of two. This progression draws a verbal bull's-eye around the listener.

How does it make you feel to know that God is in search of a fully restored relationship with you? What is holding you back from fully believing and receiving his unconditional love?

Mark 15

¹ As soon as it was morning, having held a meeting with the elders, scribes, and the whole Sanhedrin, the chief priests tied Jesus up, led him away, and handed him over to Pilate.

² So Pilate asked him, "Are you the King of the Jews?"

He answered him, "You say so."

³ And the chief priests accused him of many things. ⁴ Pilate questioned him again, "Aren't you going to answer? Look how many things they are accusing you of!" ⁵ But Jesus still did not answer, and so Pilate was amazed.

⁶ At the festival Pilate used to release for the people a prisoner whom they requested. ⁷ There was one named Barabbas, who was in prison with rebels who had committed murder during the rebellion. ⁸ The crowd came up and began to ask Pilate to do for them as was his custom. ⁹ Pilate answered them, "Do you want me to release the King of the Jews for you?" ¹⁰ For he knew it was because of envy that the chief priests had handed him over. ¹¹ But the chief priests stirred up the crowd so that he would release Barabbas to them instead. ¹² Pilate asked them again, "Then what do you want me to do with the one you call the King of the Jews?"

¹³ Again they shouted, "Crucify him!"

¹⁴ Pilate said to them, "Why? What has he done wrong?"

But they shouted all the more, "Crucify him!"

¹⁵ Wanting to satisfy the crowd, Pilate released Barabbas to them; and after having Jesus flogged, he handed him over to be crucified.

¹⁶ The soldiers led him away into the palace (that is, the governor's residence) and called the whole company together. ¹⁷ They dressed him in a purple robe, twisted together a crown of thorns, and put it on him. ¹⁸ And they began to salute him, "Hail, King of the Jews!" ¹⁹ They were hitting him on the head with a stick and spitting on him. Getting down on their knees, they were paying him homage. ²⁰ After they had mocked him, they stripped him of the purple robe and put his clothes on him.

They led him out to crucify him. ²¹ They forced a man coming in from the country, who was passing by, to carry Jesus's cross. He was Simon of Cyrene, the father of Alexander and Rufus.

²² They brought Jesus to the place called *Golgotha* (which means Place of the Skull). ²³ They tried to give him wine mixed with myrrh, but he did not take it.

²⁴ Then they crucified him and divided his clothes, casting lots for them to decide what each would get. ²⁵ Now it was nine in the morning when they crucified him. ²⁶ The inscription of the charge written against him was: THE KING OF THE JEWS. ²⁷ They crucified two criminals with him, one on his right and one on his left.

²⁹ Those who passed by were yelling insults at him, shaking their heads, and saying, "Ha! The one who would destroy the temple and rebuild it in three days, ³⁰ save yourself by coming down from the cross!" ³¹ In the same way, the chief priests with the scribes were mocking him among themselves and saying, "He saved others, but he cannot save himself! ³² Let the Messiah, the King of Israel, come down now from the cross, so that we may see and believe." Even those who were crucified with him taunted him.

³³ When it was noon, darkness came over the whole land until three in the afternoon. ³⁴ And at three Jesus cried out with a loud voice, "*Eloi, Eloi, lemá sabachtháni?*" which is translated, "My God, my God, why have you abandoned me?"

³⁵ When some of those standing there heard this, they said, "See, he's calling for Elijah."

³⁶ Someone ran and filled a sponge with sour wine, fixed it on a stick, offered him a drink, and said, "Let's see if Elijah comes to take him down."

³⁷ Jesus let out a loud cry and breathed his last. ³⁸ Then the curtain of the temple was torn in two from top to bottom. ³⁹ When the centurion, who was standing opposite him, saw the way he breathed his last, he said, "Truly this man was the Son of God!"

⁴⁰ There were also women watching from a distance. Among them were Mary Magdalene, Mary the mother of James the younger and of Joses, and Salome. ⁴¹ In Galilee these women followed him and took care of him. Many other women had come up with him to Jerusalem.

⁴² When it was already evening, because it was the day of preparation (that is, the day before the Sabbath), ⁴³ Joseph of Arimathea, a prominent member of the Sanhedrin who was himself looking forward to the kingdom of God, came and boldly went to Pilate and asked for Jesus's body. ⁴⁴ Pilate was surprised that he was already dead. Summoning the centurion, he asked him whether he had already died. ⁴⁵ When he found

out from the centurion, he gave the corpse to Joseph. [46] After he bought some linen cloth, Joseph took him down and wrapped him in the linen. Then he laid him in a tomb cut out of the rock and rolled a stone against the entrance to the tomb. [47] Mary Magdalene and Mary the mother of Joses were watching where he was laid.

29

Every Scar Tells a Story
Mark 15

I was thirteen years old. My memory is fuzzy on a few points. One moment I was riding atop my red ten-speed bicycle, and the next moment I was facedown on the pavement, pain coursing through my right arm. Asphalt and skin don't pair well. In this case I opened up the flesh of my arm almost to the bone. Even today when I see the scar on my elbow, I remember the emergency-room visit, the nausea, and, of course, the pain.

I have other scars too. I bear the marks of my gallbladder surgery. A blemish on my leg brings to mind an old puncture wound. I wonder what marks your body bears. I imagine there's a tale behind every scratch and blemish on your body.

Every scar tells a story.

Jesus, too, was scarred. The Romans didn't invent crucifixion, but they did perfect it. Reserved for the worst of criminals, crucifixion's goal was to test the extremes of torture and the endurance of pain. When death appears attractive, torture has achieved its aim. Dr. William Edwards conducted an important study on the physical effects of Roman crucifixion. Reading his report, one can more accurately imagine the excruciating pain of this form of death.[1] (*Excruciating* itself is a word that literally means "out of the cross.")

All four gospels embrace the reality of Jesus's death. While the book of Mark might not be the most thorough account, in my opinion it's the most thoughtful. Mark was deliberate in his description. His account moves the eye of the reader in a purposeful direction. Mark began by mentioning events above the cross. He then detailed events occurring on the cross. And finally he focuses our attention on happenings at the foot of the cross.

Above the cross. "When it was noon, darkness came over the whole land until three in the afternoon" (Mark 15:33). The darkening skies communicated that the events on the cross had cosmic ramifications. Creation itself experienced the effect of Jesus's self-sacrifice. The darkness at midday was a sign of the day of the Lord (see Amos 5:18). The day of the Lord was God's chosen moment of dealing with the distance between himself and humanity.

Our Milky Way galaxy is on a collision course with its next nearest neighbor, the Andromeda galaxy. The two galaxies are racing toward each other at 250,000 miles per hour. A collision is inevitable. The good news is that this collision won't occur for another four billion years. But it will happen; you can be sure of it.[2]

Humanity and God's judgment were certain to collide. Jesus, as humanity's representative, took the full brunt of God's punishment for sin. The cross was the site of this cosmic collision.

On the cross. "At three Jesus cried out with a loud voice, '*Eloi, Eloi, lemá sabachtháni?*' which is translated, 'My God, my God, why have you abandoned me?'" (Mark 15:34).

The four gospels tell us Jesus spoke from the cross seven times. Mark mentions only this one statement. Jesus offered a prayer. His prayer was in the form of a question. This prayer-question was as dark as the skies above him. What was happening to Jesus that he would express deep feelings that God had abandoned him?

The apostle Paul summarized this moment well: "[God] made the one who did not know sin [Christ] to be sin for us" (2 Cor. 5:21). We can all identify with feelings of guilt and regret when we make a mistake. And if our mistake hurts another person, we likely experience estrangement from the person we wronged. The emotions in the aftermath of sin can be overwhelming. So imagine, if you can, bearing the overwhelming weight and strain of sin from all humanity. Jesus felt the effects from the sin of all who lived before him, all who were his contemporaries, and every person in future history, including us. "[God] made the one who did not know sin to be sin for us." Our dysfunction resulted in Jesus's disconnection from God the Father. Jesus, who had enjoyed uninterrupted communion with God, could no longer sense God's presence or feel his love.

Tony Wilson was a British light-heavyweight boxer, and in 1989, one bout was going poorly for Wilson. His mother was sitting in a ringside seat, and in the middle of the fight, no longer able to contain herself, she lunged into the ring and pummeled her son's opponent with her shoe. She injured the opposing boxer so badly that he was forced to withdraw from the fight.[3]

It's good to know that someone is always in your corner (even if it's your mother). Jesus enjoyed an uninterrupted relationship with God the Father. But at this moment, he couldn't sense God's presence. Although God was present at the cross, Jesus could no longer sense God in his corner. Jesus felt completely alone.

At the foot of the cross. The opening statement of the gospel of Mark is "The beginning of the gospel of Jesus Christ, *the Son of God*" (1:1). Mark's purpose was to introduce his readers to Jesus as he really is—God's Son. At the foot of the cross, Mark's gospel comes full circle: "When the centurion, who was standing opposite [Jesus], saw the way he breathed his last, he said, 'Truly this man was *the Son of God!*'" (15:39).

Here stood the last person in the world we would expect to see the truth about Jesus. This soldier was a Gentile. (Gentiles were people notorious for being far from God.) Centurions were hardened soldiers characteristically calloused by life's harshest realities—war and death. But something happened to the centurion's heart at the foot of the cross. His wonder led to the revelation that the person on the cross was no ordinary man.

What does Jesus's death tell us? His sacrifice was significant. But how?

We live in a world of pain and death. We are affected by these two realities in abundance on a regular basis. Jesus doesn't attempt to explain away the suffering of the world. Instead, on the cross, he chose to experience the suffering of the world. Jesus doesn't offer us feel-good answers, telling us to shake off our pain. Instead, at the cross Jesus shared in our pain. Whatever else death is, because of the cross we now know we no longer face it alone. Jesus is no stranger to sorrow. Even in our deepest crisis, we can be confident of the company of Christ.

Mark makes us privy to another event that took place some distance from the cross. The Jewish temple stood within the city of Jerusalem. At the center of the temple a place was reserved for the ark of the covenant, which represented the ultimate presence of God. By God's command, the ark was kept in a special room, sealed off with a large curtain. Furthermore, only the highest-ranking priest would dare enter this room and then only one day a year. The Holy of Holies was more than a special place. It was *the* special place.

Mark informs us that at the moment of Jesus's death, the dividing curtain ripped in two—from top to bottom. The message is unmistakable. The way to God now stands wide open. His presence is available to all. The Ultimate is now Intimate.

At the Mexico City Olympics in 1968, John Stephen Akhwari ran the marathon for Tanzania. Early in the race he suffered a fall and badly injured his leg. Akhwari continued the race, knowing he wouldn't win. In fact, he was the last runner to cross the finish line. Someone asked him why he continued the race, since he knew he wouldn't earn a medal. He replied, "My country did not send me seven thousand miles to start the race. They sent me seven thousand miles to finish it."[4]

God sent Jesus to complete a task. From eternity, Jesus entered our time with something to finish. And finish it he did! Jesus accomplished something of cosmic significance. He took on your sin and mine. He opened the way to God. And in addition to temple curtains tearing from top to bottom, the hearts of many people, like that of the Roman centurion, began to turn inside out.

Jesus's scars tell these stories. The wounds on his hands, feet, head, and side show the extent and extreme of God's great love for humanity.

FOR REFLECTION

Visualize yourself at the foot of the cross. You may even imagine yourself in the place of the Roman soldier. What would you have told Jesus at the moment of his crucifixion? Why not tell him now? Perhaps the most fitting statement would be to join the centurion and confess that you too recognize Jesus as the true Son of God.

Matthew 28

¹ After the Sabbath, as the first day of the week was dawning, Mary Magdalene and the other Mary went to view the tomb. ² There was a violent earthquake, because an angel of the Lord descended from heaven and approached the tomb. He rolled back the stone and was sitting on it. ³ His appearance was like lightning, and his clothing was as white as snow. ⁴ The guards were so shaken by fear of him that they became like dead men.

⁵ The angel told the women, "Don't be afraid, because I know you are looking for Jesus who was crucified. ⁶ He is not here. For he has risen, just as he said. Come and see the place where he lay. ⁷ Then go quickly and tell his disciples, 'He has risen from the dead and indeed he is going ahead of you to Galilee; you will see him there.' Listen, I have told you."

⁸ So, departing quickly from the tomb with fear and great joy, they ran to tell his disciples the news. ⁹ Just then Jesus met them and said, "Greetings!" They came up, took hold of his feet, and worshiped him. ¹⁰ Then Jesus told them, "Do not be afraid. Go and tell my brothers to leave for Galilee, and they will see me there."

¹¹ As they were on their way, some of the guards came into the city and reported to the chief priests everything that had happened. ¹² After the priests had assembled with the elders and agreed on a plan, they gave the soldiers a large sum of money ¹³ and told them, "Say this, 'His disciples came during the night and stole him while we were sleeping.' ¹⁴ If this reaches the governor's ears, we will deal with him and keep you out of trouble." ¹⁵ They took the money and did as they were instructed, and this story has been spread among Jewish people to this day.

¹⁶ The eleven disciples traveled to Galilee, to the mountain where Jesus had directed them. ¹⁷ When they saw him, they worshiped, but some doubted. ¹⁸ Jesus came near and said to them, "All authority has been given to me in heaven and on earth. ¹⁹ Go, therefore, and make disciples of all nations, baptizing them in the name of the Father and of the Son and of the Holy Spirit, ²⁰ teaching them to observe everything I have commanded you. And remember, I am with you always, to the end of the age."

30

Beating Death
Matthew 28

The resurrection of Jesus changed everything.

Joni Eareckson Tada, popular author, artist, and radio host, was a teenage girl when a diving accident left her a quadriplegic. During her recovery she attended a conference where the speaker invited those present to kneel in prayer. Of course, Joni was unable to move. She began to weep uncontrollably, though not from self-pity. Tada explained her emotions in these words:

> Sitting there, I was reminded that in heaven I will be free to jump up, dance, kick and do aerobics. And ... sometime before the guests are called to the banquet table at the Wedding Feast of the Lamb, the first thing I plan to do on resurrected legs is to drop on grateful, glorified knees. I will quietly kneel at the feet of Jesus.[1]

The resurrection of Jesus changes everything. All of life, no matter your current circumstances, is infused with an eternal hope. If this life prevents you from being able to dance, in the resurrection you will dance flawlessly. If you're lonely in this life, in the resurrection you will be perfectly and completely loved. If you're empty, in the resurrection you will be fully satisfied. The resurrection of Jesus brings a promise to all his followers of a new heart, a clear mind, a strong body, and a life unending in quality and quantity. The Bible doesn't merely teach life *after* death; the Bible teaches life *instead* of death.

Matthew 28 describes the resurrection of Jesus as a real, historic event. While there were no witnesses to the resurrection itself—no one saw Jesus physically emerge from the tomb—there were four groups that were witnesses to the wake of the resurrection. Each group serves in a unique way to remind us that the resurrection changes everything.

The angels. Early on the first Easter morning, angels appeared at the empty tomb of Jesus. The word *angel* means "messenger." No angel was ever charged to deliver a message as important as the message delivered on this occasion. "The angel told the women, 'Don't be afraid, because I know you are looking for Jesus who was crucified. He is not here. For he has risen'" (vv. 5–6).

The King James Version of the Bible was first printed in 1611. This four-hundred-year-old translation has had a great impact on the English language. Many of the idioms and expressions common to our language were popularized by the King James Version. This version of Scripture has these phrases: my brother's keeper, a coat of many colors, a fly in the ointment, fire and brimstone, milk and honey, to harden your heart, to be at your wit's end, to walk through the valley of the shadow of death, and to put your house in order. But of all the phrases in all the pages of the Bible, the eight words of Matthew 28:6 are the greatest in impact and eternal importance: "He is not here. For he has risen."

The angel in Matthew 28 reveals the resurrection for what it is—a fact that infuses life with the hope of an eternal future.

The resurrection changes everything.

The women. The second group of witnesses to the resurrection were the women who visited the tomb on this first Easter morning. They were coming to the tomb to complete the burial customs demanded in their culture. They had come to do dignity to the body of Jesus.

The announcement of the angel sent them running in fear and excitement. They fled from the angel only to run directly across the path of Jesus: "Just then Jesus met [the women] and said, 'Greetings!' They came up, took hold of his feet, and worshiped him. Then Jesus told them, 'Do not be afraid. Go and tell my brothers to leave for Galilee, and they will see me there'" (vv. 9–10).

The first human witnesses of the resurrection of Jesus were women, a fact not to be overlooked. In the first-century Jewish world, women weren't to be trusted. A woman's word was considered so untrustworthy that it wasn't accepted in any reputable court of law. A common prayer of a Jewish man in those days was "God, thank you I was not born a Gentile, a dog, or a woman." Not very flattering. But these are just the facts.

With this worldview in place, why would Jesus permit women to be the first witnesses to the reality of the resurrection? Why would he choose women to be the first to preach the good news? Perhaps Jesus is forcing us to consider what was truly important at this moment. It is as though he was stating boldly and for all time, "This isn't about you; this is about me. Regardless of our views of the source, the story is sound. No matter who is doing the telling, the truth of my resurrection still holds."

The resurrection of Jesus changes everything.

The guards. Another group that shouldn't be overlooked is the guards. At the first sight of the angel these rugged men fainted. When they finally came to, they reported the strange events to the Jewish leaders. The Jewish officials responded by giving the guards hush money and a cover story.

I've often wondered how these men reconciled themselves to what they had witnessed. They must have been young—perhaps in their late twenties or early thirties. They had a lot of life ahead of them. In all of their subsequent years, did not even one of them ponder the unprecedented events of that morning? Did this group of men ever discuss the happenings of the day in an attempt to understand the meaning of it all? Or was the tomb guarding just another gig? Did the guards simply move on with life and forget the whole thing?

The guards' silence should give us pause to seriously reflect on the resurrection. If the resurrection really happened, how could the business or busyness of the day be considered more important than this eternal reality?

The resurrection changes everything.

The disciples. The final group to deal with the reality of the resurrection was the disciples—the first followers of Jesus.

> When [the disciples] saw [Jesus], they worshiped, but some doubted. Jesus came near and said to them, "All authority has been given to me in heaven and on earth. Go, therefore, and make disciples of all nations, baptizing them in the name of the Father and of the Son and of the Holy Spirit, teaching them to observe everything I have commanded you. And remember, I am with you always, to the end of the age." (vv. 17–20)

The resurrection changed the purpose and direction of the disciples' lives. No longer was life a matter of making money, earning respect, or competing for success. Life was now redefined around knowing Jesus and making him known to the world. No longer could the disciples claim their destinies as their own. The future of every true Christ follower is firmly in the hands of God. No longer should any follower of Jesus fear the prospect of being alone. Jesus isn't a past memory but a permanent personal presence.

Marine biologists employ a deep-sea vehicle called a bathysphere. This round submersible has a steel hull an inch and a half thick designed to survive the crushing depths of the ocean. From the safety of the bathysphere, marine biologists study life in the deepest waters. Among the inhabitants of this extreme environment are thin-skinned fish. Lacking thick skin, they survive by generating an internal pressure equal and opposite to the pressure of their ocean environment.

The world is a place of pressure. Circumstances constantly threaten to crush us. Popular wisdom encourages us to wear a thick skin to survive. But with Jesus's power and presence inside us, we have the substance to hold strong under even the most crushing forces. The final words of Jesus comfort us and grant us courage: "Remember, I am with you always, to the end of the age" (v. 20).

Indeed, the resurrection of Jesus changes everything.

FOR REFLECTION

For the Jewish people, God designated the seventh day (Saturday) as a day of rest and worship. With the resurrection of Jesus occurring on a Sunday, the focus of worship shifted to this, the first day of the week. Every week when Christians gather for worship, it's an open celebration of the resurrection of Jesus.

Have you forgotten this? Have you gotten into a rut with worship? What one thing can you do to personally transform worship from a mindless routine to a meaningful recognition of Jesus's resurrection?

FOLLOWING JESUS

Acts 1

¹ I wrote the first narrative, Theophilus, about all that Jesus began to do and teach ² until the day he was taken up, after he had given instructions through the Holy Spirit to the apostles he had chosen. ³ After he had suffered, he also presented himself alive to them by many convincing proofs, appearing to them over a period of forty days and speaking about the kingdom of God.

⁴ While he was with them, he commanded them not to leave Jerusalem, but to wait for the Father's promise. "Which," he said, "you have heard me speak about; ⁵ for John baptized with water, but you will be baptized with the Holy Spirit in a few days."

⁶ So when they had come together, they asked him, "Lord, are you restoring the kingdom to Israel at this time?"

⁷ He said to them, "It is not for you to know times or periods that the Father has set by his own authority. ⁸ But you will receive power when the Holy Spirit has come on you, and you will be my witnesses in Jerusalem, in all Judea and Samaria, and to the end of the earth."

⁹ After he had said this, he was taken up as they were watching, and a cloud took him out of their sight. ¹⁰ While he was going, they were gazing into heaven, and suddenly two men in white clothes stood by them. ¹¹ They said, "Men of Galilee, why do you stand looking up into heaven? This same Jesus, who has been taken from you into heaven, will come in the same way that you have seen him going into heaven."

¹² Then they returned to Jerusalem from the Mount of Olives, which is near Jerusalem — a Sabbath day's journey away. ¹³ When they arrived, they went to the room upstairs where they were staying: Peter, John, James, Andrew, Philip, Thomas, Bartholomew, Matthew, James the son of Alphaeus, Simon the Zealot, and Judas the son of James. ¹⁴ They all were continually united in prayer, along with the women, including Mary the mother of Jesus, and his brothers.

¹⁵ In those days Peter stood up among the brothers and sisters — the number of people who were together was about a hundred and twenty — and said: ¹⁶ "Brothers and sisters, it was necessary that the Scripture be fulfilled that the Holy Spirit through the mouth of David foretold

about Judas, who became a guide to those who arrested Jesus. [17] For he was one of our number and shared in this ministry." [18] Now this man acquired a field with his unrighteous wages. He fell headfirst, his body burst open and his intestines spilled out. [19] This became known to all the residents of Jerusalem, so that in their own language that field is called *Hakeldama* (that is, Field of Blood). [20] "For it is written in the Book of Psalms:

Let his dwelling become desolate;
let no one live in it; and
Let someone else take his position.

[21] "Therefore, from among the men who have accompanied us during the whole time the Lord Jesus went in and out among us — [22] beginning from the baptism of John until the day he was taken up from us — from among these, it is necessary that one become a witness with us of his resurrection."

[23] So they proposed two: Joseph, called Barsabbas, who was also known as Justus, and Matthias. [24] Then they prayed, "You, Lord, know everyone's hearts; show which of these two you have chosen [25] to take the place in this apostolic ministry that Judas left to go where he belongs." [26] Then they cast lots for them, and the lot fell to Matthias and he was added to the eleven apostles.

31

Where Is Jesus Now?
Acts 1

If Jesus survived death, where is he now? If his resurrection was a physical reality, why can't we see him today? If he is still alive, why aren't we permitted to touch and talk to him?

The book of Acts begins with these words: "I wrote the first narrative, Theophilus, about all that Jesus began to do and teach until the day he was taken up" (vv. 1–2). I find a small delight in reading these opening words, because the book is written to someone named Theophilus. His name literally translates as "lover of God." So, in a way, the book of Acts is written to all of us—to you and me as lovers of God.

The author of Acts was a man named Luke, the same Luke who wrote the gospel named after him. Luke wasn't content to conclude his well-researched account of the life of Jesus with the resurrection. He wanted to tell the whole story. What Jesus had started to do on earth, he would continue doing through his people, the church. The resurrection caused ripple effects, which Luke explored in the book of Acts.

I can remember visiting the Caverns of Sonora as a ten-year-old boy. Buried deep in West Texas, this underground network of watery caves is a stark contrast to the dry, lifeless desert above. For millennia, slow-dripping water has deposited minerals that have created colorful subterranean sculptures. As an awestruck visitor to this strange underground world of stalagmites and stalactites, I was even more amazed when the tour guide handed me a small piece of stalactite that had broken away from a rock formation. These rocks grow at the rate of one inch per thousand years. Thus, the two-inch piece of rock I held in my hand represented two millennia of deposits.

I still have that rock, and whenever I look at it, I'm mindful that it dates back to the time of Jesus. Likewise, the church dates its origins to the life of Jesus and continues to thrive all these centuries later. But the larger issue remains: *If Jesus isn't on earth, then just where is he?* Acts 1 tells us that Jesus was alive and visible on earth after his resurrection, spending a period of time with his closest followers: "After he had suffered, he also presented himself alive to them by many convincing proofs, appearing to them over a period of forty days and speaking about the kingdom of God" (v. 3).

During this period of visibility, Jesus seemed consumed with one topic of conversation: the kingdom of God. This phrase shows up in the pages of the New Testament a total of sixty-four times. A minor variant of this phrase—*the kingdom of heaven*, which is another way of saying *the kingdom of God*—appears an additional thirty-two times. Before his crucifixion, Jesus talked often about this topic; after his resurrection, he talked about it all the time.

If this topic was important to Jesus, then it should be important to us. The *kingdom of God* simply means "God's rule in the hearts of his people." The term is Jesus's way of referring to God's kingship in our lives and in our world. God wants to rule our hearts and minds. That's how his kingdom spreads.

I remember visiting two important houses within the space of a few hours. First was the White House. A close friend who worked on staff gave me the grand tour. I was in awe as I stood on the threshold of the Oval Office and gazed inside. I felt moved when I stood in the basement and touched the smoke damage still visible from the British attempt to burn down the White House during the War of 1812.

Shortly after the White House tour, I boarded a flight home. But severe weather stranded me overnight in Memphis, Tennessee. The layover was an inconvenience, but I couldn't pass up the opportunity to visit Graceland, the former estate of Elvis Presley. The White House and Graceland are both spectacular, but they bear a noteworthy distinction. Though the White House is home to the president, Graceland is the home of a king. While presidents come and go, Graceland recognizes only one rightful resident.

As Jesus followers, our lives are to resemble Graceland more than the White House because our lives serve as the home of a king.

For forty days Jesus spoke about the kingdom of God to his followers. At the end of these forty days, things changed: Jesus told them, "'You will receive power when the Holy Spirit has come on you, and you will be my witnesses in Jerusalem, in all Judea and Samaria, and to the end of the earth.' After he had said this, he was taken up as they were watching, and a cloud took him out of their sight" (vv. 8–9).

The theological word for this final event of Jesus's earthly ministry is *ascension*. Far from being a fringe event, this last episode in the visible life of Jesus is important to those who choose to follow him. Among many potential meanings, the ascension has three practical applications.

First, Jesus went to a real place. His ascension gives us hope that we too will join him in the presence of God in a place called heaven. There will come a time when we'll see him again. Our story doesn't end with our deaths. In a similar way that the book of Acts serves as a sequel to the gospel of Luke, heaven will be the eternal sequel to our earthly existence.

In the final scene of the last book in The Chronicles of Narnia, C. S. Lewis shared a compelling picture of heaven, saying, "All their life in this world and all their adventures in Narnia had only been the cover and the title page: now at last they were beginning Chapter One of the Great Story which no one on earth has read: which goes on forever: in which every chapter is better than the one before."[1]

The ascension assures us that existence in Christ is eternal, that death is a beginning more than an end, and that both a place and a person await us in eternity.

Second, Jesus went to a place called heaven as a full person. It's true to say that Jesus *was* human. It's equally true to say that Jesus still *is* human. Into the presence of God, Jesus took the full person-hood of his humanity. He now represents all of us before the presence of God forever. God never loses sight of humanity; Jesus's presence serves as a perpetual reminder.

Finally, the ascension of Jesus into heaven serves as a reminder of his certain return. Two angels made this quite clear. "They said, 'Men of Galilee, why do you stand looking up into heaven? This same Jesus, who has been taken from you into heaven, will come in the same way that you have seen him going into heaven'" (v. 11). In the same manner Jesus departed, he'll return. As sure as Jesus disappeared, he is certain to reappear. Our part is to remain watchful and make sure we're ready for his return.

When Canada joined the Allied forces in World War II, Canadian soldiers often served as spotters and lookouts for advancing armies. They were good at this because many of them had grown up in wide-open country. City dwellers don't need to focus on the horizon. Buildings and buses, skyscrapers and storefronts eliminate any hope of seeing around the next corner, much less to the next hill. But those raised in the endless tracts of Canadian countryside were skilled at focusing on that which was far away.

As followers of Jesus, we're invited to focus on the far horizon of Jesus's return. To live faithfully between the ascension and his second coming requires us to develop the ability to see beyond the events of today and the struggles of tomorrow, ever on the lookout for the Savior who has promised to return.

When that happens, Jesus will complete what he began. The kingdom he spoke of for forty days will become a tangible reality.

He will bring the kingdom of God—the full rule and reign of the Almighty—into our realm forever.

FOR REFLECTION

Jesus, in his fullness as a person, is in God's heavenly presence right now. Scripture makes it clear that he is praying for us at this moment (Rom. 8:34). Since this is so, take time today to let him know how you would like him to pray for you. What do you want Jesus to communicate to God on your behalf today? There is nothing like having a friend in high places!

Acts 2

¹ When the day of Pentecost had arrived, they were all together in one place. ² Suddenly a sound like that of a violent rushing wind came from heaven, and it filled the whole house where they were staying. ³ They saw tongues like flames of fire that separated and rested on each one of them. ⁴ Then they were all filled with the Holy Spirit and began to speak in different tongues, as the Spirit enabled them.

⁵ Now there were Jews staying in Jerusalem, devout people from every nation under heaven. ⁶ When this sound occurred, a crowd came together and was confused because each one heard them speaking in his own language. ⁷ They were astounded and amazed, saying, "Look, aren't all these who are speaking Galileans? ⁸ How is it that each of us can hear them in our own native language? ⁹ Parthians, Medes, Elamites; those who live in Mesopotamia, in Judea and Cappadocia, Pontus and Asia, ¹⁰ Phrygia and Pamphylia, Egypt and the parts of Libya near Cyrene; visitors from Rome (both Jews and converts), ¹¹ Cretans and Arabs — we hear them declaring the magnificent acts of God in our own tongues." ¹² They were all astounded and perplexed, saying to one another, "What does this mean?" ¹³ But some sneered and said, "They're drunk on new wine."

¹⁴ Peter stood up with the Eleven, raised his voice, and proclaimed to them: "Fellow Jews and all you residents of Jerusalem, let me explain this to you and pay attention to my words. ¹⁵ For these people are not drunk, as you suppose, since it's only nine in the morning. ¹⁶ On the contrary, this is what was spoken through the prophet Joel:

¹⁷ And it will be in the last days, says God,
that I will pour out my Spirit on all people;
then your sons and your daughters will prophesy,
your young men will see visions,
and your old men will dream dreams.
¹⁸ I will even pour out my Spirit
on my servants in those days, both men and women
and they will prophesy.
¹⁹ I will display wonders in the heaven above
and signs on the earth below:
blood and fire and a cloud of smoke.

²⁰ The sun will be turned to darkness
and the moon to blood
before the great and glorious day of the Lord comes.
²¹ Then everyone who calls
on the name of the Lord will be saved.

²² "Fellow Israelites, listen to these words: This Jesus of Nazareth was a man attested to you by God with miracles, wonders, and signs that God did among you through him, just as you yourselves know. ²³ Though he was delivered up according to God's determined plan and foreknowledge, you used lawless people to nail him to a cross and kill him. ²⁴ God raised him up, ending the pains of death, because it was not possible for him to be held by death. ²⁵ For David says of him:

I saw the Lord ever before me;
because he is at my right hand,
I will not be shaken.
²⁶ Therefore my heart is glad
and my tongue rejoices.
Moreover, my flesh will rest in hope,
²⁷ because you will not abandon me in Hades
or allow your holy one to see decay.
²⁸ You have revealed the paths of life to me;
you will fill me with gladness
in your presence.

²⁹ "Brothers and sisters, I can confidently speak to you about the patriarch David: He is both dead and buried, and his tomb is with us to this day. ³⁰ Since he was a prophet, he knew that God had sworn an oath to him to seat one of his descendants on his throne. ³¹ Seeing what was to come, he spoke concerning the resurrection of the Messiah: He was not abandoned in Hades, and his flesh did not experience decay.
³² "God has raised this Jesus; we are all witnesses of this. ³³ Therefore, since he has been exalted to the right hand of God and has received from the Father the promised Holy Spirit, he has poured out what you both see and hear. ³⁴ For it was not David who ascended into the heavens, but he himself says:

The Lord declared to my Lord,
'Sit at my right hand

[35] until I make your enemies your footstool.'

[36] "Therefore let all the house of Israel know with certainty that God has made this Jesus, whom you crucified, both Lord and Messiah."

[37] When they heard this, they were pierced to the heart and said to Peter and the rest of the apostles: "Brothers, what should we do?"

[38] Peter replied, "Repent and be baptized, each of you, in the name of Jesus Christ for the forgiveness of your sins, and you will receive the gift of the Holy Spirit. [39] For the promise is for you and for your children, and for all who are far off, as many as the Lord our God will call." [40] With many other words he testified and strongly urged them, saying, "Be saved from this corrupt generation!" [41] So those who accepted his message were baptized, and that day about three thousand people were added to them.

[42] They devoted themselves to the apostles' teaching, to the fellowship, to the breaking of bread, and to prayer.

[43] Everyone was filled with awe, and many wonders and signs were being performed through the apostles. [44] Now all the believers were together and held all things in common. [45] They sold their possessions and property and distributed the proceeds to all, as any had need. [46] Every day they devoted themselves to meeting together in the temple, and broke bread from house to house. They ate their food with joyful and sincere hearts, [47] praising God and enjoying the favor of all the people. Every day the Lord added to their number those who were being saved.

32

Happy Birthday to Us
Acts 2

I was present at the birth of all three of my children and observed my wife experience the extremes of emotion—pain one moment and joy the next. Anguish and exultation intertwined in the messiness of the event. But that's just the way birth works.

Acts 2 describes the birth of the church. The emotions in this passage of Scripture span the spectrum. And the events recorded here were messy indeed. But remember, this was a birth.

For the purpose of clarity, when I speak of the church, I'm not referring to the steepled structures where worshippers gather on Sunday morning. The Bible without exception uses the word *church* in terms of people, not buildings. The church is a group of people who follow Jesus and choose to live according to his teaching.

As we read earlier, after Jesus's resurrection, he spent forty days with his disciples, instructing them how to live under God's rule. As Jesus departed for heaven, he instructed his followers to wait in Jerusalem for a special gift from the Father. Acts tells us that "when the day of Pentecost had arrived, [the disciples] were all together in one place" (2:1). Pentecost was the Jewish holiday celebrating God's physical blessing of the annual harvest and God's spiritual blessing of giving the Law to Moses on Mount Sinai. (Remember the Ten Commandments?) But this particular Pentecost would be more than a celebration; it would be an invasion. Instead of God sending his instructions to his chosen people, he poured out his Holy Spirit on his followers: "Suddenly a sound like that of a violent rushing wind came from heaven, and it filled the whole house where [the disciples] were staying. They saw tongues like flames of fire that separated and rested on each one of them" (vv. 2–3).

Two important images help us understand what was about to take place.

First was the image of wind. In the Hebrew language, wind and breath are the same word: *ruach*. We have an echo of this in a modern idiom. To "knock the wind out of someone" is to strike a person so hard that he loses his breath. In Genesis 2, God formed Adam from the dust of the earth and then blew breath into his body, thereby lending him the gift of life. God knocked the wind *into* someone. Acts 2 is God's act of breathing life into the church.

The second image is that of fire, which is a symbol of power. Roger Clemens, the sizzling right-hander for the Boston Red Sox, pitched the first innings of the 1986 All-Star Game. Because the game was played without designated hitters, Clemens was forced to bat against his opponent, Dwight Gooden. A recent Cy Young Award winner, Gooden threw a red-hot fastball down the middle of the strike zone. Dazed, Clemens turned to catcher Gary Carter and asked, "Is that what my pitches look like?"

"You bet it is!" replied Carter.[1]

For Clemens, this was an epiphany. He took the mound to pitch three perfect innings. He had gained a new appreciation for the overwhelming power of his pitches.

The church, at its inception, was given the gift of power. Yet life and power were just the beginning of God's generosity to the newborn church. His ultimate gift to the church was the Holy Spirit. At Pentecost, "[the disciples] were all filled with the Holy Spirit and began to speak in different tongues, as the Spirit enabled them" (v. 4). These unusual events have prompted discussion, debate, and division among many different groups of Christians. But we can all agree on at least two things.

First, Acts 2 defies full explanation. But notice that the disciples weren't concerned with explaining God; they were too caught up in experiencing him. Explanations are sterile; experiences are sensate. Explanations offer no intimacy; experiences do. Can we appreciate this encounter without understanding all the details? I believe so. More than answers, we need encounters with God.

Second, the disciples were filled with the personal, powerful presence of God, which we call the Holy Spirit. J. Oswald Sanders offered this insight regarding what it means to be filled with God's Spirit: "To be filled with the Spirit is to be controlled by the Spirit. The Christian leader's mind, emotions, will, and physical strength all become available for the Spirit to guide and use."[2] Oh, that we would all allow the Spirit to fill us!

The question the original audience asked is a question all readers of Acts 2 find themselves asking: "What does this mean?" (v. 12). In interpreting these events, it's essential to remember that Pentecost was a celebration of God's gift of the Law to the Jewish people. To send the gift of his Holy Spirit on this particular date conveyed a message. God was doing more than offering rules to one group of people; now he was offering himself to all who would choose to be his followers. More than giving a structure of rules to be obeyed, he was giving his Spirit to be enjoyed. The Holy Spirit is the one who gives life and power to the church.

Acts 2 ends with a snapshot of this fully alive and newly empowered church. This depiction of the church opens with the phrase, "They devoted themselves ..." (v. 42).

In 1987, Henry Dempsey was piloting a commuter flight between Portland, Maine, and Boston, Massachusetts. Hearing a noise in the rear of the aircraft, he decided to investigate. He discovered the noise was the result of an improperly latched rear door. The plane hit some turbulence, and when Dempsey leaned against the door, it opened. He tumbled out and grabbed one of the stairway railings. He was upside down on the stairway, hanging "partially in the aircraft and partially out." Traveling at nearly two hundred miles per hour at four thousand feet, Dempsey held on for dear life. When the plane landed, his face was just inches from the runway tarmac.[3]

Devoted, indeed.

The early church had an ironclad grip on certain core practices and priorities. Whatever was happening around them, they didn't allow themselves to be distracted from these nonnegotiables. What were they?

The church was devoted to *worship*: "Every day they devoted themselves to meeting together in the temple" (v. 46). The church was devoted to the practice of *community*: "Now all the believers were together and held all things in common" (v. 44). And they were devoted to *service*, allowing the love of God to spill over the edges of the church into the world around them: "Every day the Lord added to their number those who were being saved" (v. 47).

The early church hung on to the practices of worship, community, and service as though life depended on it. The church was devoted to being a group of people who followed Jesus and lived life according to his teaching.

My best friend in high school, Nelson, was an adventurer. We were forever getting into trouble. Nelson was the one with all the imagination; I was the one along for the ride. One evening he picked me up from my house, and we drove to the top of the dam just south of town. West Texas has no water, so to this day I'm baffled as to why we had dams.

A storm was moving across the wide plains. Nelson set up a tripod and mounted his camera. He then opened the shutter as the storm raced overhead. After several minutes of exposing the film, Nelson closed the shutter. On the developed picture, there appeared to be five strikes of lightning happening all at once. In this one image, Nelson had captured the sum total of the storm's power.

Luke, with pen and parchment, captured the sum total of the early church's power. I believe it is worth stating again: the church is a group of people who follow Jesus and choose to live according to his teaching. To do this well, we require God's personal, powerful presence in the Holy Spirit. We also need to be devoted to being rightly related to God in worship, to others in community, and to the world through service. May our churches today be just as devoted.

FOR REFLECTION

Consider again J. Oswald Sanders's definition of the Spirit-filled person as one who surrenders to God the entirety of his or her identity—will, mind, emotions, and strength. Based on this definition, are you Spirit filled? Why or why not? Which aspect of your identity from this four-part list do you need to surrender to God today?

Acts 9

¹ Now Saul was still breathing threats and murder against the disciples of the Lord. He went to the high priest ² and requested letters from him to the synagogues in Damascus, so that if he found any men or women who belonged to the Way, he might bring them as prisoners to Jerusalem. ³ As he traveled and was nearing Damascus, a light from heaven suddenly flashed around him. ⁴ Falling to the ground, he heard a voice saying to him, "Saul, Saul, why are you persecuting me?"

⁵ "Who are you, Lord?" Saul said.

"I am Jesus, the one you are persecuting," he replied. ⁶ "But get up and go into the city, and you will be told what you must do."

⁷ The men who were traveling with him stood speechless, hearing the sound but seeing no one. ⁸ Saul got up from the ground, and though his eyes were open, he could see nothing. So they took him by the hand and led him into Damascus. ⁹ He was unable to see for three days and did not eat or drink.

¹⁰ There was a disciple in Damascus named Ananias, and the Lord said to him in a vision, "Ananias."

"Here I am, Lord," he replied.

¹¹ "Get up and go to the street called Straight," the Lord said to him, "to the house of Judas, and ask for a man from Tarsus named Saul, since he is praying there. ¹² In a vision he has seen a man named Ananias coming in and placing his hands on him so that he may regain his sight."

¹³ "Lord," Ananias answered, "I have heard from many people about this man, how much harm he has done to your saints in Jerusalem. ¹⁴ And he has authority here from the chief priests to arrest all who call on your name."

¹⁵ But the Lord said to him, "Go, for this man is my chosen instrument to take my name to Gentiles, kings, and Israelites. ¹⁶ I will show him how much he must suffer for my name."

¹⁷ Ananias went and entered the house. He placed his hands on him and said, "Brother Saul, the Lord Jesus, who appeared to you on the road you were traveling, has sent me so that you may regain your sight and be filled with the Holy Spirit."

¹⁸ At once something like scales fell from his eyes, and he regained his sight. Then he got up and was baptized. ¹⁹ And after taking some food, he regained his strength.

Saul was with the disciples in Damascus for some time. ²⁰ Immediately he began proclaiming Jesus in the synagogues: "He is the Son of God."

²¹ All who heard him were astounded and said, "Isn't this the man in Jerusalem who was causing havoc for those who called on this name and came here for the purpose of taking them as prisoners to the chief priests?"

²² But Saul grew stronger and kept confounding the Jews who lived in Damascus by proving that Jesus is the Messiah.

²³ After many days had passed, the Jews conspired to kill him, ²⁴ but Saul learned of their plot. So they were watching the gates day and night intending to kill him, ²⁵ but his disciples took him by night and lowered him in a large basket through an opening in the wall.

²⁶ When he arrived in Jerusalem, he tried to join the disciples, but they were all afraid of him, since they did not believe he was a disciple. ²⁷ Barnabas, however, took him and brought him to the apostles and explained to them how Saul had seen the Lord on the road and that the Lord had talked to him, and how in Damascus he had spoken boldly in the name of Jesus. ²⁸ Saul was coming and going with them in Jerusalem, speaking boldly in the name of the Lord. ²⁹ He conversed and debated with the Hellenistic Jews, but they tried to kill him. ³⁰ When the brothers found out, they took him down to Caesarea and sent him off to Tarsus.

³¹ So the church throughout all Judea, Galilee, and Samaria had peace and was strengthened. Living in the fear of the Lord and encouraged by the Holy Spirit, it increased in numbers.

³² As Peter was traveling from place to place, he also came down to the saints who lived in Lydda. ³³ There he found a man named Aeneas, who was paralyzed and had been bedridden for eight years. ³⁴ Peter said to him, "Aeneas, Jesus Christ heals you. Get up and make your bed," and immediately he got up. ³⁵ So all who lived in Lydda and Sharon saw him and turned to the Lord.

³⁶ In Joppa there was a disciple named Tabitha (which is translated Dorcas). She was always doing good works and acts of charity. ³⁷ About that time she became sick and died. After washing her, they placed her in a room upstairs. ³⁸ Since Lydda was near Joppa, the disciples heard that Peter was there and sent two men to him who urged him, "Don't delay in

coming with us." [39] Peter got up and went with them. When he arrived, they led him to the room upstairs. And all the widows approached him, weeping and showing him the robes and clothes that Dorcas had made while she was with them. [40] Peter sent them all out of the room. He knelt down, prayed, and turning toward the body said, "Tabitha, get up." She opened her eyes, saw Peter, and sat up. [41] He gave her his hand and helped her stand up. He called the saints and widows and presented her alive. [42] This became known throughout Joppa, and many believed in the Lord. [43] Peter stayed for some time in Joppa with Simon, a leather tanner.

33

When Jesus Interrupts Your Life
Acts 9

Armillaria ostoyae is big. In fact, it's huge. This common honey fungus is often found growing in gardens or on the stump of a dead tree. But *Armillaria ostoyae* is also the largest life-form known to science. When researchers found *Armillaria* in Oregon's Malheur National Forest, they assumed they had discovered multiple clusters of this fungus. Further study revealed that these clusters were all connected beneath the surface. This single life-form covers twenty-two hundred acres, making it the single largest organism on the planet.[1] A big life.

Acts 9 introduces us to Saul—more popularly known by the name Paul. Saul would transform from being an angry religious fundamentalist to being an able follower of Jesus. He would change from loathing Christians to leading them. Paul would eventually write more New Testament books than any other person, influencing generations of Christians for more than two thousand years. A big life indeed.

Saul, in the service of a strict sect of the Jewish religion, was dispatched to Damascus to intimidate and, if necessary, incarcerate Christians. But Jesus interrupted him on the way: "As he traveled and was nearing Damascus, a light from heaven suddenly flashed around him. Falling to the ground, he heard a voice saying to him, 'Saul, Saul, why are you persecuting me?'" (Acts 9:3–4).

When Christians are persecuted, Jesus takes it personally. From Jesus's own words, it's clear he makes no distinction between himself and his followers. The words "Why are you persecuting *me*?" assure us of Jesus's protective posture toward all his people.

Jesus put a stop to Saul's evil agenda, while at the same time offering him a fresh start. Saul had fancied himself an up-and-comer in the Jewish religion. Later in life, he would reminisce, saying, "I advanced in Judaism beyond many contemporaries among my people, because I was extremely zealous for the traditions of my ancestors" (Gal. 1:14).

But Jesus interrupted Saul's plans, and the two had a life-changing conversation.

No sooner did Jesus finish speaking with Saul than he began another conversation with a man named Ananias, who stands in noteworthy contrast to Saul. While Saul would become a major player in first-century Christianity, Ananias is mentioned only twice in the Bible—here in Acts 9 and later in Acts 22. Ananias was a nobody. He is a forgotten hero of Christianity, because without Ananias, there might have never been a Paul.

Ananias wore the title *disciple* (v. 10). When the followers of Jesus were first called "Christians," it may not have been considered a flattering title. In fact, it may very well have been a label meant to mock the early followers of Jesus.

When I was a young boy, my favorite hat was a trucker's cap with the Peterbilt logo embroidered across the front. I wore it so often that a group of "mean kids" from my neighborhood began to use the company's name as my nickname. They would call out, "Here comes Peterbilt!" It wasn't meant to honor me but to humiliate me. In the New Testament era, I believe the title *Christian* expressed the same intent.

Early Jesus followers simply referred to themselves as disciples. While *Christian* is used only 3 times in the New Testament, *disciple* is used some 263 times. This word means "learner, understudy, or apprentice." It implies an intentionality of living under Jesus's leadership.

It could be that Ananias wanted nothing more than to live a quiet, obscure existence. But as with Saul, the Lord interrupted his personal plans. When commanded to visit Saul, Ananias offered excuses. "But the Lord said to [Ananias], 'Go, for this man is my chosen instrument to take my name to Gentiles, kings, and Israelites. I will show him how much he must suffer for my name'" (vv. 15–16).

This is the second time in Acts 9 that the Lord spoke, which should lead us to ask a few questions: *How do I know if the Lord is speaking to me? How will I recognize his voice? How do I tell the difference between the voice of the Lord and me talking to myself?*

Certainly God can speak audibly, if he so chooses, but even in the pages of Scripture, this is the exception, not the norm. God typically speaks to his people in three ways.[2]

First, God speaks to his people through Scripture. As the apostle Paul wrote, "All Scripture is inspired by God and is profitable for teaching, for rebuking, for correcting, for training in righteousness, so that the man of God may be complete, equipped for every good work" (2 Tim. 3:16–17). Reading the Bible offers practice in learning to recognize God's voice.

When my wife and I first began dating, she had to identify herself when she called me on the telephone. But now, after two decades together, she no longer bothers to say who she is. Not only do I readily recognize her voice, but I can also usually tell her mood from her first few words. Scripture is a means for Christ followers to become familiar with God's way of speaking. In addition, God will never command anything contrary to what he has already revealed through Scripture.

Second, God speaks through other people. I've had the experience of wrestling with a decision when a fellow follower of Jesus, who had no idea what I was facing, said something that offered perfect insight or instruction for my situation. God speaking through people is modeled in Acts 9:17: "Ananias went and entered the house. He placed his hands on [Saul] and said, 'Brother Saul, the Lord Jesus, who appeared to you on the road you were traveling, has sent me so that you may regain your sight and be filled with the Holy Spirit.'"

Finally, God speaks through the circumstances of our lives. Herein is a great challenge. Much of our attention and focus is given to trying to discern the actions and attitudes of others. But few of us regularly and rigorously ask, "What is God doing? What is God trying to teach me through the circumstances I face today?"

It bears repeating that Scripture is to be trusted first and foremost as a source of God's voice. Donald Whitney says it well: "Scripture alone should be the standard by which all spiritual experiences are evaluated." Additionally, Whitney offers, "all other experiences with God that do not *begin* with Scripture should be *informed* by and *interpreted* by Scripture."[3] No matter how clearly I believe that God has spoken to me through prayer or circumstances, if either contradicts the plain teaching of the Bible, I would do well to ignore it.

I must confess my natural suspicion toward people who regularly say things like "God told me ..." or "God spoke to me and said ..." While I can't determine whether they have a direct line to God, I've chosen to follow a simple practice. If I believe that God has given me clear direction, I tell no one. My secrecy isn't embarrassment. My silence isn't spiritual shyness. My reason for secrecy is that I know all too well my tendency to manipulate people and impose my will to control outcomes. It's too easy to disguise my own opinions as God's will with the proclamation, "God told me." I also remain silent not because I lack faith in God but because I don't trust myself. If a matter is truly God's will, it will be accomplished without my having to say so.

Saul heard Jesus on the road. But Saul was forced to focus on what Jesus was trying to say through these unusual events. Saul had encountered Jesus and had simultaneously lost his sight. Someone had been sent to Saul to restore his vision and to reveal the truth of following God through faith in Jesus. There was no doubt that Jesus wanted to transform the life of small-visioned, mean-minded, closed-souled Saul into a big life.

And Saul wasted no time. Immediately he began to represent Jesus among those seeking God, even if they were prone to be suspicious. No matter. Saul's life would never be the same again. It was no longer his to plan. A big life had begun the moment he heard the voice of Jesus.

Charlie Frank trained elephants. Frank trained one elephant, Neeta, and then sent her to live at the San Diego Zoo. After a fifteen-year absence, Frank visited Neeta. As he entered the elephant enclosure, he called Neeta's name. At the sound of her master's voice, the elephant came running full speed, obeying each voice command as if their time apart had never existed.[4]

Great power exists in recognizing our Master's voice. Our Creator, our Maker, our Savior wishes to have a word with us. We must be disciplined enough to listen and brave enough to obey. A big life will be the natural result.

FOR REFLECTION

Ananias was called a disciple. A disciple is a person who apprentices under Jesus. In a culture where we use the title *Christian* too casually, the title *disciple* places more importance and intent on following Jesus.

Does the word *disciple* describe your relationship to Jesus? Why or why not?

Acts 10

¹ There was a man in Caesarea named Cornelius, a centurion of what was called the Italian Regiment. ² He was a devout man and feared God along with his whole household. He did many charitable deeds for the Jewish people and always prayed to God. ³ About three in the afternoon he distinctly saw in a vision an angel of God who came in and said to him, "Cornelius."

⁴ Staring at him in awe, he said, "What is it, Lord?"

The angel told him, "Your prayers and your acts of charity have ascended as a memorial offering before God. ⁵ Now send men to Joppa and call for Simon, who is also named Peter. ⁶ He is lodging with Simon, a tanner, whose house is by the sea."

⁷ When the angel who spoke to him had gone, he called two of his household servants and a devout soldier, who was one of those who attended him. ⁸ After explaining everything to them, he sent them to Joppa.

⁹ The next day, as they were traveling and nearing the city, Peter went up to pray on the roof about noon. ¹⁰ He became hungry and wanted to eat, but while they were preparing something, he fell into a trance. ¹¹ He saw heaven opened and an object that resembled a large sheet coming down, being lowered by its four corners to the earth. ¹² In it were all the four-footed animals and reptiles of the earth, and the birds of the sky. ¹³ A voice said to him, "Get up, Peter; kill and eat."

¹⁴ "No, Lord!" Peter said. "For I have never eaten anything impure and ritually unclean."

¹⁵ Again, a second time, the voice said to him, "What God has made clean, do not call impure." ¹⁶ This happened three times, and suddenly the object was taken up into heaven.

¹⁷ While Peter was deeply perplexed about what the vision he had seen might mean, right away the men who had been sent by Cornelius, having asked directions to Simon's house, stood at the gate. ¹⁸ They called out, asking if Simon, who was also named Peter, was lodging there.

¹⁹ While Peter was thinking about the vision, the Spirit told him, "Three men are here looking for you. ²⁰ Get up, go downstairs, and go with them with no doubts at all, because I have sent them."

²¹ Then Peter went down to the men and said, "Here I am, the one you're looking for. What is the reason you're here?"

²² They said, "Cornelius, a centurion, an upright and God-fearing man, who has a good reputation with the whole Jewish nation, was divinely directed by a holy angel to call you to his house and to hear a message from you." ²³ Peter then invited them in and gave them lodging.

The next day he got up and set out with them, and some of the brothers from Joppa went with him. ²⁴ The following day he entered Caesarea. Now Cornelius was expecting them and had called together his relatives and close friends. ²⁵ When Peter entered, Cornelius met him, fell at his feet, and worshiped him.

²⁶ But Peter lifted him up and said, "Stand up. I myself am also a man." ²⁷ While talking with him, he went in and found a large gathering of people. ²⁸ Peter said to them, "You know it's forbidden for a Jewish man to associate with or visit a foreigner, but God has shown me that I must not call any person impure or unclean. ²⁹ That's why I came without any objection when I was sent for. So may I ask why you sent for me?"

³⁰ Cornelius replied, "Four days ago at this hour, at three in the afternoon, I was praying in my house. Just then a man in dazzling clothing stood before me ³¹ and said, 'Cornelius, your prayer has been heard, and your acts of charity have been remembered in God's sight. ³² Therefore send someone to Joppa and invite Simon here, who is also named Peter. He is lodging in Simon the tanner's house by the sea.' ³³ So I immediately sent for you, and it was good of you to come. So now we are all in the presence of God to hear everything you have been commanded by the Lord."

³⁴ Peter began to speak: "Now I truly understand that God doesn't show favoritism, ³⁵ but in every nation the person who fears him and does what is right is acceptable to him. ³⁶ He sent the message to the Israelites, proclaiming the good news of peace through Jesus Christ — he is Lord of all. ³⁷ You know the events that took place throughout all Judea, beginning from Galilee after the baptism that John preached: ³⁸ how God anointed Jesus of Nazareth with the Holy Spirit and with power, and how he went about doing good and healing all who were under the tyranny of the devil, because God was with him. ³⁹ We ourselves are witnesses of everything he did in both the Judean country and in Jerusalem, and yet they killed him by hanging him on a tree. ⁴⁰ God raised up this man on the third day and caused him to be seen, ⁴¹ not by all the people, but by us whom God appointed as witnesses, who ate and drank with him after he rose from the dead. ⁴² He commanded us to preach to the people and

to testify that he is the one appointed by God to be the judge of the living and the dead. ⁴³ All the prophets testify about him that through his name everyone who believes in him receives forgiveness of sins."

⁴⁴ While Peter was still speaking these words, the Holy Spirit came down on all those who heard the message. ⁴⁵ The circumcised believers who had come with Peter were amazed because the gift of the Holy Spirit had been poured out even on the Gentiles. ⁴⁶ For they heard them speaking in other tongues and declaring the greatness of God.

Then Peter responded, ⁴⁷ "Can anyone withhold water and prevent these people from being baptized, who have received the Holy Spirit just as we have?" ⁴⁸ He commanded them to be baptized in the name of Jesus Christ. Then they asked him to stay for a few days.

34

God Loves the People
You Can't Stand
Acts 10

I grew up using an odd expression. Only recently have I bothered to learn its origin. The phrase is this: *I have more than I can shake a stick at.* It carries the idea of being overwhelmed by too many challenges. It is believed by some that this phrase dates back to the Middle Ages. When two warring armies took positions against each other, it was accepted practice for a soldier from one side to make menacing gestures toward his enemies on the other side. Often the taunting soldier would pick up a stick and wave it in determined defiance.

So imagine yourself being this warrior. As you begin to raise the stick skyward, brandishing and thrusting, you discover that the opposing army fills not only the adjacent hill but also the one behind it, and then spills over to yet another hill. The army is larger than you anticipated. Suddenly *you have more enemies than you can shake a stick at.*

It's too easy in life to accumulate enemies. Some of us may find we have more than we can shake a stick at. Perhaps it's time to put our sticks down and instead offer a hand of reconciliation.

For the Israelites of Jesus's day, the world was neatly divided into two categories of people: Jews and Gentiles. Jews were Hebrews descended from Abraham, the father of their race and faith. If one didn't qualify as a Jew, then by default that person was dumped into the Gentile category. By not being in, one was automatically out. Those who didn't qualify as God's chosen were automatically labeled God's enemies. The Jews lived in a world teeming with Gentiles; they had more enemies than they could shake a stick at.

Acts 10 is a brilliantly told story in which God challenged the Christ followers' attitude toward outsiders. Jesus was a Jew. His first followers were Jews. The early church was all but exclusively Jewish. Who was to say that it wasn't God's will for the church to be made up of only these chosen people? No Gentiles need apply, right? This chapter in Acts brings us to the unmistakable conclusion that God loves all the people we can't stand.

The chapter opens with a Gentile named Cornelius. He was an Italian by birth and a Roman centurion by occupation. A person doesn't get more Gentile than that! God heard Cornelius's prayers even before Cornelius considered himself a Christ follower. This is a comfort to those who are seeking God but haven't yet fully surrendered to him. Apparently God gives his full attention even to those who have yet to give their full devotion to him. God's command to Cornelius was clear: go make contact with Simon

Peter, who was a follower of Jesus and an influential leader in the early Christian movement.

Peter's opinion of outsiders was soon to be challenged. A Jew steeped in the narrow-minded Jew-Gentile worldview, Peter seldom questioned his hatred of Gentiles because, according to his upbringing, God didn't care much for them either.

In a vision, Peter saw a sheet. From the seaside home where he was staying, boat sails filled the skyline. One of these sails or sheets found its way into Peter's vision. When unfurled, Peter discovered it contained animals that were on the restricted list for a kosher Jewish diet. Three times a voice from heaven invited Peter to dine. Three times Peter declined. Three times a voice from heaven confronted Peter with these words: "What God has made clean, do not call impure" (v. 15).

While the message of the vision was yet unclear, God instructed Peter to go with the messengers Cornelius had sent to fetch Peter. In the Bible, seemingly insignificant details may hold a significant insight. Notice in Acts 10 that Peter happened to be in Joppa. Remember Jonah? When God instructed Jonah to go to Nineveh, Jonah traveled to Joppa instead, and from there he boarded a boat sailing in the opposite direction. Centuries later, Peter, who knew the story of Jonah by heart, found himself in the same city, facing a similar decision. In contrast to Jonah's reaction, Peter went willingly into unfamiliar—and un-Jewish—territory.

Before Peter even finished his conversation with Cornelius, something special began to happen. It became obvious to Peter that Gentiles could accept God's gift of forgiveness, receive the personal, powerful presence of the Holy Spirit, and be baptized just like Jewish believers.

Peter's earlier vision must have come back to mind. His vision wasn't about food but about folks. Peter's vision was less about what was edible and more about something of eternal importance to God—all the people of the earth. The words "What God has made clean, do not call impure" now took on a fuller and clearer meaning.

In other words, God loves all the people we can't stand.

Why is this chapter essential to our understanding of the Bible and Christian spirituality?

I write these words while visiting a country far away from America and its affluence. I'm serving with my daughter on a student missions team and spoke with a woman who is raising eight children in a single-room home with no electricity. By all standards of my native culture, this woman is unimportant and insignificant. But the truth is that God loves her just as much as those of us who overestimate our own importance. As this woman prayed, inviting Jesus to be her Lord, I was moved by God's love for all the races and classes of people on the earth. Acts 10 throws the doors of God's love and his heaven open to all people, regardless of background or breeding.

Peter's view of Gentiles was forever changed. The gospel is accessible to all people, even those of non-Jewish heritage. And in a world filled with Gentiles, like me, this is good news. Peter's experience may challenge the way you see people of different races or religions or people with unfamiliar backgrounds or unapproved-of behaviors. While we may disapprove of someone's looks or lifestyle, as followers of Jesus we can never dismiss a person as someone God doesn't love.

The church, which up to this point was predominately Jewish, became inclusive, welcoming those it had previously considered irredeemable outsiders. Peter's pull as a leader and the obvious evidence of God's gift of the Holy Spirit worked together to open the doors and hearts of the Jewish church to Gentile believers.

To observe the fiftieth anniversary of the Battle of Gettysburg, the federal government arranged a reunion of troops from both sides of the War between the States. The commemoration culminated with a reenactment of Pickett's Charge. Spectators watched as Union troops took up the same positions they had held a half century earlier. The Confederates emerged from the woods, breaking the silence of five decades with a rebel yell. A young spectator captured what happened next: "The Yankees, unable to restrain themselves longer, burst from behind the stone wall, and flung themselves upon their former enemies … not in mortal combat, but reunited in brotherly love and affection."[1]

The old divisions of Jews and Gentiles, Union and Confederate, us and them, my side and the wrong side no longer fit in the understanding of someone who has received the all-embracing love of God in Christ. We discover that God loves all the people we can't stand. And if he loves them, so can we.

FOR REFLECTION

Consider the truth that God loves all the people you can't stand. What group of people do you have an instant and almost instinctive dislike for? God's truth may challenge how you were raised to think. Also call to mind the name and face of your worst personal enemy.

Can you recognize the truth that God loves this person just as much as he loves you? Perhaps this is the first small step on the road to reconciliation.

Revelation 22

¹ Then he showed me the river of the water of life, clear as crystal, flowing from the throne of God and of the Lamb ² down the middle of the city's main street. The tree of life was on each side of the river, bearing twelve kinds of fruit, producing its fruit every month. The leaves of the tree are for healing the nations, ³ and there will no longer be any curse. The throne of God and of the Lamb will be in the city, and his servants will worship him. ⁴ They will see his face, and his name will be on their foreheads. ⁵ Night will be no more; people will not need the light of a lamp or the light of the sun, because the Lord God will give them light, and they will reign forever and ever.

⁶ Then he said to me, "These words are faithful and true. The Lord, the God of the spirits of the prophets, has sent his angel to show his servants what must soon take place."

⁷ "Look, I am coming soon! Blessed is the one who keeps the words of the prophecy of this book."

⁸ I, John, am the one who heard and saw these things. When I heard and saw them, I fell down to worship at the feet of the angel who had shown them to me. ⁹ But he said to me, "Don't do that! I am a fellow servant with you, your brothers the prophets, and those who keep the words of this book. Worship God!"

¹⁰ Then he said to me, "Don't seal up the words of the prophecy of this book, because the time is near. ¹¹ Let the filthy still be filthy; let the righteous go on in righteousness; let the holy still be holy."

¹² "Look, I am coming soon, and my reward is with me to repay each person according to his work. ¹³ I am the Alpha and the Omega, the first and the last, the beginning and the end.

¹⁴ "Blessed are those who wash their robes, so that they may have the right to the tree of life and may enter the city by the gates. ¹⁵ Outside are the dogs, the sorcerers, the sexually immoral, the murderers, the idolaters, and everyone who loves and practices falsehood.

¹⁶ "I, Jesus, have sent my angel to attest these things to you for the churches. I am the root and descendant of David, the bright morning star."

¹⁷ Both the Spirit and the bride say, "Come!" Let anyone who hears, say, "Come!" Let the one who is thirsty come. Let the one who desires take the water of life freely.

¹⁸ I testify to everyone who hears the words of the prophecy of this book: If anyone adds to them, God will add to him the plagues that are written in this book. ¹⁹ And if anyone takes away from the words of the book of this prophecy, God will take away his share of the tree of life and the holy city, which are written about in this book.

²⁰ He who testifies about these things says, "Yes, I am coming soon." Amen! Come, Lord Jesus!

²¹ The grace of the Lord Jesus be with everyone. Amen.

35

What Heaven Holds in Store
Revelation 22

One of my wife's treasured childhood memories is dancing around her father's living room, listening to his old forty-five-speed records. The music, the laughter, the trouble-free innocence of childhood evoke strong memories even now, decades later. When my wife's father died, her memories of these moments went from precious to priceless. So for a recent birthday, I asked my wife's stepmother for this collection of records. I displayed them in a small case, complete with a turntable.

While it was a pleasure to give my wife the gift of these memories, it was equally a joy to witness my children's discovery of vinyl records. For a brief moment, I was superior to my tech-savvy teens. They literally cocked their heads in bewilderment at the ancient black discs. (My favorite moment was the surprise of my youngest child when he discovered there were songs on *both* sides of the record!)

My children's first-time experience with vinyl records isn't unlike our experience of contemplating heaven. Talk of heaven is unfamiliar to our ears. The gilded existence of paradise is far removed from the pressures of our daily grind. We cock our heads as our imaginations overload from our inability to comprehend a place so radically different from the planet we call home.

If I could choose two words to sum up my thoughts of heaven—the eternal place of God's perfect presence—I would choose *mysterious* and *majestic*. Heaven is mysterious because there is much we don't understand. Heaven is majestic because there is much about it we simply *can't* understand. Revelation 22 offers a rare glimpse of heaven's interior. Even so, the description serves to deepen the mystery and broaden the majesty of the eternal realm. There are, however, a few things we know for sure.

Heaven has a river. "Then [an angel] showed me the river of the water of life, clear as crystal, flowing from the throne of God and of the Lamb" (v. 1). Water serves two primary purposes: drinking and bathing.

Drinking water provides refreshment. When my alarm clock goes off each morning at five o'clock, my first conscious thought on most days is *I'm so tired.* With a house full of children, a church full of obligations, and a life full of opportunities and obstacles, weariness is standard fare. But the promise of heaven brings hope that ultimately we'll never again experience strain or stress or being stretched beyond our capacity to cope. We'll drink freely of the "water of life" and find eternal refreshment. In heaven the promise of Psalm 23 will be forever fulfilled: "He renews my life" (v. 3).

When we use water on the outside of our bodies for bathing, it provides cleansing. In heaven every vestige of our sin, guilt, regret, remorse, and shame will be washed away. What is the worst thing you've ever done? I pose this question not to invoke guilt but to inspire hope. The river in heaven is a picture of God's promise to deal once and for all with our past. At long last we will fully understand that all our sins are forgiven and forgotten, as though they never existed at all.

Heaven has a street. The great river of heaven, we're told, will flow "down the middle of the city's main street" (Rev. 22:2). The street address of your home communicates something about your status in society. In my hometown in West Texas, a street address bearing the name Chatterton or Tanglewood communicates middle class. Whereas North Bryant connotes poverty, a street like Bentwood carries an overtone of affluence. The same is true of where I live in Tulsa. And I'm certain the same is true of your city or town. Yet from what we're told of heaven, it seems that we'll all live on the same street. No longer will there be segregation and separation. Heaven will be the experience of perfect community with others and perfect communion with God.

Heaven has a tree. "The tree of life was on each side of the river, bearing twelve kinds of fruit, producing its fruit every month" (v. 2). To understand the hints of heaven in Revelation 22, we must hear the echoes of Eden. The early chapters of Genesis tell of Adam and Eve and their unrestricted access to the tree of life. Their sin, however, separated them from this source of life. The appearance of the tree in heaven tells us that humanity has come full circle into a fully restored relationship with God. Furthermore, the tree of life points to two qualities of the caliber of life heaven holds.

First, life in heaven will be abundant. We're accustomed to trees bearing a single crop of fruit each year, but the tree of life bears a crop each month. Whatever our current understanding of life, our experience of life in heaven will be exponential.

Second, the tree of life communicates that life in heaven will have great variety. The subtle language used to describe the tree of life in Revelation 22 speaks of a tree that will yield twelve crops of fruit, with a different variety each month. Imagine a tree, if you can, that bears apples in January, oranges in February, bananas in March, cheeseburgers in April, and pizza in May. (I suppose you now know what I consider to be life-giving foods!)

Heaven won't be like the pale, sterile environment of an operating room. It's better to think of heaven in terms of FAO Schwarz, the toy store that was in New York City. Color, variety, and vitality are the status quo of eternity.

Heaven is centered around a throne. "The throne of God and of the Lamb will be in the city, and his servants will worship him" (v. 3). On this throne of heaven will reside the God of the universe. And we will be there—you and I. And we will experience his presence as never before—unhindered and uninterrupted.

In a recent conversation I had with a group of students, they confessed that the thought of heaven being a never-ending event "freaked" them out. What could we possibly do for all eternity? Won't we get bored?

As I encouraged this group of students, so I challenge you: Think of the perfect moment. Recall the first time you held hands with someone special. Think of that first kiss or the first time you held your newborn child. A perfect moment is an experience we wish would never end. But it always does. Holding hands is followed by disagreements. First kisses give way to first fights. Newborns become teenagers.

Heaven is akin to the perfect moment we wish would never end. But the mystery—and majesty—of heaven is that it won't. We'll enjoy the reality and presence of God for eternity, and even then, it won't be enough.

At the time of this writing, a dear friend departed for heaven. Calvin Miller was first my professor, then my mentor, and ultimately my friend. Originally from Oklahoma, he made plans to be buried in the rural community of Hunter. Because of my friendship and location, the family honored me with the request to conduct Calvin's graveside service.

At the service, I chose to read a passage Calvin himself wrote in one of his many books. He described standing in the very cemetery where he was to be buried, conducting the funeral for his father-in-law. As Calvin read his father-in-law's eulogy, he happened to stand on his own grave plot. The surreal moment surrendered a profound reflection:

> As I preached that funeral I felt an odd emotion. I looked out at my family all of whom are older than I (and I am no longer young).... I realized it would not be long before I myself was in a box, with someone else standing beside that box to read the same kinds of words over me.

Life is brief and I am counting on the miracle of heaven to extend it. Without that miracle, my life would end with no assurance. In short I am miracle-dependent. But I am among those who are counting on the miracle of resurrection. It is this miracle that makes of death only an inconvenience in the path to heaven, the greatest miracle of all.[1]

Heaven is mystery and majesty. But as I read these words over my friend's casket, I appreciated the truth that heaven is also a miracle—a sheer gift God lavishes on all who follow Jesus. And since heaven is the place of God's presence, the miracle of heaven is available to each of us at this very moment.

FOR REFLECTION

Call to mind, if you can, one important person in your life who has died and is now in heaven. In what ways are you grateful for that individual's influence in your life? Take a moment to thank God for that person's existence, which continues in heaven, and the impact that continues in your life. Also take time to consider how you can have a positive impact on others. What we do with our time may well affect eternity.

GOD'S MESSAGE
FOR YOU

Romans 8

¹ Therefore, there is now no condemnation for those in Christ Jesus, ² because the law of the Spirit of life in Christ Jesus has set you free from the law of sin and death. ³ What the law could not do since it was weakened by the flesh, God did. He condemned sin in the flesh by sending his own Son in the likeness of sinful flesh as a sin offering, ⁴ in order that the law's requirement would be fulfilled in us who do not walk according to the flesh but according to the Spirit. ⁵ For those who live according to the flesh have their minds set on the things of the flesh, but those who live according to the Spirit have their minds set on the things of the Spirit. ⁶ Now the mind-set of the flesh is death, but the mind-set of the Spirit is life and peace. ⁷ The mind-set of the flesh is hostile to God because it does not submit to God's law. Indeed, it is unable to do so. ⁸ Those who are in the flesh cannot please God. ⁹ You, however, are not in the flesh, but in the Spirit, if indeed the Spirit of God lives in you. If anyone does not have the Spirit of Christ, he does not belong to him. ¹⁰ Now if Christ is in you, the body is dead because of sin, but the Spirit gives life because of righteousness. ¹¹ And if the Spirit of him who raised Jesus from the dead lives in you, then he who raised Christ from the dead will also bring your mortal bodies to life through his Spirit who lives in you.

¹² So then, brothers and sisters, we are not obligated to the flesh to live according to the flesh, ¹³ because if you live according to the flesh, you are going to die. But if by the Spirit you put to death the deeds of the body, you will live. ¹⁴ For all those led by God's Spirit are God's sons. ¹⁵ You did not receive a spirit of slavery to fall back into fear. Instead, you received the Spirit of adoption, by whom we cry out, "*Abba*, Father!" ¹⁶ The Spirit himself testifies together with our spirit that we are God's children, ¹⁷ and if children, also heirs — heirs of God and coheirs with Christ — if indeed we suffer with him so that we may also be glorified with him.

¹⁸ For I consider that the sufferings of this present time are not worth comparing with the glory that is going to be revealed to us. ¹⁹ For the creation eagerly waits with anticipation for God's sons to be revealed. ²⁰ For the creation was subjected to futility — not willingly, but because of him who subjected it — in the hope ²¹ that the creation itself will also be set free from the bondage to decay into the glorious freedom of God's children. ²² For we know that the whole creation has been groaning

together with labor pains until now. ²³ Not only that, but we ourselves who have the Spirit as the firstfruits — we also groan within ourselves, eagerly waiting for adoption, the redemption of our bodies. ²⁴ Now in this hope we were saved, but hope that is seen is not hope, because who hopes for what he sees? ²⁵ Now if we hope for what we do not see, we eagerly wait for it with patience.

²⁶ In the same way the Spirit also helps us in our weakness, because we do not know what to pray for as we should, but the Spirit himself intercedes for us with unspoken groanings. ²⁷ And he who searches our hearts knows the mind of the Spirit, because he intercedes for the saints according to the will of God.

²⁸ We know that all things work together for the good of those who love God, who are called according to his purpose. ²⁹ For those he foreknew he also predestined to be conformed to the image of his Son, so that he would be the firstborn among many brothers and sisters. ³⁰ And those he predestined, he also called; and those he called, he also justified; and those he justified, he also glorified.

³¹ What then are we to say about these things? If God is for us, who is against us? ³² He did not even spare his own Son but offered him up for us all. How will he not also with him grant us everything? ³³ Who can bring an accusation against God's elect? God is the one who justifies. ³⁴ Who is the one who condemns? Christ Jesus is the one who died, but even more, has been raised; he also is at the right hand of God and intercedes for us. ³⁵ Who can separate us from the love of Christ? Can affliction or distress or persecution or famine or nakedness or danger or sword? ³⁶ As it is written:

Because of you
we are being put to death all day long;
we are counted as sheep to be slaughtered.

³⁷ No, in all these things we are more than conquerors through him who loved us. ³⁸ For I am persuaded that neither death nor life, nor angels nor rulers, nor things present nor things to come, nor powers, ³⁹ nor height nor depth, nor any other created thing will be able to separate us from the love of God that is in Christ Jesus our Lord.

36

Is God Ever Mean?
Romans 8

I'm usually comfortable speaking to large groups. But one particular audience presented a real challenge. I was worried because I knew I would soon be facing one of the toughest encounters a speaker can face. How could I get through to a group of eight-, nine-, and ten-year-olds? What were they thinking? What did they need to hear? How could I keep their attention?

So I sent an SOS to friends. Here's how my post read: "What is one thing you wish you would have learned about God as a child?" One person quickly responded with Romans 8:1: "Therefore, there is now no condemnation for those in Christ Jesus."

I thought about how many preachers have misused their pulpits, pounding a falsehood into the hearts of their hearers. The falsehood is this: God can hardly stand to look at you. How many people, I wondered, have walked away from faith out of distrust and disgust for a God who holds grudges, who looks on everyone with disdain?

What if I could find a way to communicate God's real love to these children before they absorbed a narrow and negative view of God? With this question in mind, I chose the topic of my talk: *Is God Mean?*

As I began to speak to this group of kids, I noticed something strange. The room became perfectly still. Five hundred children who had been whispering and wiggling had quieted down completely. The word *miraculous* came to my mind. I sensed they needed to hear the profound truth of God's love for them. Perhaps we all do.

But is there proof that God loves us and doesn't loathe us? How do we experience the reality of God minus the meanness we've often assumed? What is the evidence that God isn't malicious or spiteful toward us, his creation?

Paul, an early follower of Jesus, wrote a letter to a gathering of Christians in Rome—most of whom he had never met. He penned a series of truths that hold for all followers of Jesus at all times. Romans 8 revolves around this one theme that God is bent on loving every person he ever created. To detail each promise contained in this chapter of Romans would require a book in itself, so I've selected a handful of my favorites.

Romans 8:14 offers this promise: "All those led by God's Spirit are God's sons." In Paul's first-century culture, a typical Roman household was occupied by both slaves and children. On a few occasions, a slave was so valued and loved that the master would offer to adopt the slave as a son or daughter. That slave's relationship to the master would no longer be one of duty but one of dignity as a full member of the family. Once the legal diligence was done, the new son or daughter would never again be a slave. The relationship had fundamentally changed.

When we become children of God, the promotion brings with it a promise: God will watch over us, leading us faithfully through the events and circumstances of this life. Because of our new status, we have this assurance.

God can lead us even when we find ourselves in the most unpleasant of places. Esther Ahn Kim was harshly imprisoned as a Christian political prisoner in her native Korea when the Japanese occupied her country during World War II. She managed to survive by focusing on the physical and spiritual needs of those imprisoned around her. Every morning Kim would wake up in her prison cell and pray, *"[Jesus,] who do You want me to love for You today?"*[1] Kim was acting as a child of God, allowing him to lead her.

To the question "Is God Mean?" we can say a resounding no. A mean God would never invite a slave to become his child. Instead of keeping us under his thumb, God has chosen to hold us next to his heart.

Do you need more evidence? Let's consider Romans 8:29: "Those [God] foreknew he also predestined to be conformed to the image of his Son." Two rich words from this verse deserve careful exploration: *foreknew* and *predestined*.

Foreknew. The verb *to know* is often used as a euphemism in the Bible for intimacy—even sexual intimacy. If *to know* means "to love," then *to foreknow* translates to "fore-love." What could this possibly mean?

Think about it this way. I was privileged to see my daughter before she was born. As her cranium crowned the birth canal, I was allowed to see and even touch her yet-to-be-born head. I consider this event one of the most profound and moving experiences of my life. I loved my daughter even before I knew her.

Before you existed, God had already made the decision to love you. The matter was settled. God sees no reason to reconsider this matter. Even in that time of your preexistence, you were preloved.

Predestined. The prelove of God brings with it a benefit: he has granted you a predestiny. And what is your destiny? To become exactly like Jesus Christ.

Remember Michelangelo? After carving his nearly seventeen-foot-tall likeness of David from a single block of marble, someone asked how he had managed this impressive feat. Michelangelo explained that he had chiseled away everything from the rock that didn't look like David. David was already in the stone; Michelangelo simply had to liberate his form. Our destiny is to become like Jesus in our actions and attitudes. God will bring about this destiny by chiseling away from our character and personality everything that doesn't resemble Christ. The result will be total freedom for the follower of Jesus.

Indeed, God isn't mean. His decision to love us and his desire to give us a destiny are clear evidence of his love for us.

Perhaps one more passage from Romans 8 will serve as proof of God's love for humanity. I liken this chapter to the Himalaya Mountains. The Himalayas are the most majestic range of mountains found anywhere on our planet. Likewise, Romans 8 is one of the most beautiful depictions of God's love found anywhere in the Bible. If Romans 8 is the Himalayas, then verse 28 is Mount Everest. It's the high point of the high point. Romans 8:28 says, "We know that all things work together for the good of those who love God, who are called according to his purpose."

Here we have a promise that holds true no matter our immediate situation. A real-life example: cancer isn't good, but God can bring good even from this diagnosis, either by healing our bodies, thus allowing us to inspire others, or by allowing our deaths to have a positive and purposeful impact on those around us. This promise means that fear is defeated as we face the future as Jesus followers. God can use any circumstance or crisis to make us more like Christ.

When I lived in Alabama, I had a friend who owned a furniture store. Each time I bought a piece of furniture from Mark, I'd ask about an antique rolltop desk in need of restoration that sat forgotten in a back room. Each time I inquired about the desk, Mark would inform me that it wasn't for sale.

As my family prepared to move to Tulsa, I went to Mark's store one final time to ask about the desk. He told me he hadn't sold it to me all those years because he knew at some point he wanted to give it to me. So that became my going-away gift. Even now I sit at this fully restored desk and write these words.

The best gifts of God are free. He offers us a place in his family. He gives us his guidance. He offers us a destiny to become like Jesus. And he guarantees that every event will result in our benefit. Paul said it best when he boldly proclaimed, "For I am persuaded that neither death nor life, nor angels nor rulers, nor things present nor things to come, nor powers, nor height nor depth, nor any other created thing will be able to separate us from the love of God that is in Christ Jesus our Lord" (Rom. 8:38–39).

What can we draw from all this? Yes, I think we know it by now: God isn't mean.

FOR REFLECTION

As you read through Romans 8 again, what other evidence do you see that highlights the truth that God isn't mean? In what other ways does he show his love to you?

1 Corinthians 13

¹ If I speak human or angelic tongues but do not have love, I am a noisy gong or a clanging cymbal. ² If I have the gift of prophecy and understand all mysteries and all knowledge, and if I have all faith so that I can move mountains but do not have love, I am nothing. ³ And if I give away all my possessions, and if I give over my body in order to boast but do not have love, I gain nothing.

⁴ Love is patient, love is kind. Love does not envy, is not boastful, is not arrogant, ⁵ is not rude, is not self-seeking, is not irritable, and does not keep a record of wrongs. ⁶ Love finds no joy in unrighteousness but rejoices in the truth. ⁷ It bears all things, believes all things, hopes all things, endures all things.

⁸ Love never ends. But as for prophecies, they will come to an end; as for tongues, they will cease; as for knowledge, it will come to an end. ⁹ For we know in part, and we prophesy in part, ¹⁰ but when the perfect comes, the partial will come to an end. ¹¹ When I was a child, I spoke like a child, I thought like a child, I reasoned like a child. When I became a man, I put aside childish things. ¹² For now we see only a reflection as in a mirror, but then face to face. Now I know in part, but then I will know fully, as I am fully known. ¹³ Now these three remain: faith, hope, and love —but the greatest of these is love.

37

More Than a Feeling
1 Corinthians 13

Adolf von Harnack, a deep-thinking theologian from days long past, considered 1 Corinthians 13 "the greatest, strongest, deepest thing Paul ever wrote."[1] I wholeheartedly agree. At the core of this chapter is the powerful theme of love.

Before we can fully appreciate this chapter, we must clearly understand what love is. At the very least, we should dispel some of our misunderstandings about it. Love is common to the human experience. At one time or another, almost everyone has experienced love to some degree. But love is also uncommonly powerful. Love has been the source of both great sacrifice and great stupidity throughout the ages. To love is to experience one of the strongest forces in creation.

In the Greek language, the original language of the New Testament, there isn't a single word for love but several. Collectively these words provide a panoramic view of the emotion and the experience of love.

Eros is the Greek word for physical love or sexual attraction, which is where our word *erotic* comes from. If you've ever found yourself drawn to someone physically, you've experienced *eros*.

Philia is the Greek word for brotherly friendship. We all have people with whom we share an unforced and unexplainable bond. *Philia* is a relationship that simply fits.

Storge is the Greek word for love within a family. Even families that fight internally unite aggressively against any outside threats. *Storge* is a nobody-messes-with-my-sister type of love.

And then there is *agape*. Of the Greek words that describe love, *agape* is the standout. In one form or another, *agape* appears more than 250 times in the New Testament. This word describes an unconditional love. *Agape* love isn't based on physical attraction or natural affection or family connection or even emotion. Stripped of all selfishness, *agape* is the highest and purest form of love. *Agape*—and this is my working definition for *love*—is "to will and work for someone's best interest." While this is simple to say, it's difficult to do.

Every time the word *love* appears in 1 Corinthians 13, Paul reflexively used *agape*. He opened the chapter with this thought: love is something that without it, everything is nothing. He wrote,

> If I speak human or angelic tongues but do not have love, I am a noisy gong or a clanging cymbal. If I have the gift of prophecy and understand all mysteries and all knowledge, and if I have all faith so that I can move mountains but do not have love, I am nothing. And if I give away all my

possessions, and if I give over my body in order
to boast but do not have love, I gain nothing.
(vv. 1–3)

Paul spoke in extremes, and yet he didn't overstate reality. If we were fluent in all known languages and were even able to converse with angels, or if we could retain all the accumulated knowledge from the past and accurately predict every event of the future, or if we possessed a faith that could impress all people but lacked love, it's as though we would have nothing at all. Without love, all skills and gifts, resources and rewards are ultimately empty.

Love is something that without it, everything is nothing.

The same is true today, isn't it? Entertainment news is littered with people who achieve worldwide fame only to find themselves lonely. We know people of great wealth who have little self-worth because they have no one in life they can trust. And even closer to home, many of us are surrounded by stuff and yet are starving for lack of authentic love.

Love is something that without it, everything is nothing.

In words that were great, strong, deep, and true, Paul provided a well-rounded picture of *agape* love:

Love is patient, love is kind. Love does not envy, is not boastful, is not arrogant, is not rude, is not self-seeking, is not irritable, and does not keep a record of wrongs. Love finds no joy in unrighteousness but rejoices in the truth. It bears all things, believes all things, hopes all things, endures all things.

Love never ends. (vv. 4–8)

Genuine love isn't something complicated or sophisticated. Love, in fact, is quite simple.

My parents recently celebrated their fiftieth wedding anniversary. My wife and I and all my siblings, along with their spouses, gathered in our hometown to celebrate. Being from West Texas, we, of course, held the celebration at a steak house. For a Texan, nothing captures the essence of joy like large cuts of red meat.

The high point of the celebration took place as the entire family assembled around the banquet table. We listened in reverent silence as our parents talked of their half-century affection for each other. They reminisced over the easy years. It turns out the 1970s was their favorite decade, kids filling the home with laughter and activity. The lack of fashion sense aside, the seventies were the best of times. My parents also recalled the lean years. The family move to New Mexico was a disaster from the get-go. Several years were marked by unemployment. These were the worst of times.

Whatever the circumstances, my parents made the decision to love each other—to will and work for each other's best interests. Neither of my parents ever earned anything beyond a high school diploma. But in my estimation, they both hold a PhD in love— uncomplicated, unsophisticated love.

Love is learning to say and mean certain words. If love is patient, then we learn to say, "I can wait; you go first." If love is kind, we teach ourselves to confess to others, "I'm sorry. I was wrong." If love knows no boasting or pride, then we strike the words "I told you so" from our vocabularies. If love isn't easily angered, then we develop the discipline to say nothing at all when we most want to retaliate.

Legendary golfer Gary Player once joked that if he had to choose between his favorite club and his wife, he'd miss her. When he returned home that night, his wife had left a club wrapped in a slinky negligee on the bed.[2]

Love is learning to say good things and mean them; love is also learning when to choose silence.

My favorite insight from 1 Corinthians 13 comes from verse 5, where Paul said that love "does not keep a record of wrongs." If love keeps no record of wrongs, then it stands to reason that love likewise keeps no records of rights. Love doesn't keep a running tally of favors or sacrifices made for the purpose of holding another person in our permanent debt. To keep a record of all the rights we've done for someone else, only to use it later as a tool of manipulation or guilt, is far from *agape* love.

As mentioned earlier, it's a helpful tool in Bible reading to notice repeated words and phrases. Typically these repetitions signal a main point in a particular passage. In the New International Version, a popular translation of the Bible, 1 Corinthians 13:7 uses the word *always* four times: Love "always protects, always trusts, always hopes, always perseveres." Always, always, always, always. True love is no stranger to endurance. Love is sacrificial in its protection, optimistic in its trust, positive in its hope, and unflinching in its resolve. Far beyond mere emotion, love is a decision to will and work for someone's best interests—always.

In a retirement center in Northport, New York, a resident named Augie Angerame walks down the hall every day to check on another resident, Frank Dibella. This is unusual given that both Augie and Frank suffer from advanced dementia. Neither is able to communicate verbally, yet a silent bond developed between the two men.

The staff members at the retirement center were so moved by Augie's concern for Frank that they placed the two men in the same room. Only then did Augie's son, John, make a surprising discovery. By way of some old photos, John realized that Augie and Frank had served together in the same outfit during the Korean War. When Frank was injured, Augie was the army medic who patched Frank up and kept him alive. Even now, sixty years later, Augie is still checking on Frank.[3]

This is *agape* love: to will and work for someone's best interests. Great, strong, and deep indeed.

FOR REFLECTION

Reread 1 Corinthians 13:4–7. Each time you encounter the word *love*, substitute the name of Jesus. Jesus is the perfect expression of God's love for humanity. Now reread these same verses, substituting your name for the word *love*. How does it sound? Is it true? Where do you need to allow Christ to help you improve in your practice of love for others?

Galatians 5

¹ For freedom, Christ set us free. Stand firm then and don't submit again to a yoke of slavery. ² Take note! I, Paul, am telling you that if you get yourselves circumcised, Christ will not benefit you at all. ³ Again I testify to every man who gets himself circumcised that he is obligated to do the entire law. ⁴ You who are trying to be justified by the law are alienated from Christ; you have fallen from grace. ⁵ For we eagerly await through the Spirit, by faith, the hope of righteousness. ⁶ For in Christ Jesus neither circumcision nor uncircumcision accomplishes anything; what matters is faith working through love.

⁷ You were running well. Who prevented you from being persuaded regarding the truth? ⁸ This persuasion does not come from the one who calls you. ⁹ A little leaven leavens the whole batch of dough. ¹⁰ I myself am persuaded in the Lord you will not accept any other view. But whoever it is that is confusing you will pay the penalty. ¹¹ Now brothers and sisters, if I still preach circumcision, why am I still persecuted? In that case the offense of the cross has been abolished. ¹² I wish those who are disturbing you might also let themselves be mutilated!

¹³ For you were called to be free, brothers and sisters; only don't use this freedom as an opportunity for the flesh, but serve one another through love. ¹⁴ For the whole law is fulfilled in one statement: Love your neighbor as yourself. ¹⁵ But if you bite and devour one another, watch out, or you will be consumed by one another.

¹⁶ I say then, walk by the Spirit and you will certainly not carry out the desire of the flesh. ¹⁷ For the flesh desires what is against the Spirit, and the Spirit desires what is against the flesh; these are opposed to each other, so that you don't do what you want. ¹⁸ But if you are led by the Spirit, you are not under the law.

¹⁹ Now the works of the flesh are obvious: sexual immorality, moral impurity, promiscuity, ²⁰ idolatry, sorcery, hatreds, strife, jealousy, outbursts of anger, selfish ambitions, dissensions, factions, ²¹ envy, drunkenness, carousing, and anything similar. I am warning you about these things — as I warned you before — that those who practice such things will not inherit the kingdom of God.

²² But the fruit of the Spirit is love, joy, peace, patience, kindness, goodness, faithfulness, ²³ gentleness, and self-control. The law is not

against such things. [24] Now those who belong to Christ Jesus have crucified the flesh with its passions and desires. [25] If we live by the Spirit, let us also keep in step with the Spirit. [26] Let us not become conceited, provoking one another, envying one another.

38

Can God Change
Your Character?
Galatians 5

Have you ever penned an angry letter? Abraham Lincoln had a
practice worth imitating. After writing an angry note, he would set
it aside for several days. After his emotions had cooled, he would
rewrite the letter, revising any rough tones in his correspondence.
In many cases, Lincoln never sent the letter at all. In a day when
we're tempted to fire off an angry electronic message, we need to
develop this kind of restraint. However, there are occasions when
we need to let others know exactly how we feel.

Galatians is the angry letter of the New Testament. The apostle
Paul, its author, was a passionate follower of Jesus and a bold leader
in the early Christian community. Paul's teaching about the love
of God was simple and direct. Paul used the word *grace* to describe
God's act of initiating a relationship with humanity. And the term
faith was used to describe our best reaction to the love of God.
God reaches. We respond. The result is relationship.

Simple, right?

Well, in early Christianity, as in many times throughout Christian history, some people were determined to confuse this uncomplicated connection with God. A faction within the early church taught that a relationship with God required rules. Lots of rules. Grace and faith were too soft. According to this group, what people really needed were hard and fast guidelines—a long list of dos and an even longer list of don'ts—to stay in good standing with God.

Paul had reason to fume. This rule-based religion was tainting entire churches. Paul believed that Jesus doesn't want to make us more religious; he wants to see us become more alive! Grace and faith were being trivialized. Something must be said.

Paul's anger boiled over when he said, "You foolish Galatians! Who has cast a spell on you?" (Gal. 3:1). He was angry at the legalists for their propaganda, at the church for paying attention to their lies, and perhaps even at himself for not having been a better teacher for these young Christians.

As Paul's angry lecture continued, he exhausted his emotion. Late in the letter, he began to write in gentler tones of encouragement. One of the most memorable passages from the pen of Paul is found in Galatians 5:22–23, which says, "The fruit of the Spirit is love, joy, peace, patience, kindness, goodness, faithfulness, gentleness, and self-control."

I grow jalapeños. My love for cultivating peppers is a product of my Texas upbringing. I enjoy every aspect of the pepper-growing experience. The starter plants must be pruned and planted deep. The backyard must be guarded against rabbits—protection is provided courtesy of my schnauzer. The first white buds that appear on the plants inform me that the hot pain of peppers is but a few weeks away. And because I plant a dozen or so plants, it isn't long before the production of peppers outpaces my capacity to eat them. That's when the pickling begins.

I don't grow jalapeños because I enjoy the plants themselves. Nor do I grow jalapeños for the beauty of the blossoms. I grow them because I want the produce; I want the fruit.

Likewise, God wants to produce something in your life. He's looking for fruit. You may attend church, join a community of people learning to follow Jesus, and even engage in service that improves the lives of others. All these activities look good and smell nice. Yet they're not the results God is looking for in a Christ follower's life. God wants to produce something more internal and eternal.

Galatians 5 details the character change the Holy Spirit will produce in the life of a Jesus follower when given permission: "love, joy, peace, patience, kindness, goodness, faithfulness, gentleness, and self-control." These nine character traits are the fruit of the Spirit.

Paul, in other writings (Romans 12 and 1 Corinthians 12), discusses the gifts of the Spirit. Spiritual gifts must not be confused with spiritual fruit. The gifts (plural) of the Spirit are abilities God grants to Christ followers; the fruit (singular) of the Spirit is the character God instills within them.

We aren't expected to have all the gifts of the Spirit. For example, one person may have the ability to lead, while another person may have the gift of administration or service. Yet a follower of Jesus is expected to have all the fruit of the Spirit—no exceptions. Followers of Jesus can never say that God doesn't expect them to have love or joy or kindness.

Most important, the best measure of spiritual maturity isn't one's spiritual gifts but one's spiritual fruit. A person may be a wonderful singer and yet lack self-control. The fruit, not the gifts, is the true mark of maturity. If I'm a gifted preacher and yet lack patience (and I do), my lack of fruit, not the abundance of my gifts, is the true test of my spiritual health.

John Stott, a wonderful Christian thinker and writer, offered a brilliant insight that can help us better understand the nine aspects of the fruit of the Spirit in this chapter. Stott divided the nine characteristics into three categories: our relationship with God, our relationships with other people, and our relationship with ourselves.[1]

Our relationship with God: love, joy, peace. For each fruit God wants to produce in our lives, the world offers a shabby substitute. Peace is a good example. God offers peace; the world offers numbness. Consider how many things are designed not to help us feel good but to ensure we feel nothing. We spend hours in front of the television. Numbness. We drink too much. Numbness. Many even resort to using illegal substances, not to feel peace, but to experience the absence of pain. But with our cooperation, God has the power to produce continuous peace in our lives.

Our relationship with others: patience, kindness, goodness. On several occasions I've led small-group discussions on the fruit of the Spirit. I ask participants to close their eyes as I read through the list of the fruit of the Spirit. Before reciting the list, I say, "Listen for the characteristic that 'pops.' Listen for the character trait of the Spirit you believe you most lack." Almost without exception, patience tops people's lists.

Even my hero Winston Churchill was plagued with a lack of patience. Among the members of the British Parliament was Lady Nancy Astor. Their love-hate relationship was more hate than love. In her frustration she once told the prime minister, "Winston, if I were your wife I'd put poison in your coffee." Churchill calmly replied, "Nancy, if I were your husband, I'd drink it."[2] Even the greatest among us lack patience. But all of us can have patience by granting God full access to our character.

Our relationship with ourselves: faithfulness, gentleness, self-control. Who among us doesn't wish for greater self-control? Among the many difficult people in life, it seems we wrestle with ourselves most. The shelf life of our resolve is shorter than we would wish. Even when we're resolute to change our ways, old habits return with irresistible force. We choose the chocolate instead of the broccoli. The couch triumphs over the treadmill. Slothful silence wins out over the healthy conversations we need with our spouses.

The Holy Spirit is the only one who can instill self-control as a permanent part of our character. The same holds true for every fruit of the Spirit. And this may be the best insight of all. We can't produce any fruit by our own decision or will. That's why these character traits are known as the fruit of the *Spirit*. God's

Spirit is the source and sustenance of any lasting change in our personalities as we follow the person of Jesus.

FOR REFLECTION

Sir Edmund Hillary and his Sherpa guide, Tenzing Norgay, were the first humans to successfully ascend Mount Everest. Hillary, having failed to reach the summit on a previous attempt, addressed the mountain in the presence of a crowd. He reportedly said, "Mount Everest, you beat me the first time, but I'll beat you the next time because you've grown all you are going to grow … but I'm still growing!"[3] A year later, Hillary proved himself larger than the mountain.

Are you still growing? Reread the characteristics that the Holy Spirit wants to produce in your life. Are you seeing more of these traits with each passing year? In each area of your relationships with God, others, and yourself, are you continuing the ascent? There is no letting up. There is no relaxing. There is no relenting. We provide the willingness, and the Spirit provides the results of a changed character.

James 1

¹ James, a servant of God and of the Lord Jesus Christ:
To the twelve tribes dispersed abroad.
Greetings.

² Consider it a great joy, my brothers and sisters, whenever you experience various trials, ³ because you know that the testing of your faith produces endurance. ⁴ And let endurance have its full effect, so that you may be mature and complete, lacking nothing.

⁵ Now if any of you lacks wisdom, he should ask God—who gives to all generously and ungrudgingly—and it will be given to him. ⁶ But let him ask in faith without doubting. For the doubter is like the surging sea, driven and tossed by the wind. ⁷ That person should not expect to receive anything from the Lord, ⁸ being double-minded and unstable in all his ways.

⁹ Let the brother of humble circumstances boast in his exaltation, ¹⁰ but let the rich boast in his humiliation because he will pass away like a flower of the field. ¹¹ For the sun rises and, together with the scorching wind, dries up the grass; its flower falls off, and its beautiful appearance perishes. In the same way, the rich person will wither away while pursuing his activities.

¹² Blessed is the one who endures trials, because when he has stood the test he will receive the crown of life that God has promised to those who love him.

¹³ No one undergoing a trial should say, "I am being tempted by God," since God is not tempted by evil, and he himself doesn't tempt anyone. ¹⁴ But each person is tempted when he is drawn away and enticed by his own evil desire. ¹⁵ Then after desire has conceived, it gives birth to sin, and when sin is fully grown, it gives birth to death.

¹⁶ Don't be deceived, my dear brothers and sisters. ¹⁷ Every good and perfect gift is from above, coming down from the Father of lights, who does not change like shifting shadows. ¹⁸ By his own choice, he gave us birth by the word of truth so that we would be a kind of firstfruits of his creatures.

¹⁹ My dear brothers and sisters, understand this: Everyone should be quick to listen, slow to speak, and slow to anger, ²⁰ for human anger does not accomplish God's righteousness. ²¹ Therefore, ridding yourselves

of all moral filth and the evil that is so prevalent, humbly receive the implanted word, which is able to save your souls.

²² But be doers of the word and not hearers only, deceiving yourselves. ²³ Because if anyone is a hearer of the word and not a doer, he is like someone looking at his own face in a mirror. ²⁴ For he looks at himself, goes away, and immediately forgets what kind of person he was. ²⁵ But the one who looks intently into the perfect law of freedom and perseveres in it, and is not a forgetful hearer but a doer who works — this person will be blessed in what he does.

²⁶ If anyone thinks he is religious without controlling his tongue, his religion is useless and he deceives himself. ²⁷ Pure and undefiled religion before God the Father is this: to look after orphans and widows in their distress and to keep oneself unstained from the world

39

Straight Talk
James 1

James is my favorite book of the Bible. When I first discovered it in college, I read it voraciously. My copy of the Bible from those days, which I still possess, bears the scars of my frequent visits to this small letter. The spine is broken, and the pages of James have long since separated from the binding.

For me, James can be summed up in two words: *bold* and *blunt*. I'm naturally drawn to people who will tell me what I need to hear rather than what I want to hear. And I appreciate people who couple this quality of frankness with love. The truth they say may be hard, but I know their love for me is deep. I sense these same qualities of candor and care when I read James.

James, the author of this short volume, was none other than the half brother of Jesus. Jesus was the son of Mary and the Holy Spirit, while James was the son of Mary and Joseph. Knowing James shared a biological connection to Jesus makes his self-introduction all the more impressive: "James, a servant of God and of the Lord

Jesus Christ" (1:1). James could have just as easily touted himself as "James, the brother of Jesus." But to James, his most significant connection to Jesus wasn't biological but spiritual. Jesus is Lord of all. James saw himself as Jesus's servant. (Actually, James used the word *slave*.) James belonged to Jesus in ways no family relationship could adequately express.

The book of James is a personal letter. When I write a letter to my wife, I don't think in terms of an outline with a logical sequence of thoughts. I'm not writing a research paper; I'm having a one-sided conversation. The letter of James is very much stream of consciousness. The current of the conversation, as it flows from one topic to the next, is strong and meaningful.

James opened his letter by addressing something we experience in great abundance and something else we greatly lack.

We all have an overabundance of suffering, or so it seems. Instead of offering pity, James put suffering in perspective: "Consider it a great joy, my brothers and sisters, whenever you experience various trials, because you know that the testing of your faith produces endurance. And let endurance have its full effect, so that you may be mature and complete, lacking nothing" (vv. 2–4).

Who else talks like this? When we face difficult times, many people tell us that everything will be all right or that our trying times will soon end. But not James. He doesn't fill our heads with false hopes of easier days ahead. He doesn't tell us what we *want* to hear; he tells us what we *need* to hear. James invites us to see difficult times not only as good but also as instrumental to God for our spiritual development—that we would be "mature and complete, lacking nothing." Challenges bring with them the opportunity of developing maturity.

Satchel Paige, the once-famous baseball player, grew up not knowing his birthday. Because of inadequate record keeping, Paige was denied the privilege of knowing his exact age. It was Paige who asked the iconic question, "How old would you be if you didn't know how old you are?" If you didn't have the reference point of your birthday or birth year, how old would you say you are, judging only by the way you act and feel and behave? Physically the challenge is to stay young. Spiritually the challenge is to grow wise. No matter what the calendar says, Jesus followers can have maturity beyond their number of years.

So when you encounter your next difficult season, resist the urge to pray, *God, get me out of this!* Instead, choose to pray, *God, what do you want me to get out of this?* Suffering is certainly no fun, but it may be an opportunity for God to transform us.

As we experience an abundance of suffering in life, we also experience a shortage of wisdom. Many are the times when life baffles us and we're at a loss for determining the best course of action. During our study of Proverbs 1, I suggested this definition of *wisdom*: wisdom is doing the right thing at the right time for the right reasons. James tells us, "Now if any of you lacks wisdom, he should ask God—who gives to all generously and ungrudgingly—and it will be given to him. But let him ask in faith without doubting. For the doubter is like the surging sea, driven and tossed by the wind" (vv. 5–6).

Certainly, wisdom takes time and experience to develop. I don't panic in certain circumstances the way I did twenty years ago. Experience grants us the ability to act, not react, to crisis. Experience is a great teacher. If wisdom is our goal, we must recognize that God is the ultimate giver of this gift.

James went on to address a wide variety of topics, such as wealth and humility, the source of temptation, the value of listening over speaking, and the benefit of avoiding anger. Toward the end of this chapter, he addressed the great value of Scripture:

> Be doers of the word and not hearers only, deceiving yourselves. Because if anyone is a hearer of the word and not a doer, he is like someone looking at his own face in a mirror. For he looks at himself, goes away, and immediately forgets what kind of person he was. But the one who looks intently into the perfect law of freedom and perseveres in it, and is not a forgetful hearer but a doer who works—this person will be blessed in what he does. (vv. 22–25)

We face two great challenges when allowing Scripture to change us. First is the challenge of listening to it.

Franklin D. Roosevelt disliked the long receiving lines at White House receptions. The guests were so busy talking and trying to impress one another that no one listened. One evening as he greeted guests, he reportedly shook hands with each person and said, "I murdered my grandmother this morning." Guest after guest smiled and offered the usual niceties in return. One dignitary, however, heard the president and understood the humor of the moment. He replied, "I'm sure she had it coming to her."[1]

Understanding Scripture starts with listening. James invites us to do more than listen, but listening is still a must!

The second challenge of accepting Scripture, once we hear it, is to obey. Consider a few radical statements from the teachings of Jesus: "Love your enemies" (Matt. 5:44). "Don't worry" (6:25). "Do not judge" (7:1). Are you willing to convert these words into works? Once we hear, we must purpose to practice. If we do, we're promised great blessings from God.

In the mid-twentieth century, J. B. Phillips rendered an English translation of the Greek New Testament that is lively and insightful. Looking back on the translation process, Phillips said he felt like an electrician working on the wiring of his house with the electricity left on.

The Bible contains great power for the follower of Jesus. Listening and doing—converting the Bible into behavior—bring their own rewards of growth and freedom. For those who dare to listen and obey, James promised that "this person will be blessed in what he does" (James 1:25).

FOR REFLECTION

I consider the final statement of James 1 a high point of the entire letter: "Pure and undefiled religion before God the Father is this:

to look after orphans and widows in their distress and to keep oneself unstained from the world" (v. 27).

The chapter ends with the perfect opportunity to listen and obey the words of the Scriptures. This verse calls us to defend the defenseless. At the same time, we're to intentionally practice purity in an impure world. Is there someone you need to stand up for today? Who comes to mind? In what area do you need to purposefully practice purity?

1 John 3

¹ See what great love the Father has given us that we should be called God's children — and we are! The reason the world does not know us is that it didn't know him. ² Dear friends, we are God's children now, and what we will be has not yet been revealed. We know that when he appears, we will be like him because we will see him as he is. ³ And everyone who has this hope in him purifies himself just as he is pure.

⁴ Everyone who commits sin practices lawlessness; and sin is lawlessness. ⁵ You know that he was revealed so that he might take away sins, and there is no sin in him. ⁶ Everyone who remains in him does not sin; everyone who sins has not seen him or known him.

⁷ Children, let no one deceive you. The one who does what is right is righteous, just as he is righteous. ⁸ The one who commits sin is of the devil, for the devil has sinned from the beginning. The Son of God was revealed for this purpose: to destroy the devil's works. ⁹ Everyone who has been born of God does not sin, because his seed remains in him; he is not able to sin, because he has been born of God. ¹⁰ This is how God's children and the devil's children become obvious. Whoever does not do what is right is not of God, especially the one who does not love his brother or sister.

¹¹ For this is the message you have heard from the beginning: We should love one another, ¹² unlike Cain, who was of the evil one and murdered his brother. And why did he murder him? Because his deeds were evil, and his brother's were righteous.

¹³ Do not be surprised, brothers and sisters, if the world hates you. ¹⁴ We know that we have passed from death to life because we love our brothers and sisters. The one who does not love remains in death. ¹⁵ Everyone who hates his brother or sister is a murderer, and you know that no murderer has eternal life residing in him. ¹⁶ This is how we have come to know love: He laid down his life for us. We should also lay down our lives for our brothers and sisters. ¹⁷ If anyone has this world's goods and sees a fellow believer in need but withholds compassion from him — how does God's love reside in him? ¹⁸ Little children, let us not love in word or speech, but in action and in truth.

¹⁹ This is how we will know that we belong to the truth and will reassure our hearts before him ²⁰ whenever our hearts condemn us; for God is greater than our hearts, and he knows all things.

²¹ Dear friends, if our hearts don't condemn us, we have confidence before God ²² and receive whatever we ask from him because we keep his commands and do what is pleasing in his sight. ²³ Now this is his command: that we believe in the name of his Son Jesus Christ, and love one another as he commanded us. ²⁴ The one who keeps his commands remains in him, and he in him. And the way we know that he remains in us is from the Spirit he has given us.

40

Becoming Your True Self
1 John 3

A wise friend once observed that only two things can be said for certain about the future: First, what you don't expect to happen *will*. And second, what you do expect to happen *won't*. Time and again I've found these statements to be true.

Our future in Christ is the focus of 1 John 3, and we can accept these words as promises from God. What we're told here is certain to transpire. Yet at the same time, the future won't be entirely what we assume it will be. Whatever we might expect our future in Christ to be, it's sure to be even *better*.

John, when he met Jesus, was the youngest of the twelve original disciples. Tradition tells us that John was no more than a teenager when he first followed Jesus. By the time he wrote the trilogy of books that bear his name—1, 2, and 3 John—he was an old man. John's heart overflowed into his pen as he wrote of God's great affection for us: "See what great love the Father has given us that we should be called God's children—and we are!

The reason the world does not know us is that it didn't know him" (1 John 3:1).

The phrase John used to speak of God's "great love" is an idiom that poses the question, *Of what country is this?*[1] God's love is foreign to our understanding. In a world where love is equated with shallow feelings and a "What have you done for me lately?" mentality, the love of God is unconditional to the point of being altogether alien.

With God's love in mind, John gives us a glimpse of tomorrow: "Dear friends, we are God's children now, and what we will be has not yet been revealed. We know that when he appears, we will be like him because we will see him as he is. And everyone who has this hope in him purifies himself just as he is pure" (vv. 2–3).

What powerful words! A few simple phrases embedded in these verses deserve our attention.

When he appears. Everything in the Bible points to a visible, physical, bodily return of Jesus Christ from heaven to earth. No sooner had the disciples witnessed Jesus's departure than angels appeared to give them a promise. "They said, 'Men of Galilee, why do you stand looking up into heaven? This same Jesus, who has been taken from you into heaven, will come in the same way that you have seen him going into heaven'" (Acts 1:11). John was present at the ascension and heard these words. Decades later he held firm to the truth that Jesus is certain to appear again.

We will see him. Some might imagine the future return of Jesus as a dreadful event. And for some it may be. But for the Jesus follower, Jesus's return is a thing of honor and beauty, not horror and dread.

Robert Louis Stevenson wrote of a storm at sea. According to subsequent versions of the story, the passengers huddled below deck were wet from the rain and fearful from the pitch and roll of the sailing vessel. One passenger, no longer able to live with the unknown, fought his way to the hatch. As he ascended above deck, he saw that the pilot had lashed himself with a rope to the wheel of the ship to avoid being washed overboard. As the boat lurched, the passenger and pilot locked eyes. In a moment the passenger caught the confidence and courage of the man guiding the ship through the gale. The man returned to the terror-stricken passengers and gave his report: "I have seen the face of the pilot.... All is well."[2]

When, at long last, we finally see the face of Jesus—the one we've followed through the span and spasms of life—we'll know for certain and forever that, indeed, all is well.

We will be like him. Jesus's appearance will result in our final transformation into the persons God intended us to be from the beginning. Our completion in Christ will be fully realized. Our character will be cleansed of all sin, guilt, remorse, and regret. Every imperfection and inferiority will be expunged from our identity as though these things had never existed in the first place. What freedom there will be in our completeness! And what pleasure God will take in seeing his children become exactly like his Son.

As a young child, I visited the Alamo in San Antonio, Texas, for the first time. (Seeing the Alamo is a required pilgrimage for every young Texan.) I vividly recall the red hat my parents purchased for me. Texans are taught to revere those who died defending the Spanish mission from the advance of Santa Anna's army. A commonly repeated story contends that in the Alamo's portrait gallery, one portrait bears an inscription below it that reads, "James Butler Bonham. No picture of him exists. This portrait is of his nephew, Major James Bonham, deceased, who greatly resembled his uncle. It is placed here by the family that people may know the appearance of the man who died for freedom."[3]

Whether this story is true, I cannot say. But this I do know: resembling Jesus is a daily challenge. It is also our destiny. When we see Jesus, we'll be changed into his perfect image. Until this experience, our daily experiment is to *continue to become until we completely become like Christ*. For all eternity, we'll bear a striking resemblance to the man who died for our freedom.

The first three verses of 1 John 3 raise our hopes as Jesus followers. The balance of the chapter speaks of our existence until then. Understanding eternity, we must also appreciate the interim.

Twice in this chapter, John talks about the arrival of Jesus. On both occasions he connected Jesus's first coming with the sin in our lives. In the first instance he wrote, "You know that [Jesus] was revealed so that he might take away sins, and there is no sin in him" (v. 5). And the second reference states, "The Son of God was revealed for this purpose: to destroy the devil's works. Everyone who has been born of God does not sin, because his seed remains in him; he is not able to sin, because he has been born of God" (vv. 8–9).

The bottom line is this: we take sin far too lightly. God doesn't. Jesus went out of his way to deal with the Devil's destructive actions and our self-destructive habits. How dare we take so lightly what Jesus takes so seriously and personally! No longer can we excuse, ignore, or explain away our sin. We must be intentional about removing every sin that finds its way into our character.

At the other extreme of taking sin too lightly is the habit of holding guilt too tightly. To all the guilt-prone personalities who habitually condemn themselves, John said, "God is greater than our hearts, and he knows all things" (v. 20).

Guilt isn't bad. In fact, guilt is an underappreciated gift from God because it serves as a clue that something is dangerously wrong in our lives.

On March 18, 1937, an explosion shook the silence of the small town of New London, Texas. A cloud of natural gas ignited in a schoolhouse basement, killing 294 people, mostly children. The gas leak was undetected because natural gas is naturally odorless. The unpleasant odor we associate with natural gas today is due to additives. The smell of mercaptan or thiophane serves to alert us to a potential natural-gas leak. Their smell tells us something may be very wrong.

In the same way, guilt is an additive that God has given to sin. It's the distinctive odor of wrongdoing. Guilt alerts us to the need to change and repent. But for some, the scent of guilt lingers even after the sin is gone.

Once sin has been dealt with, the work of guilt is done, and we may in good conscience let it go. This is why John ended with the encouraging words, "Dear friends, if our hearts don't condemn us, we have confidence before God" (v. 21).

What freedom we have knowing that God doesn't want to condemn us. Neither does he encourage us to beat ourselves up with pointless guilt. Rather, he gives us bold confidence as we experience his complete forgiveness.

FOR REFLECTION

Guilt is a state, not a feeling. One can *be* guilty and yet not *feel* guilty. Also, one may not be guilty at all but wrestle with overwhelming feelings of regret and remorse. Hear the truth again: guilt is a state, not a feeling. Once we have repented of a sin, guilt's work is done, and we're permitted to let go of it.

What unnecessary guilt are you holding today? Guilt grows stronger when we keep it a secret. Share your guilty feelings openly with God—and perhaps with someone you trust—and ask God for the grace to let go. Allow him to speak directly to you through the words of 1 John 3:20: "God is greater than our hearts, and he knows all things."

Epilogue

Some years ago my wife and I somehow got it into our heads to watch the American Film Institutes's one hundred greatest movies of all time. With one hundred years of moviemaking to its name, the film industry selected what it deemed to be the best of all motion pictures ever made. The oldest movie to appear on the list at the time was *Intolerance* (1916), and the most recent was *The Fellowship of the Ring* (2001). Some of the movies we had seen. Most we had not.

We began to work and watch our way through these movies, only to find ourselves consistently sidetracked by other productions that had something in common with one of the films on the official list. For instance, no sooner had we watched *It's a Wonderful Life* with Jimmy Stewart than we also found ourselves wanting to watch other Stewart classics, such as *Harvey* and *Shenandoah*. We couldn't watch the original *The Godfather* without also watching *The Godfather: Part II* (which is on the list) and *The Godfather: Part III* (which is not).

Growing up, my wife and I had both loved the television series *M*A*S*H* with Alan Alda, so we decided to watch the 1970 movie starring Donald Sutherland. The movie itself whet our appetite for the nostalgia of the television series, which now occupies considerable space on our DVR.

At this pace we'll never make it through all one hundred films.

Simply put, these essential movies provided us with a starting place. They served as sure footing to step away from our predictable patterns of movie watching into the larger world of filmography.

The forty chapters contained in this book are intended to serve you in much the same way as you walk into the larger universe of the Bible. I mean no irreverence by comparing movies to the Scriptures. I only mean to capture the effect that I hope you've experienced from becoming familiar with these forty chapters of the Bible.

Perhaps as you read Proverbs 1, something about its punchy and practical wisdom hit home for you. Now, taking what you know of this single chapter, you may stride into the entire book of Proverbs with a bit more confidence and curiosity. Or possibly, as you read the foundational teachings of Jesus in Matthew 5, 6, and 7, your interest has grown stronger than your sense of intimidation, and now you're better prepared to explore the greater expanse of Jesus's instruction.

So will you make it through the entire Bible? I hope so.

But more than completion, the goal of Bible reading is clarity. The Bible makes more sense each time we read it. Ultimately, our clarity goes beyond the Scriptures to God himself. As you read the Bible, may you see God in crisper detail. Indeed, there is no substitute for Scripture in its ability to help us perceive God's face, his hand, and—best of all—his heart.

My son Caleb is quietly observant. Even as a very young child, he learned to recognize the McDonald's sign anytime we were on a family road trip. From the far reaches of the minivan, he would point with a chubby finger and exclaim in urgent tones, "I see it! I see it!" Limited though his vocabulary was, his recognition produced excitement. Indeed, he couldn't fathom why we didn't pull over each time we saw this double-arched sign of culinary delight.

As you explore the pages of the Bible, may you sense more and more the reality of God's presence until you can exclaim with conviction and clarity, "I see him! I see him!"

Notes

INTRODUCTION

1. George G. Hunter III, *How to Reach Secular People* (Nashville: Abingdon, 1992), 41.

2. Robert L. Sumner, *The Wonder of the Word of God* (Murfreesboro, TN: Biblical Evangelism Press, 1969), 12, cited in Donald S. Whitney, *Spiritual Disciplines for the Christian Life*, rev. ed. (Colorado Springs: NavPress, 2014), 30–31.

CHAPTER 1

1. Paul Brand and Philip Yancey, *Fearfully and Wonderfully Made* (Grand Rapids: Zondervan, 1980), 179.

2. Leonard Sweet, *AquaChurch* (Loveland, CO: Group Publishing, 1999), 115.

CHAPTER 2

1. Brad Dunn and Daniel Hood, *New York: The Unknown City* (Vancouver: Arsenal Pulp, 2004), 16.

2. Environmental Protection Agency data, cited in Dunn and Hood, *New York*.

CHAPTER 3

1. Brian Clark Howard, "How Ants Survive Flooding by Forming Giant Rafts," *National Geographic*, October 6, 2015, http://news.nationalgeographic.com/2015/10/151006-fire-ants-rafts-south-carolina-flooding/.

2. See Rachel Nuwer, "When Fire Ants Build Rafts, There Are No Free Loaders," Smithsonian.com, June 13, 2014, www.smithsonianmag.com/smart-news/when-fire-ants-build-rafts-there-are-no-free-loaders-180951738/?no-ist.

CHAPTER 4

1. Efrem Smith, *Jump: Into a Life of Further and Higher* (Colorado Springs: David C Cook, 2010), 19–20.

CHAPTER 5

1. Richard Woods, *Meister Eckhart: Master of Mystics* (London: Continuum International, 2011), 130.

2. William C. Frey, *The Dance of Hope: Finding Ourselves in the Rhythm of God's Great Story* (Colorado Springs: WaterBrook, 2003), 174.

CHAPTER 6

1. Philip Yancey, *Prayer: Does It Make Any Difference?* (Grand Rapids: Zondervan, 2006), 92.

CHAPTER 7

1. Lloyd J. Ogilvie, *Facing the Future without Fear: Prescriptions for Courageous Living in the New Millennium* (Ann Arbor, MI: Servant Publications, 1999), 22.

2. Gordon Livingston, *And Never Stop Dancing: Thirty More True Things You Need to Know Now* (Cambridge, MA: Da Capo, 2008), 52–53.

3. Frank Newport, "More Than 9 in 10 Americans Continue to Believe in God," Gallup, June 3, 2011, www.gallup.com/poll/147887/Americans -Continue-Believe-God.aspx.

4. "Religion among the Millennials," Pew Research Center, February 17, 2010, www.pewforum.org/2010/02/17/religion-among-the-millennials/.

5. Charles H. Spurgeon, *Morning and Evening II: A Second Year of Daily Devotions*, The Devotional Classics of C. H. Spurgeon (Lafayette, IN: Sovereign Grace Publishers, 1990), 27.

CHAPTER 9

1. Frederick Buechner, *Beyond Words: Daily Readings in the ABC's of Faith* (San Francisco: HarperSanFrancisco, 2004), 365.

CHAPTER 10

1. University of California, study cited in John Ortberg, *If You Want to Walk on Water, You've Got to Get Out of the Boat* (Grand Rapids: Zondervan, 2001), 47.

CHAPTER 11

1. John F. Kavanaugh, *The Word Engaged: Meditations on the Sunday Scriptures; Cycle C* (Maryknoll, NY: Orbis Books, 1997), 91.

CHAPTER 13

1. J. F. Campbell, ed. and trans., *Popular Tales of the West Highlands* (London: Alexander Gardner, 1890; Abela, 2009), 1:250.

2. Mark Buchanan, *Spiritual Rhythm: Being with Jesus Every Season of Your Soul* (Grand Rapids: Zondervan, 2010), 213.

3. Walter Brueggemann, *The Message of the Psalms: A Theological Commentary* (Minneapolis: Augsburg, 1984), chaps. 2–4.

4. Shawn W. Larson, "10 Bizarre Eating Habits," Listverse, August 16, 2013, http://listverse.com/2013/08/16/10-bizarre-eating-habits/.

CHAPTER 14

1. Paul Brand and Philip Yancey, *Fearfully and Wonderfully Made* (Grand Rapids: Zondervan, 1980), 45–46n.

2. There are many variations of Saint Patrick's prayer "The Deer's Cry." For an example, see Saint Patrick, *St. Patrick: His Writings and Life*, ed. and trans. Newport J. D. White (New York: Macmillan, 1920), 66–67.

CHAPTER 15

1. Stephen R. Covey and Keith A. Gulledge, "Principle-Centered Leadership," *Journal for Quality and Participation* (July/August 1992): 70, www.leadcentre.info/wp-content/uploads/2014/02/01h.-Principle -centered-leadership.pdf.

2. I'm indebted to Kenneth Boa's definition of *wisdom*—"the ability to use the best means at the best time to accomplish the best ends"—for helping me greatly in crafting my own definition. See Kenneth Boa, *Conformed to*

His Image: Biblical and Practical Approaches to Spiritual Formation (Grand Rapids: Zondervan, 2001), 205.

3. Homer, *The Odyssey of Homer*, vol. 1, trans. Alexander Pope (London: C. Whittingham, 1809).

4. Leslie A. Bryan, Jesse W. Stonecipher, and Karl Aron, "180-Degree Turn Experiment," *University of Illinois Bulletin* 52, no. 11 (September 1954): 16, http://aviation.illinois.edu/avimain/papers/research/pub_pdfs /journalpubs/180%20Degree%20Turn.pdf.

CHAPTER 16

1. Mike Fallin, "The Real Face of Jesus," *Popular Mechanics*, January 23, 2015, www.popularmechanics.com/science/health/a234/1282186/.

2. Philip Yancey, *Prayer: Does It Make Any Difference?* (Grand Rapids: Zondervan, 2006), 24.

CHAPTER 17

1. Winston S. Churchill, *The Gathering Storm* (New York: RosettaBooks, 2009), 601.

CHAPTER 19

1. Paul Delatte, *The Rule of Saint Benedict*, trans. Justin McCann (Eugene, OR: Wipf and Stock, 2000), 71. This quote, in its fuller form, is one of my favorites: "Happy those who have nothing to hide … who live full in the day. Happy those who have brought all their being to a perfect simplicity, and who, before God and before men, are what they are, without duality, stiffness, or effort, but with flexibility and ease."

2. Neal Bascomb, *The Perfect Mile: Three Athletes, One Goal, and Less Than Four Minutes to Achieve It* (Boston: Mariner Books, 2005), 104–5.

3. Jonathan Edwards, *Jonathan Edwards on Evangelism*, ed. Carl J. C. Wolf (Eugene, OR: Wipf and Stock, 2013), ix.

4. John R. W. Stott, *Issues Facing Christians Today*, 4th ed. (Grand Rapids: Zondervan, 2006), 487.

CHAPTER 20

1. Don Everts and Doug Schaupp, *I Once Was Lost: What Postmodern Skeptics Taught Us about Their Path to Jesus* (Downers Grove, IL: InterVarsity, 2008), 31.

WHY TWO TESTAMENTS?

1. Bio Staff, "Bob Ross: 13 Happy Little Facts about the Iconic PBS Painter," October 29, 2015, Biography.com, www.biography.com/news/bob-ross -biography-facts.

CHAPTER 21

1. D. Elton Trueblood, AZ Quotes, accessed October 27, 2016, www.azquotes .com/quote/749754.

CHAPTER 23

1. Clifton Fadiman and André Bernard, eds., *Bartlett's Book of Anecdotes*, rev. ed. (Boston: Little, Brown, 2000), 118.

CHAPTER 24

1. Dallas Willard, *The Divine Conspiracy: Rediscovering Our Hidden Life in God* (San Francisco: HarperSanFrancisco, 1998), 200.

2. Philip Yancey, *Prayer: Does It Make Any Difference?* (Grand Rapids: Zondervan, 2006), 191.

3. "Hail Scale," TORRO, accessed August 25, 2016, http://torro.org.uk/hscale.php.

4. Christopher C. Burt, "World's Largest Hailstones," *WunderBlog*, www.wunderground.com/blog/weatherhistorian/worlds-largest-hailstones.

CHAPTER 25

1. Collis Huntington, quoted in Stephen E. Ambrose, *Nothing Like It in the World: The Men Who Built the Transcontinental Railroad 1863–1869* (New York: Touchstone, 2001), 117.

2. Richard J. Foster, *Prayer: Finding the Heart's True Home* (San Francisco: HarperSanFrancisco, 1992), 8–9.

3. John C. Waugh, *Kansai International Airport: Airport in the Sea* (Danbury, CT: Children's Press, 2004), 28.

CHAPTER 26

1. J. B. Phillips, *Your God Is Too Small: A Guide for Believers and Skeptics Alike* (New York: Touchstone, 2004), 56.

CHAPTER 27

1. Michelle Starr, "Mystery Solved: The Sailing Stones of Death Valley," CNET, August 27, 2014, www.cnet.com/news/mystery-solved -the-sailing-stones-of-death-valley/.

CHAPTER 28

1. Alon Harish, "Texas Man Finds Stolen Car 42 Years Later," ABC News, July 11, 2012, http://abcnews.go.com/US/texas-man-reunites-car-42-years -stolen/story?id=16757179#.UARCb_XAHak.

2. "Prosthetic Leg Found at Alton Towers," UltimateRollerCoaster.com, October 31, 2008, www.ultimaterollercoaster.com/forums/europe -roller-coasters-parks/30605.

3. Timothy Keller, *The Prodigal God: Recovering the Heart of the Christian Faith* (New York: Dutton, 2008), xii–xiii.

CHAPTER 29

1. William D. Edwards, "On the Physical Death of Jesus Christ," *JAMA* 255, no. 11 (1986): 1455–63, http://jama.jamanetwork.com/article.aspx ?articleid=403315.

2. "Crash of the Titans: Milky Way Is Destined for Head-On Collision with Andromeda Galaxy," Science Daily, March 31, 2012, www.sciencedaily .com/releases/2012/05/120531135438.htm.

3. "Victory Is Upheld," *New York Times*, October 13, 1989, www.nytimes.com /1989/10/13/sports/sports-people-boxing-victory-is-upheld.html.

4. Suzanne Lainson, "What Are You Trying to Accomplish as an Athlete?," *The Creative Athlete*, June 1997, http://onlinesports.com/sportstrust/creative1.html, cited in Fred Lowery, *Covenant Marriage: Staying Together for Life* (New York: Howard Books, 2003), 124.

CHAPTER 30

1. Joni Eareckson Tada, *Heaven: Your Real Home,* devotional ed. (Grand Rapids: Zondervan, 1996), 47.

CHAPTER 31

1. C. S. Lewis, *The Last Battle* (New York: Harper Trophy, 1984), 230.

CHAPTER 32

1. "Wednesday, Week 20," *Men of Integrity: A Daily Guide to the Bible and Prayer* (Nashville: W Publishing, 1999).

2. J. Oswald Sanders, *Spiritual Leadership: A Commitment to Excellence for Every Believer* (Chicago: Moody, 2007), 80.

3. "Pilot Is Survivor in Freakish Mishap," *New York Times*, September 4, 1987, www.nytimes.com/1987/09/04/us/pilot-is-survivor-in-freakish -mishap.html.

CHAPTER 33

1. John Lloyd and John Mitchinson, *The Book of General Ignorance: Everything You Think You Know Is Wrong* (New York: Harmony Books, 2006), 5.

2. Notice I say *typically*, not *always*. For a near-exhaustive look at the means through which God speaks, I recommend Henry and Richard Blackaby's book, *Hearing God's Voice* (Nashville: B&H, 2002).

3. Donald S. Whitney, *Simplify Your Spiritual Life: Spiritual Disciplines for the Overwhelmed* (Colorado Springs: NavPress, 2003), 31, 32.

4. Dallas Willard, *Hearing God: Developing a Conversational Relationship with God* (Downers Grove, IL: InterVarsity, 2012), 218–19.

CHAPTER 34

1. Geoffrey C. Ward, with Ric Burns and Ken Burns, *Ken Burns's The Civil War Deluxe eBook: An Illustrated History* (New York: Knopf, 2011).

CHAPTER 35

1. Calvin Miller, *Miracles and Wonders: How God Changes His Natural Laws to Benefit You* (New York: Warner Books, 2003), 23–24.

CHAPTER 36

1. Francis Chan, *Forgotten God: Reversing Our Tragic Neglect of the Holy Spirit* (Colorado Springs: David C Cook, 2009), 97–99.

CHAPTER 37

1. Adolf von Harnack, quoted in Frederick F. Shannon, *The New Personality and Other Sermons* (London: Revell, 1915), 159.

2. Gary Player, quoted in "A Life Long Player: A Clinic with Gary Player," *Golf Today*, accessed August 27, 2016, www.golftoday.co.uk/golf_international _mag/features/gary_player_clinic.html.

3. Steve Hartman, "Even in Dementia, Korean War Medic Cares for His Men," CBS News, August 31, 2012, www.cbsnews.com/8301-18563 _162-57504593/even-in-dementia-korean-war-medic-cares-for-his -men/?tag=mncol;lst;1.

CHAPTER 38

1. John Stott, *Baptism and Fullness: The Work of the Holy Spirit Today* (Downers Grove, IL: InterVarsity, 2006), 99.

2. Stephen Mansfield, *Never Give In: The Extraordinary Character of Winston Churchill* (Nashville: Cumberland House, 1995), 139.

3. Sir Edmund Hillary, quoted in Jack Canfield and Mark Victor Hansen, *Chicken Soup for the Soul: Unlocking the Secrets to Living Your Dreams* (Deerfield Beach, FL: Health Communications, 2003), 321.

CHAPTER 39

1. Franklin D. Roosevelt, quoted in Clifton Fadiman and André Bernard, eds., *Bartlett's Book of Anecdotes* (Boston: Little, Brown, 2000), 465.

CHAPTER 40

1. See John R. W. Stott, *The Letters of John*, Tyndale New Testament Commentaries (Grand Rapids: Eerdmans, 1988), 122.

2. Robert Louis Stevenson, cited in E. M. Bounds, *The Classic Collection on Prayer* (Orlando: Bridge-Logos, 2001), 567.

3. William Crook, "Week 43: Tuesday; Coming to Resemble Christ," in *God Is Faithful: My Daily Devotional* (Nashville: Thomas Nelson, 2014), 255.

About the Author

Deron Spoo became pastor of First Baptist Church in Tulsa, Oklahoma, in the year 2000 at the age of twenty-nine. Since then, Deron has helped his church transition from being a downtown church to a regional church committed to urban ministry. He also reaches one hundred thousand people each week through his televised devotionals, *First Things First*. Deron is a graduate of Southwestern Baptist Theological Seminary, where he received his master of divinity degree. He and his wife, Paula, have three children—Kira, Caleb, and Seth.

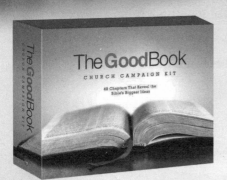